WESTERN MARXISM

western MARXISM

HOW IT WAS BORN, HOW IT DIED,
HOW IT CAN BE REBORN

by DOMENICO LOSURDO

edited by GABRIEL ROCKHILL

with an introduction by JENNIFER PONCE DE LEÓN
and GABRIEL ROCKHILL

translated by STEVEN COLATRELLA
with GEORGE DE STEFANO

MONTHLY REVIEW PRESS
New York

Copyright © 2024 by Monthly Review Press
All Rights Reserved

Originally published as *Il marxismo occidentale: Come nacque, come morì, come può rinascere* by Domenico Losurdo by Gius, Laterza & Figli S.p.A, Bari, Italy (2017). English translation by Steven Colatrella with George De Stefano published by Monthly Review Press 2024 © by Monthly Review Press

ISBN Paper 978-1-68590-062-5
ISBN Cloth 978-1-68590-063-2

Typeset in Bulmer Monotype

Monthly Review Press, New York
monthlyreview.org

5 4 3 2

Contents

Introduction
Socialism as Anticolonial Liberation:
Contemporary Lessons from Losurdo
by Jennifer Ponce de León and Gabriel Rockhill | 9
Note from the Translators and Editors | 35

ACKNOWLEDGMENTS | 36
PREMISE: WHAT IS WESTERN MARXISM? | 37

PART I
1914 AND 1917: THE BIRTH OF WESTERN
AND EASTERN MARXISM | 42
  1 The Turning Point of August 1914 in the West | 42
  2 The Turning Point of October 1917 in the East | 45
  3 State and Nation in the West and the East | 48
  4 The Money Economy in the West and the East | 53
  5 Science, Imperialist War, and Anticolonial Revolution | 56
  6 Western Marxism and Messianism | 60
  7 The Struggle against Inequality in the West and the East | 63
  8 The Blurred Boundaries between Western Marxism and Eastern Marxism | 66
  9 The Difficult Reciprocal Recognition between Two Struggles for Recognition | 69

PART II
SOCIALISM VERSUS CAPITALISM, OR ANTICOLONIALISM VERSUS COLONIALISM? | 73
  1 From the Only Proletarian Revolution to the Anticolonial Revolution | 73
  2 The National and Colonial Question in the Heart of Europe | 77
  3 The Socialist Countries in the Epoch of the Napoleonic Wars | 79

    4 Danielson's Dilemma and the Two Marxisms | 83
    5 The Two Marxisms at the Beginning and End
       of the Second Thirty Years' War | 88

PART III
WESTERN MARXISM AND THE ANTICOLONIAL REVOLUTION:
A MEETING THAT DIDN'T HAPPEN | 92
    1 The Bobbio-Togliatti Debate in the Year of Dien Bien Phu | 92
    2 Marx, Cut in Half by Della Volpe and Colletti | 95
    3 "Workerism" and the Condemnation of Third Worldism | 98
    4 Althusser, Anti-humanism, and Anticolonialism | 102
    5 Althusser's Idealist and Eurocentric Regression | 105
    6 Bloch's Legacy and the Transfiguration of Liberalism | 108
    7 Horkheimer: From Anti-authoritarianism
       to Philo-colonialism | 111
    8 Adorno's Imperial Universalism | 116
    9 Whoever Is Unwilling to Talk about Colonialism Should
       also Keep Quiet about Capitalism and Fascism | 119
   10 Marcuse and the Difficult Rediscovery of Imperialism | 123
   11 The August 4th of Critical Theory and of
       the Concrete Utopia | 126
   12 1968 and the Mass Equivocation of Western Marxism | 130
   13 Sartre's Populist and Idealist Anticolonialism | 134
   14 Timpanaro, Anticolonialism, and Anarchism | 137
   15 The Isolation of Lukács | 139

PART IV
THE TRIUMPH AND DEATH OF
WESTERN MARXISM | 141
    1 *Ex Occidente Lux et Salus!*
       (Light and Salvation from the West!) | 141
    2 The Cult of Arendt and the Erasure of
       the Colonialism-Nazism Nexus | 144
    3 The Third Reich from the History of Colonialism
       to the History of Madness | 152
    4 On Trial: Colonialism or Its Victims? | 157
    5 With Arendt, from the Third World to
       the Western Hemisphere | 160

6   Foucault and the Removal of Colonial Peoples from History | 163
7   Foucault and the Esoteric History of Racism | 165
8   On Biopolitics | 171
9   From Foucault to Agamben (via Levinas) | 177
10 Negri and Hardt and the Esoteric Celebration of Empire | 182

PART V
REVIVAL, OR THE LAST GASP
OF WESTERN MARXISM? | 186
1   Žižek's Anti-imperialism | 186
2   Žižek, the Degradation of the Anticolonial Revolution, and the Demonization of Mao | 190
3   Harvey and the Absolutization of Inter-imperialist Rivalry | 193
4   Ah, if Only Badiou Had Read Togliatti! | 195
5   Transformation of Power into Love, Critical Theory, the Fused Group, and the Renunciation of Power | 199
6   The Struggle against the Phrase, from Robespierre to Lenin | 203
7   War and the Death Certificate of Western Marxism | 207

PART VI
HOW MARXISM IN THE WEST CAN BE REBORN | 212
1   Marx and the Future in Four Acts | 212
2   The Long Struggle against the World Colonial-Slavery System | 215
3   Two Marxisms and Two Different Temporalities | 221
4   Restoring the Relationship with the World Anticolonial Revolution | 224
5   The Lessons of Hegel and the Rebirth of Marxism in the West | 227
6   East and West: From Christianity to Marxism | 231

APPENDIX
How "Western Marxism" Was Born and How It Died | 235

Notes | 264
Index | 299

INTRODUCTION

Socialism as Anticolonial Liberation: Contemporary Lessons from Losurdo

by Jennifer Ponce de León and Gabriel Rockhill

> [To] imagine that social revolution is *conceivable* without revolts by small nations in the colonies and in Europe... is to *repudiate social revolution*. Whoever expects a "pure" social revolution will *never* live to see it. Such a person pays lip-service to revolution without understanding what revolution is.[1]
>
> — LENIN

According to Domenico Losurdo, the Russian Revolution inaugurated a new phase of global anticolonial struggle, providing an example to the world of how to break the chains of imperialism.[2] After fending off fourteen capitalist countries that immediately sought to "strangle the Bolshevik baby in its crib," according to the choice words of Winston Churchill, the USSR proceeded to construct the first socialist state.[3] The Third Reich picked up where these fourteen countries had left off. Funded by the capitalist ruling class, it attempted to conquer and colonize the USSR in order to put an end, once and for all, to this beacon of anticolonial liberation.

The international fascist onslaught, of which Nazism formed a decisive part, was defeated, primarily due to the strength and monumental sacrifices of the Soviet and Chinese peoples. This opened what Losurdo refers to as a second phase of anticolonial struggle in the age of imperialism. Commonly known as the Cold War, this era was marked early on by an expansion of the socialist world and a triumphant wave of anti-colonial revolutions, as well as horrific imperial aggression against the efforts of people in the regions of the world underdeveloped by capitalism to throw off the yoke of colonialism and neocolonialism. The United States not only took a leading role in endeavoring to enforce neocolonialism across the Global South; it also subordinated other imperialist powers, bringing many of their colonial and semi-colonial possessions under its control.[4]

The dismantling of the USSR in 1991 opened a third phase of struggle, which commenced with a relatively short-lived moment of imperialist triumphalism. However, capitalist states proved incapable of overcoming their contradictions and repressing revolutionary projects. The resilience and subsequent rise of China is one clear sign among many others that the anti-imperialist project of building a socialist world is alive and well.

Losurdo was born in Italy in 1941, at the onset of the Nazis' Operation Barbarossa against the USSR, and thus at the tail end of the first phase of anticolonial struggle. Living through its second phase, the Cold War, he saw Italy polarized between what was at the time one of the strongest communist parties in Europe, the Partito Comunista Italiano (PCI), and imperial forces intent on rehabilitating fascism to combat communism in order to make Italy into a lackey of the United States and the capitalist camp.[5]

A lifelong militant, Losurdo joined the PCI in 1960 at the age of nineteen.[6] Originally founded under a slightly different name by Antonio Gramsci and others as a section of the burgeoning Third International (1919–1943), the PCI had spearheaded the anti-fascist resistance and then emerged as the second-largest party in Italy in the wake of the Second World War. The U.S. government was so fearful that it would win the 1948 election that it poured more than 10 million dollars into funding anti-PCI groups, and the CIA made plans for a fascist coup d'état if the Communists won.[7] Even though they ended up losing this particular election, due in large part to imperialist meddling, they remained a powerful political, economic, and cultural force.

Losurdo's militant engagements testify to his dedication to what he refers to in his work on Gramsci as a "critical communism," which eschews dogmatism in favor of an ongoing process of learning rooted in a concrete analysis of specific historical conjunctures. In the context of the Sino-Soviet split, Losurdo left the PCI in 1969 and then joined the China-oriented Partito Comunista d'Italia (PCd'I), an organization named after the original Italian section of the Third International. Through the course of the 1970s, he wrote weekly commentaries and analyses for their newspaper. He continued to maintain his dedication to the international project of anti-colonial liberation through some of the darkest years of counter-revolutionary revanchism and the neoliberal assault on the working class. When the USSR was eventually dismantled in 1991, marking the onset of the third phase of struggle, many Western intellectuals feted the end of communism. Losurdo instead joined the Partito della Rifondazione Comunista (PRC), which repudiated the PCI's social-democratic or liberal-democratic dissolution into the Partito Democratico della Sinistra (PDS). He later continued his Marxist militancy with the Partito dei Comunisti Italiani (PdCI), which recovered the old name of the PCI in 2016 in an attempt to revive the legacy of this tradition.

Losurdo's political commitments and intellectual practice were shaped by his close collaboration with German scholar Erdmute Brielmayer (b. 1943), who was also actively engaged in communist party politics. The two had met while students at the University of Tübingen, where Losurdo studied as an exchange student. They later married and moved together to Italy. There, Losurdo worked as a professor of philosophy at the University of Urbino, where he had earlier obtained his doctorate. Brielmayer's work with him made possible his publication of some fifty books on the history of bourgeois thought, Marxism, and the communist movement. As Andreas Wehr explains, Brielmayer "proofread his texts, took care of quotations, and procured necessary literature.... She was his most important advisor and at the same time took care of the daily things that had to be done at home, which meant that she had his back. Only because of this was it possible for Domenico to be so productive academically and in publishing."[8] Brielmayer's translation of nearly all of Losurdo's books into German also contributed crucially to the international circulation of his scholarship.

It is noteworthy that, in spite of Losurdo's international recognition as a leading intellectual, fewer than ten of his books are currently available in English. We are thus very pleased to present his penultimate monograph, *Western Marxism* (2017), as well as the first English translation of an important lecture he presented on the topic in 2007.[9] This work is the culmination of decades of research on the history of the Marxist tradition and its internal struggles. It elucidates one of the major splits in global Marxist debates that marked Losurdo's generation and continues to structure many contemporary controversies. He described the emergence of this schism in the 1970s in an interview with Stefano Azzarà, a scholar who has authored an insightful book on Losurdo's work.[10] The Eastern Marxists, as he explained, were identified as those who actually exercised power, as in the USSR, Vietnam, Korea, China, Cuba, and so forth.[11] The Western Marxists, by contrast, were intellectuals who opposed these efforts to construct socialism, rejecting the quest for power in favor of diverse forms of critical theory, while sometimes presenting their distance from power as an epistemological advantage for discovering so-called authentic Marxism. Losurdo's geographic references to the West and the East thereby tend to abide by the same logic elucidated by Evald Ilyenkov: "The 'Western World' is the part of the world based on private property while the other part that is on the road to collectivization, that is, on the road to socialism and communism, is the 'Eastern World.'"[12]

Far from being strictly geographic terms, however, Eastern and Western are used more generally to refer to two different political orientations, both of which have manifested themselves around the world. One of them is dedicated to the difficult and drawn-out process of building socialism in a capitalist-dominated world and, in particular, across the Global South, which has been the principal site for such endeavors thus far. The other is generally dismissive of such practical undertakings, often belittling concrete struggles against imperialism because they do not live up to an imagined standard of theoretical or moral purity.[13]

It is important to recognize that Losurdo is diagnosing a historical phenomenon that extends well beyond the work of self-declared Marxists. He focuses on philosophical currents coming out of the Frankfurt School and French theory, as well as some of the work that is in dialogue with them. While these traditions often draw on Marxism, they tend to treat it as one discourse among others, which they freely combine, in idealist fashion, with bourgeois or even radically aristocratic theories of various sorts.[14] This has led some thinkers associated with Marxism to take explicitly anti-Marxist positions, as we shall see. What the Western Marxists examined in this book share in common, then, is not their dedication to Marxism per se. Rather, it is their promotion by the U.S.-driven theory industry as the most radical theory on offer. As a result, their work provides the historical foundation and referential basis for so many of the commodities produced by the business of contemporary theory in the imperial core. Much of what Losurdo diagnoses in this book therefore applies *mutatis mutandis* to many other trends promoted by the theory industry, some of which are openly anti-Marxist, including postcolonial theory, decolonial theory, liberal feminist and queer theory, Afro-pessimism, and so forth.[15]

WESTERN MARXISM AND THE POLITICS OF DEFEAT

> Despair is typical of those who do not understand the causes of evil, see no way out, and are incapable of struggle.
>
> —LENIN[16]

This book is a rejoinder to Perry Anderson's *Considerations on Western Marxism* (1976). The latter's Trotskyist assessment, written in dialogue with the editorial staff of the *New Left Review*, identifies some key aspects of Western Marxism. However, it is simultaneously symptomatic of many of the problems that Losurdo highlights in this tradition, including its patronizing Eurocentrism, idealism, and complicity with imperialism. Anderson's understanding of Western Marxism (in which he bizarrely includes Communist Party militants György Lukács and Antonio Gramsci) is that it is a "product of *defeat*": "The failure of the socialist revolution to spread outside Russia, cause and consequence of its corruption inside Russia, is the common background to the entire theoretical tradition of this period."[17] This purported failure contributed to Western Marxists' withdrawal from parties and into the academy, their shift away from political and economic issues in favor of philosophic and aesthetic concerns, and their injection of pre- and extra-Marxist theoretical elements into historical materialism.[18]

At the same time, Anderson asserts that the "Stalinization" of the communist movement transformed the USSR into "a semi-literate backwater" and led to an "overall weakness of socialist culture," whereas "major sectors of bourgeois thought regained a relative vitality and superiority over socialist thought."[19] In this regard, he repeatedly celebrates the "radical novelty" of the Western Marxists, who indulge in bourgeois culture while abandoning praxis, producing theories that have little to no use value for the struggles of the working and oppressed masses.[20] In perfect line with the precepts of bourgeois culture, and as an apparent rebuttal to the Marxist position that the validity of any claim depends on the primacy of practice, Anderson insists that "the pertinent criterion here is not the validity of these innovations, or their compatibility with the basic principles of Marxism: it is their originality."[21] Drawing on the historical experience of Europe, which he describes as "in certain critical respects the most *advanced* in the world," Anderson goes on to assert that the innovative spirit of Western Marxism has been able to achieve "a sophistication greater than that of any previous phase of historical materialism."[22]

Anderson's work was published by New Left Books (later renamed Verso Books) only a year after the Vietnamese people, under the leadership of Ho Chi Minh and the Communist Party, had handed a spectacular defeat to the most powerful imperialist army in the world.

Introduction 15

However, there is no reference in it to "Ho Chi Minh thought" and little to no discussion of Vietnam or other socialist revolutions, aside from the peremptory assertion that they have failed to construct socialism.[23] Lest we forget, which would be easy to do when reading Anderson's book, the socialist world actually witnessed a massive expansion between the Second World War and the mid-1970s. Eastern Europe, liberated from fascism and authoritarian regimes, was integrated into the socialist camp, and revolutionary governments took power in Korea and Vietnam, both of which were drawn-out processes due to brutal imperialist interventions. After the Chinese Revolution of 1949 and China's formal alliance with the USSR in 1950, approximately one-third of the world's population was living in socialist countries. This trend continued, in fits and starts, through the following three decades as there was a veritable global surge in socialist revolutions and national liberation struggles, from Cuba to Guinea-Bissau and beyond. This was the precise period during which Anderson penned his jeremiad on political defeat. It is important to add, moreover, that these socialist advances also contributed to both social welfare compromises and a relative strengthening of revolutionary socialism within the capitalist core. This is easily visible when compared to the subsequent era of counter-revolutionary revanchism known as neoliberalism.

The supposed defeat that is the hallmark of Western Marxism, according to Anderson, actually only applies to Europe and, more precisely, Western Europe. Moreover, it only really means that communists did not succeed in seizing state power in the West, as they nonetheless exercised significant political, economic, and cultural influence. From the point of view of the global working class, this period was one of major advances and some remarkable victories, including the incredible rout of fascism, the global weakening of imperialism through successful anticolonial struggles, and the imposition of democratic reforms and social welfare provisions in the West. From Anderson's vantage point as a prominent theorist in the imperial core, these achievements were apparently of little import, presumably because they did not bring about theoretical innovations of the sort cherished by intellectuals of his ilk. With the exception of the early

Lenin, read as a progenitor of Trotsky, Anderson suggests that Eastern Marxists did not make any major theoretical contributions.[24] The fact that they actually *made revolutions*—mobilizing theoretical and practical knowledge to raise millions of people out of abject conditions of slavery, exploitation, and oppression—pales in comparison to the intellectual novelties of Western theorists promoted as major commodity producers by Anderson's publication platforms. From the perspective of this grandee of the Western theory industry, it appears that the exchange value of Marxist theory, which is augmented by novelty and originality, is more important than its use value for human liberation.

These positions are typical of Western Marxism, as it is understood and analyzed by Losurdo. Anderson's book is, in fact, a repository for many of its major themes: idealism and the primacy of theory, Eurocentric social chauvinism in the sense of an attitude of patronizing cultural superiority, the dogmatic rejection of actually existing socialism, a politics of defeat based on historical misrepresentations, a willful dilution of Marxism with bourgeois theory and petty-bourgeois theoretical practices, a celebration of marketable novelty at the expense of practical relevance, and self-promotional opportunism that perpetuates cultural imperialism and disdain for Marxism in the Global South.[25] In the Postscript to his 1983 quasi-sequel to *Considerations on Western Marxism*, Anderson laid his cards on the table by peremptorily asserting that socialism did not exist anywhere in the world, but that it should nonetheless remain an object of theoretical debate (ironically, this was the same year as the socialist revolution in Burkina Faso led by Thomas Sankara).[26] The reason for this is because of the purported need for a third way, meaning "a social order beyond both capital and bureaucracy [i.e., actually existing socialism]."[27] The closest he comes to describing this anti-socialist intellectual orientation is by claiming that an "open and inventive Marxism" should simply no longer be Marxist but instead "find its province in a flexible balance" between "anarchism and fabianism."[28]

Third-way politics of this sort has regularly been criticized by Marxists, who have identified it as an expression of a petty-bourgeois class position, particularly within the imperialist core. Nicos

Poulantzas (whom we do not necessarily follow on all issues) provided a lapidary summary of these critiques: "The petty bourgeoisie actually has, in the long run, no autonomous class political position of its own. This simply means that, in a capitalist social formation, there is only the bourgeois way and the proletarian way (the socialist way): there is no such thing as the 'third way,' which various theories of the 'middle class' insist on."[29] Regarding Anderson's specific third-way endorsement of Fabianism and anarchism, it is worth briefly recalling the long-standing Marxist critiques of both of these traditions. As Anderson presumably knows, Fabianism opposed the Socialist League, which was strongly supported by Engels and "distinguished itself from the start by declaring anti-imperialism central to the definition of socialism in the Marxian conception."[30] In its manifesto, the Fabian Society openly embraced imperialism and rejected the principle of the self-determination of nations, which was central to Lenin and the Bolsheviks.[31] As Zak Cope explains, "The ideologically predominant Fabian section of the British Independent Labour Party . . . was in the majority imperialist. . . . Fabianism sought to weld 'socialism' (narrowly defined as a more egalitarian redistribution of Britain's wealth) to the expansionist nationalism of British imperialism."[32] As early as 1902, J. A. Hobson had underscored the existence of "Fabian imperialists," a point that Lenin emphasized as well in his critique of the "social-imperialists" more generally, meaning those who, like "the opportunist Fabian Society," were "socialists in words and imperialists in deeds."[33] Moreover, Lenin's foundational critique of "*petty-bourgeois revolutionism*, which smacks of, or borrows something from, anarchism," includes a perfect summary of Anderson's overall orientation: "The petty bourgeois 'driven to frenzy' by the horrors of capitalism is a social phenomenon which, like anarchism, is characteristic of all capitalist countries. The instability of such revolutionism, its barrenness, its liability to become swiftly transformed into submission, apathy, fantasy, and even a 'frenzied' infatuation with one or another bourgeois 'fad'— all this is a matter of common knowledge."[34] Losurdo, we can see here, is clearly following in Lenin's footsteps by redeploying and updating his insightful critiques of petty-bourgeois radicalism à la Anderson.

Unlike Anderson and other Western Marxists, Losurdo begins with the primacy of practice and always centers the colonial question. His study of Western Marxism is not an ideological analysis that focuses solely on superstructural elements, nor is it an immanent critique or an ad hominem attack that lambasts these thinkers for their individual ideas. On the contrary, as in his other work, he elucidates the objective forces driving the ideology of Western Marxism, which he sees as a cultural product of the imperialist core. This is surely one of the reasons why he uses geographic terminology. It is not to imply that *all* Marxists in a particular region necessarily suffer from the same ideology, which would be reductivist. It is rather that there are very real material forces that foster within the imperialist center a particular ideology that can—and should be—resisted. One of the goals of the book, as the subtitle specifies, is precisely to reinvent Western Marxism beyond this anti-socialist ideology.

Unlike many of the thinkers analyzed in this work, and in counter-distinction to Anderson's glorification of intellectual originality unmoored from practical validity, Losurdo does not concoct theories out of whole cloth. He also does not indulge in discursive chicanery or proliferate references to the latest theoretical commodities in order to market his work. On the contrary, all of his writings are characterized by a sober analysis of concrete reality that is profoundly historical. He clearly sought to understand and learn from material practice in such a way that his theoretical work is first and foremost grounded in the elucidation of the objective world. For it is practice itself that is the ultimate arbiter of truth, not the so-called marketplace of ideas or some imaginary realm of pure thought.

Objective Ideological Critique of the Western Left

> One cannot live in society and be free from society. The freedom of the bourgeois writer, artist or actress is simply masked (or hypocritically masked) dependence on the money-bag, on corruption, on prostitution.
>
> —Lenin[35]

In a letter to Franz Mehring in 1893, Friedrich Engels wrote:

> Ideology is a process which is, it is true, carried out consciously by what we call a thinker, but with false consciousness. The actual motives by which he is impelled remain hidden from him, for otherwise it would not be an ideological process. Hence the motives he supposes himself to have are either false or illusory.[36]

These illusory motives, Engels goes on to explain, are those of pure thought, meaning that the thinker in question assumes that their ideas originate in a conceptual realm, independently of concrete, material reality. Rejecting this idealist approach, he proposes instead a materialist analysis of the objective forces that condition one's subjective thoughts while simultaneously impeding one's conceptual apprehension of said forces.

This account of ideology as false consciousness is central to Losurdo's work. In a telling passage in one of his books, he invokes Christopher Columbus's plan to reach the East Indies by sailing West from Europe as a useful metaphor.[37] Although the Italian explorer's subjective aspirations were to discover a western passage to the East Indies, the objective nature of the world made it such that he actually landed in the West Indies. From a dialectical point of view, subjective thoughts always need to be situated within the objective material world. The latter is primary, as the example of Columbus shows, since his subjective will could not bend objective reality to it. However, the relationship between these two dimensions is dialectical. They mutually inform one another because our apprehension of objective reality is itself mediated by subjective factors. Columbus thought the world was different than it actually is (insofar as we currently understand it). Ultimately, there is no God's-eye view, so any apprehension of objective reality is mediated by subjective experience, which is itself conditioned by this very same reality.

Losurdo's analysis in this book seeks to bring to the fore the objective social forces that have produced Western Marxism as a remarkably consistent ideology in imperialist countries (as well as in class strata in the periphery that aspire to imperialist rewards). At the same time, it eschews mechanical explanations or reductivisms in favor of a complex and nuanced account of the dialectical play of forces between subjects and objective reality. This is attested to, among other things, by the fact that Losurdo himself was a Marxist working in the Western world who critically diagnosed and rejected its dominant ideologies in favor of supporting the anticolonial struggle to build socialism.

Losurdo draws extensively on V. I. Lenin's resounding diagnosis and trenchant indictment of chauvinism and racism in the socialist movement within imperialist states. Many of Lenin's searing critiques of revisionism, meaning the gutting of Marxism's revolutionary core, center on a condemnation of the social chauvinism that plagued European members of the Second International (1889–1916). The Bolshevik leader criticized as opportunists those who supported the First World War, lining up on the imperial agendas of their national bourgeoisies against the interests of the global working class. In his 1915 text on the "Collapse of the Second International," he explained:

> By social-chauvinism we mean acceptance of the idea of the defense of the fatherland in the present imperialist war, justification of an alliance between socialists and the bourgeoisie and the governments of their "own" countries in this war, a refusal to propagate and support proletarian-revolutionary action against one's "own" bourgeoisie, etc. It is perfectly obvious that social-chauvinism's basic ideological and political content fully coincides with the foundations of opportunism. It is *one and the same* tendency. In the conditions of the war of 1914–15, opportunism leads to social-chauvinism. The idea of class collaboration is opportunism's main feature.[38]

Lenin not only critiqued social chauvinism among European workers; he also identified its material basis in the imperialist world system. In his 1916 essay on imperialism, which set much of the political agenda for the Third International, he argued that the imperialist extraction of monopolist super-profits from peripheral societies had created a labor aristocracy among the European working class, resulting in their embourgeoisement—that is, their identification with the interests of their own national bourgeoisies, over and against those of their fellow proletarians in other countries.[39] Lenin's foundational elucidation of imperialism's tendency to exacerbate uneven development and the stratification of the global working class, as well as his insistence on the right of nations to self-determination, have served as a basis for countless subsequent analyses that seek to identify the material foundations of racism and chauvinism. It should be noted, moreover, that his theorization of dependency, super-exploitation, and the regional differentiation of labor has also been widely used to analyze racialized social and labor hierarchies that obtain *within* single nation-states, including in what has been subsequently identified as internal colonialism.[40]

Losurdo demonstrates how the social chauvinism of many Western Marxists expresses itself in paternalistic attitudes toward the efforts of workers and peasants in the peripheries to struggle against imperialism. Like Lenin, he situates this condescending mindset as a legacy of the Second International, whose material basis is found in the socioeconomic relations of the imperialist world system. Those who enjoy the wages of imperialism are more likely to have disdain for, or disinterest in, the complex struggles for national liberation in the periphery, which is dismissed as "the savage barbarism of the East," in the choice words of Max Horkheimer (which equally represented the views of his close collaborator Theodor Adorno).[41]

This chauvinistic attitude has become so foundational to Western Marxism that theorists in this tradition often behave as if there were no need to actually study the history of socialist states in any serious manner. In fact, the attempt to do so is often looked upon with suspicion, as a sign that one might be a boor siding with the slaves, rather than a professional intellectual with a keen sense of what is worthy of scholarly inquiry. Michel Foucault is a case in point since he rejected what he referred to as the totalizing approach of Marxism in favor of occupying the position of a specific intellectual who only addresses topics within his or her areas of expertise. Yet the author of *The Order of Things* readily pontificated about the death of socialism, even though he had little to no knowledge of its international history. According to this specific intellectual, who was purportedly opposed to totalizing narratives: "*Everything* that this socialist tradition has produced in history is to be condemned."[42] The colonial geography underlying Foucault's chauvinism and ultracrepidarianism could not be clearer, and it is to be found in the work of many of his fellow Western intellectual grandees: while the history of Western Europe—his privileged object of study—is infinitely complex and requires expert knowledge, the class struggles of workers and peasants in the imperial periphery can be dismissed out of hand as misguided without even studying them.

Many Western Marxists have therefore come to embrace a form of critical theory that is skeptical of *all* forms of power and domination, while simultaneously celebrating the moral excellence of those who are oppressed and bereft of power (whom Foucault, like his anticommunist ally André Glucksmann, referred to as "the pleb," Jacques Rancière calls "the demos," and so on). Losurdo refers to this tendency as "populism," and he identifies it as one of the major leitmotifs in Western Marxism. Thinkers like Antonio Negri and Michael Hardt, for instance, express their sympathy for the oppressed but refuse to side with them if they gain real power and, in particular, control of the state. Citing their clear positions on this issue, Losurdo points out with trenchant irony that this ultimately means that they are on the side of the oppressed *as long as they are losing*.[43] He shrewdly recalls that this is the same position that G. W. F. Hegel criticized in Christians who, in order to accomplish their obligation to serve the poor, needed the institution of poverty to persist indefinitely.

Those intellectuals Losurdo refers to as populists are generally skeptical of—if not opposed to—political parties, as well as the exercise of state power. For them, getting organized through the party form, like seeking to take over the state apparatus, inexorably leads to new forms of oppression that besmirch the moral excellence of the downtrodden. This is one of the reasons why rebellionism is another leitmotif in Western Marxism. Celebrating insurgency and revolt for their own sake, often devoid of context or concrete political content, many Western Marxists exalt the figure of the rebel, whom they present as anti-dogmatic, radically free, and morally superior to those denigrated as authoritarian, state-centric socialists and party intellectuals.

Yet this libertarian orientation, which segues in key ways with liberal ideology, only amounts to what Losurdo calls a "dogmatism of the subject": a thoughtless embrace of the figure-in-revolt, which is an obvious projection of Western Marxists' own self-image qua petty-bourgeois *enfants terribles*. As he explains, drawing on important insights from Gramsci, rebellionism can lend itself to distinct, and even opposed, political projects. The deep and expansive history of dissident politics clearly demonstrates this point, since the right-wing and often philo-fascist dissidents promoted by imperialist governmental agencies like the CIA were—and are—rebels opposed to (socialist) states.

Slavoj Žižek, arguably the most contumacious of Western Marxists, first came to public attention as an anti-communist dissident. "In [the] late 1980s," he candidly explained, "I myself was personally engaged in undermining the Yugoslav Socialist order."[44] Although much of what this pro-Western parvenu from the East writes is an unhealthy hodgepodge of sophistic chicanery, anecdotal triviality, and puerile provocation, he does indeed have a well-documented history of working as a dissident against the Communist government of Yugoslavia. He was the main political columnist for a prominent dissident magazine that the Yugoslav Communist Party accused of being backed by the CIA.[45] He also co-founded the Liberal Democratic Party and ran for president of Slovenia against the Communists, advocating for "planned privatizations" and proclaiming, like a dutiful capitalist ideologue, "more capitalism in our case would mean more social security."[46]

Those Western Marxists who do appear to propose some kind of alternative to the extant order often traffic in magical thinking and a belief in the most suspect forms of idealist, utopian salvation. Losurdo details how this type of Marxism has grafted itself onto religious ideologies deeply rooted in the Judeo-Christian tradition. Messianism is their lifeblood, and it is another motif of Western Marxism. Although the precise forms it takes vary considerably, there is a general tendency to project a vision of the future as totally other than what currently exists. Such a future cannot, therefore, be arrived at through the telluric path of extant institutions, including the rule of law, parliaments, parties, states, and so forth. In extreme ultra-leftist cases, all of this and much more needs to be abolished. The new world aspired to, since it is totally other, must break with everything and arrive on the scene more or less miraculously.

In Alain Badiou's version of messianic Marxism, to take but one obvious example, this occurs through an inexplicable event that calls upon individuals to convert themselves into subjects by asserting their faith in its reality and taking it upon themselves to reconfigure the extant situation based on their fidelity to the unexplainable. Anyone with even scant familiarity with the story of Christ cannot fail to grasp the ideological progenitor of what Badiou has marketed as his grand new "Idea of communism" qua constitution of a community of the faithful under the banner of his philosophic brand.

Losurdo is a realist who advocates for scientific socialism over and against the utopian socialism, anarchism, and defeatism of the Western Marxists. Socialism does not fall from the sky, nor is it simply the desideratum of an individual or, for that matter, a combination of both à la Badiou. Communism is not merely an idea or a desire, as figures like Badiou and Žižek have contended. Losurdo opposes theories and discourses of this sort, which combine wish fulfillment with what one can only hope is willful ignorance. Communism, he maintains with Marx and Engels, is "the *real* movement which abolishes [*aufhebt*] the present state of things. The conditions of this movement result from the now existing premise."[47] The verb *aufheben* here does not refer to a total negation of capitalist society, as he reminds us in the present book, but to a negation that is also, crucially, an assumption of certain aspects of extant society.

The Bourgeois Cultural Apparatus and the Compatible Left

> All revolutions fail [*foirent*]. Everyone knows it: we pretend to rediscover it here [with the anti-communist writings of André Glucksmann and François Furet]. You have to be a complete idiot [*débile*] [not to know that]!"
>
> —Gilles Deleuze[48]

It is not the least bit surprising that Losurdo, while a prominent and important thinker, has by no means been promoted by the imperial theory industry in a manner comparable to the Western Marxists, whose global class standing and ideology he diagnoses with such remarkable acumen. In capitalist societies, the bourgeoisie does not only own the overall means of production, after all, but it also owns and controls the means of intellectual production: universities, research centers, think tanks, publishing houses, the press, the mass media, and so forth. The ruling class has a vested material interest in policing the limits of acceptable discourse. If forced to accommodate some form of Marxism, its preference for idealist discourses openly hostile to actually existing socialism is very well established. These discourses often promote, moreover, the dynamics of cultural imperialism, and they are promoted in turn by the bourgeois cultural apparatus, which peddles them around the globe as the only valid version of Marxism.

Western intelligence agencies have been deeply involved in this project by running expansive and extremely well-funded propaganda campaigns aimed at redefining the very nature of the left. As CIA officer Thomas Braden candidly admitted, the goal of these endeavors has been to promote the compatible or respectable left, which is opposed to actually existing socialism. "In much of Europe in the 1950s," he explained, "socialists, people who called themselves 'left'...were the only people who gave a damn about fighting communism."[49] This is why the CIA lavishly funded anti-communist leftist intellectuals and promoted their work around the world. The Congress for Cultural Freedom (CCF), one of its most important front organizations, has been described by Hugh Wilford as one of the largest patrons of art and culture in the history of the world.[50] It established offices in thirty-five countries, mobilized an army of about 280 employees, published or supported some fifty prestigious journals around the world, planned or sponsored 135 international conferences and seminars, published at least 170 books, ran a press service whose reports reached five million readers, and much more. Prominent Western Marxists such as Horkheimer participated in its junkets. Others, like Adorno, had their work published and translated in its journals, while directly collaborating with CIA agent Melvin Lasky, who took the lead in the German anti-communist *Kulturkampf*. In 1975, when the Church Committee released its report on the U.S. intelligence community and its abuses, the CIA admitted that it was in contact with "many thousands" of academics in "hundreds" of institutions (and no reform since has prevented it from continuing or expanding this practice).[51]

The opportunism of the Western Marxists that Losurdo critiques must be understood via an analysis of class interest. They are all professional intellectuals ensconced in elite networks in the Global North and are part of what some call the new petty bourgeoisie, meaning the professional-managerial class stratum in the imperialist core. "Afraid of proletarianization below, attracted to the bourgeoisie above," while often being resentful of its overlords but devoid of a long-term collective political project, the new petty bourgeoisie sometimes celebrates jacqueries and supports greater access to power for its social group. However, it does not generally seek concrete system change because "it does not want to break the ladders by which it imagines it can climb."[52] It is here that it becomes clear that many of the Western Marxists within this class stratum occupy the position of radical recuperators: presenting themselves as representing the interests of the oppressed, but devoid of a practical program for social transformation, they ultimately seek to recuperate potentially insurgent forces within the capitalist order by guiding the masses toward symbolic or discursive solutions, such as consumerism within the confines of the imperial theory industry. This false solution to very real problems has the added benefit of bolstering the social standing of the petty-bourgeois producers of these intellectual consumer goods.

Most Western Marxists have understood, at least implicitly, that, in order to climb the social ladder in the capitalist world, they need to give to the system of knowledge production what it demands, in particular, opposition to actually existing socialism. In return for this, they will be festooned by the very system they feign to oppose. If they pursue their social ascendency as the *enfants terribles* of capital with the rabid alacrity of a Žižek, they might even make it, like him, into the list of the "Top 100 Global Thinkers" in *Foreign Policy* (a journal with ties to the U.S. State Department). This philosophic grifter's best idea, according to this magazine with links to the engine of U.S. imperialism, should be no cause for surprise: "The big revolution the left is waiting for will never come."[53]

Losurdo chose a different path characterized by a profound integrity and a humble dedication to the emancipation of the global working and oppressed masses. Rather than allowing himself to be determined by the objective forces of his existence as a professional intellectual in the West, he engaged in a self-critical examination of the very conditions of possibility of his intellectual production. This was surely facilitated by his being in constant dialogue with political parties and the global communist movement. His work is thereby a testament to the fact that subjective freedom is not enhanced by ignoring the objective forces that determine our thoughts and actions, but precisely by recognizing the extent to which our worldviews have been conditioned by social determinants. This form of objective ideology critique, meaning criticism of the objective determinations of our individual ideology rooted in the economic base and global class struggle, is precisely what his work demands. Those in the imperial core need to ask if their assumptions about the world are not largely a consequence of forces—like the deep history of imperialism—of which they remain, perhaps willfully, ignorant.

Socialism or Imperial Barbarism in the Twenty-First Century

> The struggle against imperialism, for liberation from colonial or neocolonial shackles, which is being carried out by means of political weapons, arms, or a combination of the two, is not separate from the struggle against backwardness and poverty. Both are stages on the same road leading toward the creation of a new society of justice and plenty.
>
> —Ernesto "Che" Guevara[54]

One of the dominant slogans of neoliberal ideology, proffered by

Margaret Thatcher, holds that "There Is No Alternative" (TINA) to capitalism. It is a historical irony that many Western Marxists who are nominally committed to building a world beyond capitalism nonetheless accept Thatcher's dictum. Ostensibly desiring an alternative to capitalism while regularly denigrating historical efforts to construct socialism has, in effect, produced an idealist version of TINA. The latter holds that the sole alternative to capitalism exists as an unrealized potential that only coheres in the *ideas* of professional intellectuals (but certainly not in the practices of people in socialist societies unless, in extreme cases, they are consigned to brief eruptions in the past). This idealist anti-capitalism, hegemonic in the West's supposedly radical intelligentsia, not only acquiesces to Western imperialism's triumphalist claims about the end of socialism; it also often accepts the ruse that imperialism no longer structures political and economic relations around the world (Hardt and Negri's *Empire* is one infamous example of such an account).[55] These two tendencies go hand-in-hand, as the dismissal of imperialism undergirds the denigration of socialist states' struggles against it, including and especially via their efforts to develop in order to avoid being turned back into colonies or semi-colonies of the imperialist powers.

The confluence between this idealist version of TINA and support for imperialism is readily visible in the work of the illustrious director of the Frankfurt School, Max Horkheimer. Although he never tired of dismissing actually existing socialism as barbaric and even fascist, he declared his unwavering support for the U.S. anti-communist intervention in Vietnam. This was his justification: "In America, when it is necessary to conduct a war,—and now listen to me ... it is not so much a question of the defense of the homeland, but it is essentially a matter of the defense of the Constitution, the defense of the rights of man."[56] Some thirty years later, the co-author of *Empire*, Michael Hardt, repeated Horkheimer's claim nearly verbatim. NATO's bombing of Yugoslavia—which was part of the neocolonial neoliberal counter-revolution and openly violated international law—was "not the deed of American imperialism," he flatly declared, but was "actually intended to safeguard human rights."[57]

Losurdo's work offers an invaluable antidote to this anti-communist and pro-imperialist tendency within Western Marxism. He demonstrates how neoliberalism, which emerged in the 1970s and continues today, has always been an imperialist project aimed not only at rolling back gains made by the global working class, but specifically at countering the efforts of colonized and formerly colonized people to resist imperialist subordination.[58] He also provides a sober historical-materialist analysis of actually existing socialism, which makes patently clear that an alternative to capitalism is not just an idea, but a practical process that may be long, but is well underway.

The People's Republic of China (PRC), the largest and most prominent socialist state-building project, is central to Losurdo's understanding of the contemporary world. He has mobilized his extensive knowledge to dismantle myths about it promulgated by the Western bourgeoisie and its ideological gatekeepers, notably that it is capitalist and imperialist.[59] He has also foregrounded China's remarkable ability to learn from the successes and failures of socialist projects, including its own and those of the Soviet Union. Its ongoing revolutionary program is thus deeply rooted in what Losurdo calls "a process of learning" and a long-term commitment to building socialism step by step. He rejects the tendency on the part of certain Western Marxists to fetishize and misrepresent the Cultural Revolution as a great but lost opportunity to create a revolution within the revolution. He also critically dismantles the widespread idea in the West that the leadership of Deng Xiaoping led to a fulsome embrace of neoliberal capitalism. Against these established Western positions, Losurdo demonstrates how China's developmental project—not unlike Lenin's New Economic Policy in the USSR—has integrated elements of capitalism in order to develop the productive forces and gain access to the advanced science and technology of the West.[60] As Losurdo argues, Deng was integral to the project of liberating Marxism-Leninism from populist and pauperizing tendencies in order to develop socialism as the project of eliminating misery and fostering "common prosperity."[61] This does not mean that he idolizes Deng or simplistically champions him over Mao, nor does it imply that he misrecognizes the important foundations laid in the early decades of Communist rule in China. It is rather that he advances a more dialectically nuanced understanding of the evolution of Chinese socialism that rejects the assumption—widely held in the West—that the reform and opening-up constituted an abandonment of its fundamental principles.

For independent nation-states that have historically been subject to colonial or neocolonial domination, their struggle for national liberation has passed from a political-military phase, Losurdo argues, to a political-economic phase wherein the development of the productive forces is of paramount importance.[62] Development is needed if these countries are to maintain independence and avoid being subordinated to imperialist powers through relations of economic dependency. It is also required to meet the needs of people who have been subject to great privation owing to the conditions of underdevelopment imposed upon them.

The PRC's gains on this front are remarkable, a fact recognized by sources that could not be suspected of pro-China bias, such as the World Bank. When the Communists came to power in 1949, China was an underdeveloped country with a largely illiterate population that had suffered from a century of humiliation, meaning foreign conquest, capitalist rapine, and subordination to imperialist powers. In over seventy years of Communist Party rule, the country has been completely transformed. Life expectancy, which was only around thirty years in the late 1940s, has been increased to seventy-seven years, surpassing life expectancy in the United States.[63] Aggregating data from multiple sources, including the World Bank, John Ross argues that "China's rate of increase of life expectancy in the three decades after 1949 was the fastest ever recorded in a major country in human history."[64] Ross also marshals extensive evidence to demonstrate that "in seven decades, China's economy will have gone from being only one-sixth the size of the U.S. to overtaking it."[65]

This has required monumental sacrifices on the part of the Chinese people, which is one of the contradictions inherent in socialist development (in part because it does not rely on colonialism like capitalist development). However, the government has also set its sights on overcoming these and other contradictions. In this regard, it has overseen the greatest poverty alleviation program in the history of humanity, lifting 850 million people out of extreme poverty (more than the entire population of Latin America).[66] The PRC also launched the Belt and Road Initiative (BRI) in 2013, an ambitious project aimed at improving global infrastructure and fostering mutually beneficial economic growth. Offering a model for development that stands in stark contrast to the neocolonial and imperialist paradigm promoted by the dominant capitalist countries, the BRI has attracted, as of fall 2023, the participation of 151 member countries.[67] China has also been a driving force behind BRICS, the Shanghai Cooperation Organization, and other international projects aimed—among other things—at developing trade and organizational infrastructure for a multipolar world.

The Chinese development model offers a crucial alternative to the capitalist West as the Chinese Communist Party seeks a form of modernization characterized by people-centered development and the "harmonious coexistence between man and nature."[68] As John Bellamy Foster notes, China has implemented major ecological reforms even as it has sought "rapid economic growth aimed at bringing China up to a level with the West."[69] These include "pollution reduction; reforestation and afforestation; development of alternative energy sources; imposing restrictions in sensitive river areas; rural revitalization; food self-sufficiency through collective means" and the reduction of reliance on coal.[70] Moreover, the PRC acknowledges that economic growth will need to be slowed in the coming decades in order for China to meet its stated goals of implementing an "ecological civilization" and reaching net-zero carbon emissions by the mid-twenty-first century.[71]

Losurdo was always careful to avoid the idealist belief in anything like a perfect model, and he acknowledged the historical contingencies of class struggles.[72] While noting ongoing battles within the Chinese Communist Party between a primarily nationalist current and one with broader communist ambitions, he did not purport to predict their outcome. Nonetheless, he had a deep understanding of the world-historical significance of China's socialist project. It is aimed at overcoming what he called the "great divergence," or the international division of humanity between the labor aristocracy in the capitalist core and the workers and peasants in the colonial or semi-colonial periphery. "China," he wrote, "is the country that more than any other is challenging the international division of labor imposed by colonialism and imperialism, and furthering the end of the Columbian epoch—a fact of enormous, progressive historical significance."[73]

Although many Western Marxists unquestioningly refer to China as authoritarian, capitalist, or even dictatorial, the PRC is a representative and consultatory "whole-process people's democracy" founded on socialist principles of party control of the state and the towering heights of the economy.[74] There is indeed a capitalist sector and even a capitalist class stratum that has been allowed to operate in China, but it does not control the state or key pillars of the economy. Having emerged within a capitalist-dominated world, and faced with the very real choice of *develop or die*, this has been a tactical decision for socialist China. Its overarching strategy of building socialism, however, has been clearly outlined and maintained, according to Losurdo, by the likes of Deng, and now Xi Jinping.

The PRC is by no means the only example of successful socialist state-building projects—and much could be added here about other important examples—but it is certainly the largest and most visible. This is precisely why the capitalist powers, and in particular the United States, are intent on subordinating China and attempting to overthrow its leadership. In spite of all of the propaganda that they pump out to demonize China, the power elite understands full well the reality behind its lies: the PRC is a very real threat to its imperial dominion. It refuses to return to the status of a colony or semi-colony, and it offers an alternative framework of international development that is more attractive to most of the world than the imperialist model imposed by the West.

Class Struggle in Theory: From Lenin to Losurdo

Socialism or barbaric imperialism with an increasing risk of human annihilation: this is the basic choice that humanity faces in the early twenty-first century, when nuclear war and complete ecological collapse are imminent possibilities. The Western Marxists, as Losurdo predicted, have continued their practice of gesturing toward a magical beyond while pursuing the terrestrial task of advancing their careers, opposing socialism in the real world, and, in numerous instances, openly supporting imperialism, as in Žižek's fulsome support for the U.S.-led proxy war in Ukraine.[75]

Losurdo invites us, instead, to contribute to the collective project of developing the rich tradition of critical communism.[76] Such an orientation endeavors to learn practical lessons from the global history of class struggle, rather than seeking refuge in the realm of ideas and purported theoretical blueprints. This requires engaging in an ongoing process of learning and humble self-critique based on objective reality and the primacy of practice, thereby contributing to the difficult but necessary project of charting uncharted territory, namely that of collectively building and supporting a world of common prosperity. For Western Marxism—and the Western Left more generally—to shift its orientation, such self-critique is absolutely necessary, and Losurdo's work is an invaluable guide to this ideological realignment.[77]

In 1918, when the recently minted USSR was being invaded and the imperialist barbarians were literally at the gates, Lenin reached not for a gun but for his pen. As if there were no more urgent task, which might seem shocking given the situation, he wrote a fiery reply to Karl Kautsky titled *The Proletarian Revolution and the Renegade Kautsky*.[78] From the vantage point of this peerless leader of the Russian Revolution, one of the most pressing tasks was to reorient the global communist movement away from Kautsky's social chauvinist support for imperialism. This required engaging in class struggle in theory, fighting for the hearts and minds of the working and oppressed of the world, likely with the hope that the revolution would spread or, at a minimum, that the imperialist armies would lose some workers from their ranks.

Although written in a very different context, Losurdo's work is characterized by a similar urgency and accountability to the needs of the struggle. In a world facing intensifying capitalist degradation and imperialist barbarism, with the increasing threats of nuclear apocalypse and the thoroughgoing destruction of the biosphere, it forces us to reply to the same straightforward question posed by Lenin: which side are you on, that of the imperialists and their well-paid ideological lackeys, or that of the people in their struggle for liberation and a sustainable world?

NOTE FROM THE TRANSLATORS AND EDITORS

Losurdo's referencing system is somewhat idiosyncratic. The translators and editors were able to fill in certain gaps: the edition of the book cited, missing page numbers, some unreferenced quotations. Generally, when an end note occurs at the end of a paragraph, the quotations within that paragraph derive from the source cited in the note. In some places, the reverse is true. An end note covers quotations in succeeding paragraphs. The context is critical in these cases. There are a few cases in which it was not possible to find the exact source. In most of these, the editors found a source that conveys the ideas expressed in the text, and they created an appropriate end note.

ACKNOWLEDGMENTS

I was helped in the bibliographical research and correction the text by Stefano Azzarà, Paolo Ercolani, Elena Fabrizio, Giorgio Grimaldi (who edited the index of names), and Aldo Trotta. To all of them, my thanks.

PREMISE

What is Western Marxism?

This book takes its title from a 1976 book in which an English philosopher, Marxist, and communist (Trotskyist) militant invited "Western Marxism" to finally declare its total distinctness and independence from the caricature of Marxism in the officially socialist and Marxist countries, all of which were in the East. The Soviet Union was particularly targeted. There, notwithstanding the October Revolution and the example of Lenin, Marxism was by now "a memory of the past"; Stalin and "collectivization" had put "an end to all serious theoretical work." Nor did "People's China" come out much better. To see it as an "alternative model" meant confirming "the political heterogeneity of Western Marxism." The condemnation included the Western Communist parties, characterized by their "absolute loyalty to Soviet positions" and, therefore, were also de facto Eastern or Easternizing.[1]

The indictment did not spare even the party of Gramsci and Togliatti, which had constantly wedded affirmation of the universal value of the October Revolution with emphasis on the profound political and cultural differences between the East and the West, and so with theorizing the necessity of developing a national path to socialism, one adequate to the needs of countries in the West. The English philosopher was implacable: "No intellectual (or worker) within a mass communist party of this period, not integrated into its leadership, could make the smallest independent pronouncement on major political issues."[2] And so: "The figure of Gramsci was converted into the official ideological icon of the Party, invoked on every public occasion, while his actual writings were manipulated or neglected."[3] How the obtuse guardians of an arid cultural desert succeeded in attracting *en masse* fierce and sophisticated intellectuals, exercised an extraordinary influence and hegemony over Italian culture, and enjoyed great international prestige remains a mystery.

Perry Anderson was not the first to note the divergence between Western and Eastern Marxism. Writing in the early years of the Cold War, an eminent French philosopher, Maurice Merleau-Ponty, observed:

> The revolutionary politics which, in the perspective of 1917, was historically to take the place of "liberal" politics—occupied with difficult organizational problems, with defense, and with improvements—has become more and more a politics for new countries, the means for semi-colonial countries (or for civilizations long since paralyzed) to change to modern modes of production. The immense apparatus that it constructed, with its disciplines and its privileges, at the moment that it shows itself to be efficacious for building an industry or for putting a new proletariat to work, evacuates the terrain of the proletariat as the ruling class and forfeits the mystery of civilization which, according to Marx, the Western proletariat carried.[4]

The previous year, at Dien Bien Phu, the powerful army of colonialist France was soundly defeated by the Vietnamese movement and the people's army led by the Communist Party. Everywhere in Asia, echoes rang of the strategic victory of anticolonialism that had brought about the founding of the People's Republic of China. Yes, communism was revealed as the leading force of the anticolonial revolution and, once in power, of the accelerated development that the "semi-colonial economies" urgently needed. These were undeniable results and successes, but, asked the French philosopher, were they part of the communism that the "Western proletariat" had the historic mission of building, at least in the eyes of Marx and of "Western Marxism"?[5]

Here we encounter the expression "Western Marxism" for the first time. It was not, however, contrasted positively to the Eastern kind. If anything, only in the context of a complex critique of Marx and communism could "Western" Marxism constitute the principal object. Once the initial hopes for a radically new society and for the "withering away of the state apparatus" vanished, one conclusion emerged: "Today's communism verges on *progressivism*," and progressivism cannot ignore the concrete conditions of the country or the area in which political action takes place.[6] Done once and for all with the messianic prospect of the total regeneration of humanity, it was necessary to go on a case-by-case basis: "Where there is a choice between famine and the communist apparatus, the decision (in favor of the latter) goes without saying," and probably for the French philosopher the decision went without saying when it was between colonial subjection and anticolonial revolution (especially led by the communists). The West, however, presented a very different picture: Was the communist revolution really necessary and beneficial, and what would be its concrete results?[7]

This stance had many weaknesses. To better refute it, the French philosopher accentuated the messianic tendency in Marx and Engels. He did not consider that they speak of "the withering away of the state" and, sometimes, of the "withering away of the state in a strictly political sense"; only the former formulation can be accused of messianism (and of anarchism).[8] Second, Merleau-Ponty avoided interrogating the possible relationship between the end of colonialism in all its forms and the building of a post-capitalist society. Third, and above all, can we consider the anticolonial struggle as an exclusive problem of the East? To support the struggles against colonial and neocolonial subordination, absolving those responsible for such policies would be inadmissible. And not only for ethical reasons. The two world wars had demonstrated that colonial expansionism flowed through ruinous inter-imperialist rivalries to have a global impact; the flames ignited a few years earlier by Hitler in his attempt to build the German colonial empire in Eastern Europe had ended by burning down the West as well, and Germany itself.

Having made this criticism, the French philosopher deserves credit for being the first to have identified the objective sociopolitical reasons that led to the bifurcation between the two Marxisms. In the East, and in practically all of the countries where communists had taken power, the principal problem of political leadership was not the "withering away of the state apparatus" but how to avoid the danger of colonial or neocolonial subjection and how, therefore, to make up for backwardness in relation to the more industrially advanced countries.

Merleau-Ponty was far from disavowing Eastern Marxism in the name of the Western version. If we want to find a precedent for Perry Anderson's attitude, we must search elsewhere. Before the British and the French philosophers, Max Horkheimer, in 1942, called attention to the turn that had occurred in the land of the October Revolution: the Soviet Communists had abandoned "the abolition of the state" to concentrate on the problem of accelerated development of the "industrially backward fatherland." It was a fitting observation, unfortunately, formulated as a contemptuous condemnation. The *Wehrmacht* was at the gates of Moscow, and to regret or be indignant over the fact that the Soviet leaders were not worrying about how to realize the ideal of the withering away was grotesque (Hitler, in his way, would have shared such regret and indignation!). The German philosopher did not realize that the behavior he reproached had enabled the Soviet Union to escape from the colonialist subjection and slavery that the Third Reich sought to impose on it. The desperate struggle waged in the East to resist a colonial war of decimation and enslavement seemed irrelevant to a philosopher who appreciated not Marx's program of the revolutionary transformation of what exists so much as the pursuit of a remote future ideal of a society free of contradictions and conflict, and therefore without the need for a state apparatus.[9]

More than a quarter of a century later, Horkheimer returned to the theme of the abolition of the state, albeit referring this time not to the authors of the *Manifesto of the Communist Party* but rather to Schopenhauer. On the one hand, he paid homage to Marx—"the

Premise 41

time has come to finally make the Marxian doctrine, in the West, one of the principal materials of teaching"; on the other, he expressed his annoyance with the idea that "in many Eastern countries [Marxism] serves as a useful ideology for making up the advantage gained by the West in industrial production."[10] The "Marxian doctrine" celebrated here bore no relation to North Vietnam's development of its productive forces, occupied as it was with defending itself against a barbaric aggression that was ready to use chemical weapons. But nevertheless, Horkheimer indulged and even supported it. As in 1942, so it was in 1968; utopia looked with disdain at the dramatic struggles in the East that were not a subjective choice but dictated by an objective situation. But without recourse to this expression, Western Marxism had already turned its back on that of the East.

We must ask: When did the bifurcation between the two Marxisms begin? With the rise of Stalin's autocracy, as Anderson maintains? And if, instead, we find it was already present the day after the turning point of 1917? And if the first cracks had already emerged when unity appeared as firm as ever, cemented by the chorus of indignation over the foul butchery of the First World War and the capitalist-imperialist system accused of provoking it? And if the cracks and the subsequent alienation, beyond those of different objective conditions and cultural traditions, are because of the theoretical and political limits from the start of Western Marxism, that most sophisticated version, battle-tested on the academic plane?

It was a long road to the manifesto in which Anderson proclaimed the excellence of Western Marxism, finally liberated from the suffocating embrace of Eastern Marxism. A bright new life seemed to be on the horizon for the former; in fact, its premise was suicidal. We are dealing with important but largely ignored political and philosophical chapters of history that my book seeks to reconstruct, with the aim also of interrogating the prospects for a rebirth, on new bases, of Western Marxism.

PART I

1914 and 1917:
The Birth of Western and Eastern Marxism

1. THE TURNING POINT OF AUGUST 1914 IN THE WEST

The history that I propose to reconstruct begins between August 1914 and October 1917, between the outbreak of the First World War and the victory of the October Revolution. On the wave of these two epochal events, Marxism experienced a global diffusion that projected it well beyond the Western borders where it had been confined since the Second International. There is, however, another side to the triumphal coin: the encounter through culture, geopolitics, and economic-social conditions among very different peoples stimulated an internal process of differentiation, with the emergence of contradictions and conflicts unknown previously. To understand these, we must interrogate the deep-seated motivations that led to one adhering to the communist and Marxist movements that took form in those years.

In the West, the radical, indeed apocalyptic historical turning point is undoubtedly represented by the scale and the flames of the First World War. The exhaustion, disgust, and indignation over the interminable slaughter promoted the rapid spread of the communist movement. What had already happened in Italy in the months or even weeks that preceded the rise of the Bolsheviks to power is symptomatic. Between February and October 1917, two delegates of the provisional government constituted in Moscow after the overthrow of the Czarist autocracy arrived in Turin to contact an allied country in the ongoing war and to counter rising pacifist tendencies. Before they had even arrived, the delegates made clear their hostility to the Bolsheviks (who demanded immediate peace). But, when Kerensky's emissaries appeared on the balcony of the Siccardi Palace, the crowd of forty-thousand workers that had been waiting for them started shouting, "Viva Lenin!"

It was, to be exact, August 13, 1917. Ten days later, barricades went up to support the antiwar opposition, resulting in Turin being declared a war zone and the creation of military tribunals.[1] We could say that the mass of protesters and rebels joined the October Revolution before it had even occurred and joined it on the wave of antiwar struggle. In our day, it is politically correct to speak of October 1917 in Russia not as a revolution but rather as a coup d'état, except that we see the protagonist of this supposed coup provoke an almost-revolution thousands of kilometers away before it had even taken power! This happened because his name and the party he guided were inextricably connected to an unequivocal condemnation of the war and the sociopolitical system accused of provoking it.

This spiritual climate explains the formidable attraction that the October Revolution exercised in the West not only on the masses but also on intellectuals of the highest level. One thinks of Georg Lukács. In his autobiography, he recalls, "My interest in ethics led me to the revolution"; this interest was one with his opposition to the war. He saw this opposition as constituted by the most elementary forms of morality:

> I was sharply opposed to it from the outset . . . my hostility to positivism was partly politically motivated. For all my condemnation of conditions in Hungary, this did not mean I was prepared to accept British Parliamentarianism as an alternative ideal. But at the time, I perceived nothing with which to replace the existing order. From that

point of view, the Revolution of 1917 was a great experience since it made clear that things could be otherwise. Whatever view one took of this "otherwise," it made a decisive difference to all our lives or at least to the lives of a considerable proportion of our generation.[2]

Analogously, Ernst Bloch writes, speaking of the young Hungarian philosopher and himself, "At the start of the war, in 1914, we felt completely lost. This war became a decisive factor in the development of each of us. For him, the link with the communist movement was both a support and a refuge."[3] Even without forming organic relationships with the party and the communist movement, on the plane of ideas, the young German philosopher reached conclusions not dissimilar to those of the young Hungarian philosopher. Later, Bloch would write that he took in "the Russian Revolution" as "an unprecedented liberating jubilee."[4] In *The Spirit of Utopia*, composed mainly during the war years, a period among the "most infamous in history," he wrote that if "Europe"—responsible for the war—"prompts eternal death," the fact that the country of the October Revolution resisted the aggression of this or that capitalist power was to be celebrated. Yes, "there stands, unbowed, a Marxist republic in Russia." In any case, more than ever, he called for "the true total revolution" invoked by Marx that will realize "freedom" and signal "the beginning of world history after prehistory."[5] The October Revolution was the truth finally discovered of how many had worked to make concrete the struggle against the war, even against the "genocide" (*Völkermord*) that was occurring. We turn, this time, to the language of two leaders of the socialist and anti-militarist movement, Rosa Luxemburg and Karl Liebknecht. The future leaders of the October Revolution (some of whom had been educated in the West) also read and experienced the First World War as the definitive demonstration of the intrinsic horror of the capitalist-imperialist system and the absolute necessity of overthrowing it. To give a few examples: Bukharin spoke of the "horrid factory of corpses," and Stalin of "mass extermination of the life forces of the people." The picture painted by Trotsky was particularly eloquent: "The work of Cain of the 'patriotic press' of the two opposed sides was the irrefutable demonstration of the moral decadence of bourgeois society." Yes, humanity had fallen back into a "blind and shameful barbarism," trying to set fire to a "contest of bloody folly" by using the most advanced technologies to militaristic ends; it was a "scientific barbarism," which raised up the greatest discoveries of humanity "only to destroy the foundations of civilized social life and annihilate the human race."

All the good that civilization had produced had been drowned in blood and the filth of the trenches: "health comfort, hygiene, the usual everyday relationships, the bonds of friendship, professional obligations and in the last analysis the apparently indestructible rules of morality." Later, but still regarding the catastrophe that broke out in 1914, the term "holocaust" emerged. On August 31, 1939, Molotov accused France and England of having rejected the Soviet policy of collective security in the hopes of unleashing the Third Reich against the USSR, without hesitating thereby to provoke "a new great massacre, a new holocaust of the nations."

2. The Turning Point of October 1917 in the East

In Asia, the First World War did not arouse the same emotions as in Europe, not only because the battlefields were thousands of kilometers away. In the colonies and semi-colonies, the capitalist-colonialist system had revealed its terrible capacity for oppression and violence well before August 1914. For China, the tragic turning point was the Opium Wars. To neutralize "the British narco traffickers" and put an end to the opium trade, whose devastating effects were by this point known to all, the Taiping Rebellion erupted between 1851 and 1864, "the bloodiest civil war in the history of the world, with an estimated twenty million to thirty million dead."[6] After powerfully contributing to provoking it, the West became its beneficiary since afterward it extended its control over a lacerated and even more defenseless country. A historical period opened that saw "China crucified" (the Western butchers were joined in the meantime by Russia and Japan). To the "foreign bombardments" and "the most terrible insurrections in her history" were added "great natural cataclysms" to which the country, falling apart, could offer no resistance. "Almost certainly, the number of victims involved had never been so high in the history of the world."[7]

Compared to this gigantic tragedy, the outbreak of the First World War is a small affair. Asked to intervene alongside Great Britain, Sun Yat-Sen, the president of the republic born of the revolution of 1911 and the overthrow of the Manchu Dynasty, replied in a famous letter to Lloyd George that "quarrels among whites did not concern the Chinese."[8] The victory of one or the other side would not have changed anything in the oppressive behavior of the capitalist and colonialist West. What did provide a scintilla of hope at the end of the tragic era that began with the Opium Wars and made Sun Yat-Sen enthusiastic was the rise of the Bolsheviks to power. That promised to put an end to the war but also, above all, to colonial slavery.

This second aspect led the Chinese leader to draw up the balance sheet on a chapter of history whose end could finally be glimpsed, thanks to the October Revolution: "The Indians in America have been almost destroyed by them," and a similar fate loomed over the other colonized peoples, including the Chinese. Their situation was desperate, except that "the 150 million Slavs have risen to speak a word of justice for the oppressed nations, and to oppose imperialism and militarism." So "without anyone expecting it, a great hope was born for humanity, the Russian Revolution." Imperialism didn't take long to respond: "The great powers attacked Lenin ... because Lenin engaged in the actual work of liberation and self-determination," but humanity would not easily renounce the possibility of liberating the oppressed peoples from colonial domination.[9]

Certainly, Sun Yat-Sen was not a Marxist nor a communist, but from the "great hope" he described in sometimes naïve but moving language we can understand the founding of the Chinese Communist Party (CCP) on July 1, 1921.

In light of all this, the characterization of the twentieth century as "a brief century" that, according to Eric Hobsbawm, began with the traumatic experience of the First World War, is affected by Eurocentrism. An *ante litteram* critic of this view emerged from the speech on

December 26, 1920, that "the delegate of Indochina" gave at the Congress of Tours of the Socialist Party of France:

> You all have known that French imperialism entered Indochina half a century ago. In its selfish interests, it conquered our country with bayonets. Since then we have not only been oppressed and exploited shamelessly, but also tortured and poisoned pitilessly. Plainly speaking, we have been poisoned with opium, alcohol, etc. I cannot, in some minutes, reveal all the atrocities that the predatory capitalists have inflicted on Indochina. Prisons outnumber schools and are always overcrowded with detainees. Any natives having socialist ideas are arrested and sometimes murdered without trial. Such is the so-called justice in Indochina. In that country, the Vietnamese are discriminated against, they do not enjoy safety like Europeans or those having European citizenship.

After making these grave accusations, "the delegate from Indochina" (who much later would become famous worldwide as Ho Chi Minh) concluded, "We have realized that the Socialist Party's joining the Third International means that it has practically promised that from now on it will correctly assess the importance of the colonial question."[10] Notwithstanding the cautious language, which was intended to avoid conflict, a point emerges clearly: The turning point in world history is not August 1914, when a tragedy that had been occurring for a long time in the colonies spread to Europe. Rather, it was October 1917, that is, the revolution, that brought hope for the end of this tragedy to the colonies. Lenin stressed the horror of colonialism: "The most liberal and radical personalities of free Britain . . . become regular Genghis Khans when appointed to govern India."[11] He had Marx's lesson on Ireland to back him up. Marx blasted liberal England's treatment of Ireland (a colony, even if located in Europe): it is a policy even more ruthless than Czarist and autocratic Russia carries out in Poland; indeed, it is a terroristic policy that is "unheard of in Europe" and can find an analogy only among "the Mongols."[12] Just as we see in the appeal launched by Ho Chi Minh to his party comrades to not lose sight of the colonial question, the lessons of Marx on the macroscopic terms of exclusion from liberal freedom find more attentive listeners in the East than in the West. It is the first such relevant difference, but it will certainly not be the last.

3. State and Nation in the West and the East

In Europe, because the rejection of the war inspired the choice of revolution, critics of the existing order aimed mainly at the state apparatus and the military. Lukács denounced obligatory conscription as "the most abject slavery that has ever existed" and condemned "the Moloch of militarism" that devoured millions of human victims.[13] Some years later, Walter Benjamin built on the critique of "obligatory military service" that was at the heart of "militarism," understood as "the obligation of the universal recourse to violence as a means for pursuing the ends of the State," to proceed to a global condemnation without the appeal of the existing order: "The last war" revealed the infamy of which it was capable.[14] In an early, unfinished 1915 essay on Dostoevsky, Lukács, horrified by total mobilization, the military code, and the execution squads, defined the state as "organized tuberculosis" and as "organized immorality," manifested "externally as will to power, as war, as conquest, as vengeance."[15]

"Yes," says Bloch, "the state reveals itself as a discrete, heathenish, satanic coercion-materiality." It was necessary to do away once and for all with this monster: "May it have a Bolshevistic function for a time as a transitionally necessary evil." It is the patriotic or chauvinistic pathos that feeds "the militaristic State," the insatiable Moloch that devours men. And against this as well, Bloch breathed words of fire: "The murderous coercion of universal conscription" served not the nation as official ideology pretends, but the capitalist "stock exchange" and the Hohenzollern dynasty. Except that, together with patriotic and chauvinistic pathos, the very idea of nation itself ended up being rejected as well: To the rhetoric of "the native soil" and "the traditionalism of *Vaterland*" are counterposed "the truly Christian . . . idea of humanity" and "medieval" universalism, which know no national (or state) borders.[16] The influence of anarchism is quite evident, just as it is evident in Benjamin, who, aside from denouncing obligatory military service, ended up identifying and jointly criticizing violence, law, and power.

It would be in vain to search for these anarchistic tones in the Marxist and Communist movement that was forming in the East in the wake of the October Revolution. It is a difference whose foundations can be discerned already in the discourses of Lenin. During the war, with his eyes fixed on Europe, the great revolutionary repeatedly denounced militarization and total mobilization as "military slavery" imposed on the population.[17] It was not only the front that was regimented by the code of war and by terror; the "rear" was transformed as well, even in "the more advanced countries," in "cases of martial law for the workers." Written and published while the butchery of war was at its most furious and on the eve of the revolution called forth to end it, *State and Revolution* formulates the thesis that the victorious proletariat "needs only a state which is withering away."[18] It is the "necessary but transitory evil" that Bloch talked about. In another vein, Lenin defined imperialism as the presumption of being "model nations" and attributing to themselves "the exclusive privilege of forming states."[19] In other words, beyond its economic sacking of other countries, he characterizes imperialism by its political oppression of nations and hierarchy. The exploited and oppressed were branded as incapable of governing themselves or constituting independent states; the struggle to shake off this stigma was a struggle for recognition. It was about liquidating colonial subjection to construct an independent national state. What inspired the revolution of colonial peoples was not the password of a "state that is withering away" but a state that is being built.

We can well understand the tones that resounded from the East. Take Sun Yat-Sen. He had long lived abroad and searched for motivations and inspiration to help overthrow the dilapidated Manchu Dynasty and found the first Chinese Republic. He, therefore, can't be accused of xenophobia. However, he summarizes the thinking of the anticolonial movement, including its communist faction: "To preserve their privileged position in oppressed countries as well as their supremacy over the world, the imperialist powers are advocating the doctrine of cosmopolitanism to make the world submissive and obedient." These do everything they can to discredit patriotism as something "narrow and illiberal."[20]

Behind Sun Yat-Sen's position, as with the founding of the Chinese Communist Party, lie two events: On July 25, 1919, Lev Mikhailovich Karakhan, Vice-People's Commissar for Foreign Affairs, declared that Soviet Russia was ready to renounce "all territorial and other acquisitions" of the Czarist empire on Chinese soil, and to annul "all unequal treaties" that China signed under threats of bombardment and invading armies.[21] That summer, the Treaty of Versailles, which ended the First World War, transferred to Japan the privileges in Shandong that Imperial Germany had stripped from the Beijing government. A great wave of protest developed in China, the May 4th Movement, from which emerged not a few of the leaders and militants of the Chinese Communist Party. By then, it was clear to all that the Western democracies, having waged war against the Central Empires, raising the banner of freedom and self-determination of peoples, would not hesitate to perpetuate the semi-colonial condition of China. The only hope came from the country and the movement arising from the October Revolution, to which Chinese Communists looked, deciding to put themselves to the test in the struggle for national liberation. As Mao Zedong put it, "It was through the Russians that the Chinese found Marxism. Before the October Revolution, the Chinese were ignorant of Lenin and Stalin and did not even know of Marx and Engels. The salvoes of the October Revolution brought us Marxism-Leninism."[22]

While he was occupied with the War of National Resistance against Japanese imperialism, which sought to "subject all of China and to make the Chinese their colonial slaves," Mao recalled his first introduction (in the last years of the Manchu Dynasty) to the cause of revolution:

> In this period, I also began to have a certain amount of political consciousness, especially after I read a pamphlet telling of the dismemberment of China.... After I read this I felt depressed about the future of my country and began to realize that it was the duty of all the people to help save it.[23]

More than a decade later, on the immediate eve of the proclamation of the People's Republic, Mao recounted the story of his country. He invoked in particular the resistance to the powers involved in the Opium Wars, the Taiping Rebellion against the Manchu Dynasty, and "against the Ching, servants of imperialism," the war against Japan in 1894–1895, "the war against the aggression of the allied forces of the eight powers" (following the Boxer Rebellion), and, finally, "the Revolution of 1911 [that] broke out against the running dog of imperialism, the Ching Dynasty." So many struggles, so many defeats. How to explain the overthrow, which finally came about? Mao observed:

> For a long time in the course of this resistance movement, that is, for over seventy years from the Opium War of 1840 to the eve of the May 4th Movement of 1919, the Chinese had no ideological weapon with which to defend themselves against imperialism. The ideological weapons of the old die-hard feudalism were defeated, had to give way and were declared bankrupt. Having no other choice, the Chinese were compelled to arm themselves with such ideological weapons and political formulas as the theory of evolution, the theory of natural rights and of the bourgeois republic, which were all borrowed from the arsenal of the revolutionary period of the bourgeoisie in the West, the native home of imperialism. The Chinese organized political parties and made revolutions, believing that they could thus resist foreign powers and build a republic. However, all these ideological weapons, like those of feudalism, proved very feeble and in their turn had to give way and were withdrawn and declared bankrupt.
>
> The Russian Revolution of 1917 awakened the Chinese, and they learned something new, Marxism-Leninism. In China, the Communist Party was born, an epoch-making event. . . . Since they learned Marxism-Leninism, the Chinese people have ceased to be passive in spirit and gained the initiative. The period of modern world history in which the Chinese and Chinese culture were looked down upon should have ended from that moment.[24]

If, in the West, communism and Marxism are the truth and the weapon to end war and pull it up by the roots, in the East, communism and Marxism-Leninism are the truth and the ideological weapon to end a situation of oppression and being "looked down upon" by colonialism and by imperialism. It is a project that began with the Opium Wars, even before the founding of Marxism-Leninism and Marxism as such (in 1840, Marx was still a university student). It was not Marxism that provoked the revolution in China; it was the age-old resistance, the ongoing revolution of the Chinese people that found and became aware of itself in Marxist or Marxist-Leninist ideology and put an end to colonial domination. A few days after giving the above-cited speech, Mao declared, "Ours will no longer be a nation subject to insult and humiliation. We have stood up. The era in which the Chinese people were regarded as uncivilized is now ended."[25]

Let's return to the "delegate from Indochina" who, in 1920, spoke at the Congress of the French Socialist Party. When asking the party to join the Communist International, he still called himself Nguyen Ai Quoc, or "Nguyen the patriot."[26] He did not see any contradiction between internationalism and patriotism; indeed, the latter, in the situation in which Indochina found itself, was felt to be a concrete expression of internationalism. Some decades later, having become the leader of Vietnam, which at least in the north had begun to taste independence, Ho Chi Minh urged the young to commit themselves to study, calling on them as follows:

> Eighty years of slavery have diminished our country's strength. Now we must retrieve the heritage bequeathed to us by our ancestors.... Will Vietnam achieve fame and glory? Will her people occupy an honorable place on par with the other peoples of the five continents?[27]

Nine years before his death, on the occasion of his seventieth birthday, while one of the most barbaric colonial wars of the twentieth century raged in Indochina, Ho Chi Minh recalled his intellectual and political journey: "At first, patriotism, not yet communism, led me to have confidence in Lenin, in the Third International."[28] What led to such an emotional reaction were the appeals and the documents that had promoted the struggle for the liberation of the colonial peoples, emphasizing their right to constitute themselves as independent national States. "The theses of Lenin (on the national and colonial question) aroused in me great emotion, enthusiasm, great faith, and helped me see the problem clearly."[29] In his *Testament*, after having called his fellow citizens to the "patriotic struggle" and to the commitment "to save the fatherland," Ho Chi Minh added up his balance sheet: "With my whole life, body and soul, I served the fatherland, I served the revolution, I served the people."[30]

4. The Money Economy in the West and the East

Seen as a consequence of the imperialist contest for market domination and for raw materials, and the capitalist hunt for profits and for super profits, but above all as a moralizing key, the product of the *auri sacra fames* [accursed hunger for gold] rather than as the result of a determinate social system, the First World War aroused in the West a spiritual climate that found its most significant expression in Ernst Bloch. In his eyes, the transcendence of capitalism must involve "liberation from the materialism of class interests as such" and the "abolition of poverty and . . . all questions of economics." To that, not even the great revolutionaries have paid sufficient attention:

> Man does not live by bread alone. As extensively important as the external may be, and must be attended to, it still only suggests, it does not create, for human beings, not things, not their powerful process, outside of us and wrongly turned over onto us, invent history. What must still come economically, the necessary economic-institutional change, is defined by Marx, but the new man, the leap, the power of love and of light, morality itself, has not yet been allotted the desirable degree of autonomy in the definitive social order.[31]

Indeed, as Bloch emphasized in the first edition of *The Spirit of Utopia*, the Soviets in power in Russia were called upon to end not only "every private economy" but also every "money economy" and, with this, the "mercantile morality that consecrates all that is most evil in man." Together with economic power, it was power as such that must be questioned; in the final analysis, the "transformation of power into love" must be accomplished.[32] Walter Benjamin observed, "The modern economy, seen as a whole, resembles much less a machine that stands idle when abandoned by its stoker than a beast that goes berserk as soon as its tamer turns his back."[33] In other words, it was not about making the "machine" of the economy more efficient or less devastating, thanks to a revolutionary upheaval; instead, it was about caging or perhaps annihilating that beast that, notwithstanding every sociopolitical transformation, continues to be the economy as such.

Among the principal protagonists of the slaughter provoked by the imperialist competition was Russia, where, after the October Revolution, there likewise spread a vision that looked with disdain at the economic world in its totality and not incidentally, therefore, screamed at the scandal of the New Economic Policy (NEP). The NEP, begun in 1921, followed on the heels of a "war communism" that brought an egalitarian but desperate and coerced asceticism. It is a very different vision from that just analyzed above regarding the West, and it was recalled by a Soviet Communist Party militant in the 1940s:

> "We young Communists had all grown up believing that money was done away with once and for all," recalled one Bolshevik in the 1940s. "If money was reappearing, wouldn't rich people reappear too? Weren't we on the slippery slope that led back to capitalism?"[34]

Only with difficulty and faced with charges of betrayal could Lenin bring to the center of attention the problem of economic development in a backward country that had exited the First World War and the civil war devastated and now had to confront an international situation thick with peril. Right before his death, Stalin felt obligated to engage in a polemic against those who, in the name of the struggle against capitalism, sought to end "commercial production" and "commodity circulation" and do away with the "money economy."[35]

The situation was very different in China. Let's look at what happened in the liberated areas governed by the Communist Party from the late 1920s. The anti-communist Kuomintang and the Nanking government sought to force the Communists to capitulate through military force and economic strangulation. During his travels, Edgar Snow observed, "Trade between Red and White districts was prohibited by Nanking, but by using small mountain roads, and by oiling the palms of border guards, the Reds at times managed to carry on a fairly lively export business. Taking raw materials from the soviet districts, the transport corps in the service of the state trade bureau or the cooperatives exchanged them for Kuomintang money and needed manufactures."[36] Demonized in Russia and in Europe as an expression of a greedy and rotten world that needed to be demolished once and for all, the "money economy" and trade were instead synonymous here with physical survival and the defense of the revolutionary project to save China and to build a new and better world.

The contrast between the East and the West was further accentuated in the succeeding years. After the rise of Fascism and Nazism in Italy, Germany, and Japan, the struggle for wages and better conditions of life challenged production and war efforts, the aggressors' war machine, and the champions of revived colonial expansion. With mass rage over the Japanese invasion of China, we find what Mao defined as "the identity between the national and the class struggle."[37] From that moment, the commitment was to production and economic development because, above all, in the liberated zones controlled by the Communist Party, these were simultaneously integral to the national and class struggle. It is understandable then, that even in the heat of battle, Mao would call on the Communist leaders to give great attention to the economic dimension of the conflict:

> In the present war conditions, all organizations, schools and army units must make great efforts to grow vegetables, breed pigs, collect firewood, make charcoal, expand handicrafts and raise part of their own grain supply. At all levels, the leading personnel in the Party, government and army organizations and schools should master

all the skills involved in leading the masses in production. No one who fails to study production carefully can be considered a good leader."[38]

5. Science, Imperialist War, and Anticolonial Revolution

Let's return to the "delegate from Indochina" at the Congress of Tours in December 1920. We saw him travel for a long time in the West. Why? Troung Chinh, who in 1930 participated with Ho Chi Minh at the founding of the Indochinese Communist Party, explains. Judging from his testimony, the future leader of Vietnam stayed in France to obtain a cultural education in that country "and also science and technical knowledge."[39] Analogously, starting with Sun Yat-Sen, so did the Chinese revolutionaries. In Europe between 1896 and 1898, Sun became "one of the most diligent frequenters of the library at the British Museum," the library so dear to Marx. Except for the future first president of the Chinese Republic, it wasn't about studying capitalist economics: "The dominant interest of Sun remained the 'secret' of the West, that is, technology in its various aspects and above all military technology." Later, intellectuals who went abroad in "work-study" programs and were committed to stealing the secrets of the West made notable contributions to the founding of the Communist Party. Some were destined to play major roles: Zhou Enlai, Deng Xiaoping, and Chen Yi. They found themselves in Paris at the same time as Ho Chi Minh, who may have helped put them "in touch with French Communists."[40]

It was a movement that was not foreign to Mao Zedong. Speaking with Snow, he referred to his decision not to travel to Europe: "I felt that I did not know enough about my own country and that my time could be more profitably spent in China." This does not mean diffidence toward those who made a different choice. Mao continued to tell his story: "Before leaving China"—referring to the students enrolled in the "work-study programs" in France—"these students planned to study French in Beijing. I helped organize the movement, and in the groups who went abroad were many students from the Hunan [Mao's home province] Normal School, most of whom later became famous radicals."[41]

This helped to create a division of labor. If Mao remained in China to deepen his knowledge of a country the size of a continent, other young revolutionaries went to France to obtain the West's culture and make themselves co-participants with their compatriots. Common to each was the conviction that to achieve national redemption, China needed to critically assimilate the science and technology of the countries that imposed the colonial and semi-colonial yoke on it. Zhou Enlai is illuminating in this regard: After being one of the leaders of the student movement of May 4, 1919, and having spent a year in prison because of it, he left for France.[42] The anticolonial movement, which had organized large protests in China's public squares, momentarily travelled to one of the most advanced Western countries to learn science and technology. Some decades later, Deng Xiaoping called on his country to not lose sight of an essential point: "Science is a great thing, and we should recognize its importance."[43]

Faith in science and technology was not shared in the West. Bukharin, who from 1911 moved back and forth between Europe and the United States (before returning to Russia in the summer of 1917), denounced the monstrous growth of the state apparatus that had occurred since the outbreak of the war: "This is the New Leviathan, beside which the fantasy of Thomas Hobbes looks like a child's toy." By now, "everything has been mobilized" and "militarized," and this fate also involved the economy, culture, morals, and religion; not even "medicine" and "bacteriology" had escaped. In fact, all of the "enormous technical, economic and ideological machine" had been transformed into an "enormous death-dealing machine."[44] We encounter a brilliant analysis of what will later be called "totalitarianism," but one has the impression that this analysis tends to connect science and technology too strictly to capitalism, imperialism, and war.

It is a recurrent tendency in the culture between the two wars in Germany, in the country that perhaps more than any other between 1914 and 1918 was involved in the development of chemical arms and in the systematic application of science to the operations of war.

Benjamin observed that for "imperialists," "technological sense" resided exclusively in "dominion over nature" (which could also be utilized for war). In this sense, "technology had betrayed humanity and transformed the nuptial bed into a bloodbath." Twelve years later, before going willingly to meet death to escape his persecutors, Benjamin, in his *Theses on the Philosophy of History*, raises a cry of alarm: "The progress in the mastery of nature and in the exploitation of nature" could only go hand in hand with a frightful "regression of society"; the formidable war machine of the Third Reich was the radical and tragic refutation of the illusion, long cultivated by the workers and socialist movement, that science and technology could be in themselves instruments of emancipation.[45]

The ideological climate described here ended up influencing an author organically linked to the communist movement: Lukács, in *History and Class Consciousness*, seems to identify "the growth of mechanization" with "dehumanization" and "reification."[46] In some ways, as has been rightly observed, the author of this work gives proof of "hostility toward the natural sciences— something entirely foreign to all previous Marxist literature,"[47] that is, to a Marxism that had not yet passed through the horrors of the application of science and of technology to the operations of war.

Independently of war, the devastating crisis of 1929 and the consequent mass unemployment are considered in the West as having demonstrated that technological progress was far from synonymous with emancipation. Leaving behind her initial sympathy for Marx, Simone Weil wrote: "The present production system, namely, big industry, reduces the worker to the position of a wheel in the factory and a mere instrument in the hands of his employers."[48] Any hopes in "technological progress" were "vain and misleading." Eight years later, referring to the Great Depression, Horkheimer observed that "machines have become means of destruction not merely in the literal sense (as happened in the First World War): they have made not work but the workers superfluous" as happened following the crisis that exploded in 1929.[49]

All in all, we can say that a concern dear to anarchism had made a comeback between the two wars. Let's read Bakunin:

And in this day and age what is it that constitutes the principle underlying the power of the State? Why, it is science. Yes, science ... and, above all, military science with all its tried and tested weaponry, these formidable instruments of destruction which "work wonders," the science of genius which has conjured up steamships, railways and telegraphy which, by turning every government into a hundred armed, a thousand-armed Briareus, giving it the power to be, act and arrest everywhere at once, has brought about the most formidable political centralization the world has ever witnessed.

In the eyes of the anarchist leader, not only on the battlefield but also in the factory, science and technology had revealed themselves to be synonymous with domination and oppression: "We need only list the machines and every workingman and honest advocate of the emancipation of labor would accept the justice of what we say." Therefore, "bourgeois science" must be rejected and combated in the same way as "bourgeois wealth," all the more so since "the advances of science and of the arts" were the cause of "intellectual slavery" beyond that of "material slavery."[50]

Defeated by Marx in his time, this historical account (which liquidated science, technology, and modernity) sees its victory (in the West) with the First World War and the Great Depression. One can understand then the point of view expressed in the middle of the twentieth century by two illustrious philosophers: "But the totalitarian order has granted unlimited rights to calculating thought and puts its trust in science as such. Its canon is its own brutal efficiency."[51] Even as it celebrates its triumphs on the battlefield, science makes its devastating effects felt at every level.

At this point, we can summarize the contrast that appeared regarding science and technology. In the West, they are an integral part of "the new Leviathan" (to use Bukharin's language), utilized by the capitalist bourgeoisie to raise profits by squeezing the waged workforce to prepare the "technological machine" and the "death machine" for the struggle for world hegemony. In the East, science and technology are essentials for developing the resistance to the politics of subjection and oppression conducted by this same "new Leviathan." If in the West, the Great War, the Great Depression, the rise of fascism and of Nazism, and the Second World War make the anarchist judgment credible, this judgment gains little ground in the East. There, the objectivity of the natural sciences, which in *History and Class Consciousness* was connected directly to the logic of calculation and of the exploitation of the capitalist economy, must instead still be accomplished to develop a modern industrial apparatus and to escape from underdevelopment and from colonial and semi-colonial dependence; and this accomplishment often implies conflicts with animistic and premodern visions that are obstacles to the application of science and technology to nature.

6. Western Marxism and Messianism

Let's try to formulate an initial summary of the different forms that Marxism takes in Europe and in Asia. According to Merleau-Ponty, Marx imagined "a noncapitalistic future" that he hoped would be an "absolute Other."[52] This vision, well-represented in Western Marxism, is absent in the East. The underdeveloped countries, before they can completely tear down capitalism, first must, and want to, enjoy the "miracle" of the wonderful development of the productive forces that the *Communist Manifesto* rightly attributes to that social system.[53] We find Mao in 1940 declaring that the revolution he was promoting, before moving on to socialism must "clear the way for capitalist development," even if a capitalism strictly controlled by a political power and by a party determined to go well beyond it in carrying out the revolutionary transformation of the existing society. For the Chinese Communist leader, the post-capitalist future is not an "absolute Other" to the regime that it is intended to replace; more than a total negation, we find ourselves before a sort of Hegelian *Aufhebung*, a negation that carries with it, even if in a radically new context, the heritage of the high points of that which is negated. It is a question of transcending capitalism but without compromising. It further strengthens the capacity for developing the productive forces to which it gives impetus.

The diversity of objective material conditions and cultural traditions drives the bifurcation of Marxism. Judeo-Christian messianism has informed the West, reinforced by the horror of the First World War. With the end of the slaughter, there is an expectation of a world redeemed from wrong and sin. One thinks of Bloch, who in August 1918 sees the First World War as a "crusade" against radical evil, represented by Germany and by the Central European Powers, a crusade whose protagonists should be the Entente but above all "Christianity in struggle, the *ecclesia militans*."[54] Immediately after the October Revolution, we see him invoke the "transformation of power into love" and transcending the "mercantile morality," the original source of evil and sin. It is true, responding to the foreseeable objections, that many times the philosopher makes clear that what he seeks is a "concrete utopia," founded on an ontology that does not confuse the existing with the factual and that does not lose sight of the "not-yet-existing." Yet this category is so large, and so lacking in reference to time, and to ways of realizing the longed-for future, that it could include even the most abstract utopia.

The messianism of Benjamin is quite explicit. In 1940 and on the eve of his suicide, after having criticized in the *Theses on the Philosophy of History* the "homogeneous and empty time" on which an evolutionism incapable of understanding, or even imagining, the qualitative leap that alone can save us is based, he turns to the "messianic time" of Jewish tradition: Here "every second" is the "straight gate through which the Messiah might enter."[55] Rather than a cold and rational analysis, the gravest tragedy ever to occur in Europe had brought about a situation so desperate as to suggest waiting for the Messiah as an alternative to the present that appeared to be without any means of escape.

Even an author like Lukács, who, in his younger years and in the period in which the horror and the indignation over the war had not yet found an articulated political response, seemed to be influenced by the climate described above. Marianne Weber sees him animated by "eschatological hope" and looking toward the "ultimate goal" of "world redemption" to be brought about thanks to a "final conflict between God and Lucifer." Even if this is a tendentious description, one is struck by the fact that in 1916, while the battlefield slaughter was raging, Lukács, taking up an expression of Fichte, speaks of his own time as an "era of complete sinfulness." Later, the Hungarian philosopher scolds Fichte for having counterposed to the "era of complete sinfulness" a "contemplated utopian future"; it is a criticism that sounds like a self-criticism and a distancing from the apocalyptic tones of his youth.[56]

It goes without saying that it would be in vain that we should search in China, in Indochina, and in Eastern Marxism in general for appeals to "*ecclesia militans*" and to "the Messiah" or to a vision that entrusts to the revolution the task of the liquidation of "radical evil," of "complete sinfulness," of the "mercantile morality" and of "power" as such. I have already discussed how different the Chinese cultural tradition was. Certainly, midway through the nineteenth century in China, the Taiping revolt broke out, which, breaking with Confucian tradition, sought a radically new order, the "Celestial Reign of Peace." Not by chance, however, the protagonist of this gigantic mass rising was convinced he was the younger brother of Jesus and was profoundly influenced by Christianity and Christian Messianism. The tragic outcome of the Taiping Revolt, which cost rivers of blood and ended up accelerating the ruin of the country, and by consequence, its colonial and semi-colonial subjection, may have further immunized Chinese culture to messianic temptations, and that could have contributed to a more "pragmatic" reception of the theory of Marx. In Europe and the West, instead, the great historical crisis—the two world wars, and, between the first and the second, the Great Depression, and the rise of Nazism and fascism—found its epicenter and flared up in a particularly traumatic way, immediately following the *Belle Époque* and the Hundred Years' Peace (1815–1914). All this, together with the Judeo-Christian tradition, promoted the Messianic reading of the tragedy of those decades.

The fact remains of the *longue durée* of the messianic and utopian tendency of Western Marxism. It reacted with irritation when Lukács self-critiqued his "messianic sectarianism" and "messianic utopian aspirations" of *History and Class Consciousness* for the tendency to represent post-capitalism as somehow "proclaiming a total break with every institution and mode of life stemming from the bourgeois world."⁵⁷ Yet in the 1960s, the ideal (dear to Herbert Marcuse) of a society founded on a substantial liberation from work and on the definitive triumph of *eros* over every form of domination (and perhaps also of power) was widely diffused and, at times, radicalized. The principal exponent of Italian "workerism," Mario Tronti, called explicitly for the "abolition of work." Decades later, he proudly proclaimed his consonance with the "millenarian heresies" of the "workers of the twentieth century."

Still more telling is the remarkable success of a book published in 2000. It concludes by evoking an extraordinary future of universal regeneration that recalls not so much the revolution of Marxian memory as the apocatastasis of which first-century Christians, and particularly enthusiastic theologians, spoke, signaling the rise of a final reconciliation not only of human beings with one another but also of humans with nature and the animal species. We think of authors like Origen or John Scotus, the prophets of the apocatastasis: Here finally, "the animals, sister moon, brother sun, the birds of the field, the poor and exploited humans, together against the will of power and corruption ... biopower and communism, cooperation and revolution remain together, in love, simplicity, and also innocence."⁵⁸

7. The Struggle Against Inequality in the West and the East

Condemning with fiery words the carnage of war and the sociopolitical system that led to it, Bloch attacked the social polarization that characterizes capitalism, notwithstanding the homage it pays to (juridical) equality:

> This, says Anatole France, is equality before the law: that it forbids rich and poor alike to steal firewood or to sleep under bridges. That so little hinders actual inequality that it actually protects it.... For since the lawyers are trained in no other way than formally, precisely the abilities of the exploiter class in calculation, mistrust, and underhanded accounting find a cognate basis in this formalism, still apart

from the fact that the contents of any possible economic system can be inserted without contradiction into the abstract amoralism of jurisprudence.... All of law, far and away the preponderance of criminal law, too, is merely the ruling class's means of maintaining a rule of law protecting its interests.[59]

As we can see, the condemnation was radical, but it was based exclusively on the conditions of the popular masses in the West. This is true as well for Benjamin: He too took up the satirical comments of the French writer on the laws of bourgeois society that "poor and rich are equally forbidden to spend the night under bridges" and that, at the political level, transfer of power is only tolerated "from the privileged to the privileged."[60] He made no reference to the conditions of the peoples of the colonies; indeed, as far as Bloch is concerned, we see immediately that, in these years, he polemicized against those who, in his eyes, excessively emphasized the colonial question.

Obviously, Ho Chi Minh, too, had the cause of equality at heart, but his priorities were different. In the speech that called on French Socialists to join the Communist International, he declared, "Such is so-called justice in Indochina. In that country, the Vietnamese are discriminated against; they do not enjoy safety like Europeans or those having European citizenship." Inequality was denounced with an eye primarily toward the conditions of the colonial peoples. For the Vietnamese revolutionary, it was not only a question of challenging the formal character of juridical equality; such legal equality was not realized in any way in the colonies. Enjoying a decidedly privileged treatment were not only the French but also those Vietnamese and Indochinese who had Europeanized, such as those who converted to Christianity, the religion of the dominant colonial power, and so, in a way, were co-opted into the civilization or into the self-styled superior race. For some time, Ho Chi Minh embraced the idea of translating the works of Montesquieu into Vietnamese, in particular, *The Spirit of the Laws*.[61] The capitalist West puffs out its chest with pride in its liberal principles, but in the colonies, they have always been careful to not put them into practice but to not even make them known!

Ho also denounced material inequality, with a view, first of all, to the colonies: The Vietnamese "live in misery when there is abundance for their executioners, and die of starvation when there is a bad harvest."[62] Material inequality intersected with legal inequality, so the colonial peoples were forced to submit simultaneously to arbitrary arrests and desperate hunger. "Algeria suffers from famine. Here is how Tunisia is ravaged by the same scourge. To remedy this situation, the Administration arrested and imprisoned many starving people. And so that the 'down and out' did not take prison for shelter, they were not given anything to eat. Some die of starvation during the imprisonment."[63] Above all, Ho didn't lose sight of perhaps the most important point: The anticolonial revolution sought to achieve emancipation at every level, not only for the individual but for the nation as well. It was necessary to end "the formal nod due to the superior race by the vanquished race."[64] In other words, it was necessary to end the deferential bowing the Vietnamese were obligated to engage in when they ran into a Frenchman.

We have seen Sun Yat-Sen attribute to the October Revolution the merit of having risen up "against inequality in defense of humanity." The inequality he referred to was global. During the Chinese Revolution, the demand for equality was constantly aimed at the humiliation suffered by the nation as a whole. Vibrant and recurring were the condemnations of the "unequal treaties" colonialism imposed on China; these had to give way to "treaties based on equality."[65] Also condemned was the "extraterritoriality" that the United States, above all, forced on China, which granted the right to U.S. citizens (and those converted to Christianity and Westernized) in that great Asian country to organize and act as a state within a state.[66] In any case, the struggle to affirm on an international basis the principle "of equality, mutual benefit and mutual respect for territorial integrity and sovereignty" was an essential aspect of the anticolonial revolution.[67]

It goes without saying that neither Mao Zedong nor Ho Chi Minh lost sight of the problem of building a society free of the social polarization that characterizes both the pre-capitalist and the capitalist world.

The fact remains that, contrary to Europe, in Asia, the communists hailed the October Revolution, taking from it the stimulus to liberate themselves from the frightful inequality that the more advanced countries, or that capitalism and imperialism, have brought to bear on the colonial peoples.

8. The Blurred Boundaries Between Western Marxism and Eastern Marxism

I have distinguished between Western and Eastern Marxism, referring to Western Europe and Asia. But where should we place Soviet Russia? All of the members of the leadership group of the Bolshevik Revolution had, to varying degrees, taken up the lessons of Lenin on the centrality of the colonial question and all to varying degrees tried to spread the revolution throughout Europe and to bring about an upheaval, a radical change without historical precedent. And so, at least for a time in Russia, there seemed to be no trace of the bifurcation between the two Marxisms. This bifurcation took form over time, as the expectation that the arrival of a worldwide society characterized by the vanishing of the mercantile economy, of the state apparatus and of national borders, of a society that eliminates every source of conflict and disharmony, lost credibility. The more this exhilarating prospect faded, the more urgent the task of governing Russia, a country in the grip of historical backwardness and the devastations of the First World War and of civil war, such that the Bolshevik leaders were forced to face, through oscillations and contradictions, a learning process that had to happen rapidly given the perils of the internal and international situations.

The case of Lenin is exemplary. For some time, while the revolution seemed to spread beyond the borders of Russia, he shared the illusions of the other Bolsheviks to the point of making a risky prediction (in the closing speech of the founding Congress of the International, March 6, 1919): "The victory of the Communist revolution is assured. The comrades present in this hall saw the founding of the first Soviet Republic; now they see the founding of the Third,

Communist International (applause), and they will all see the founding of the World Federative Republic of Soviets."[68] In the early days of October 1920, in a climate of lingering euphoria, Lenin reaffirmed, "The generation of people who are now at the age of fifty cannot expect to see a communist society. This generation will be gone before then. But the generation of those who are now fifteen will see a Communist society and will build this society. This generation should know that the entire purpose of their lives is to build a Communist society."[69] It didn't take long for the illusion of the arrival of a radically new world in the near future, under the banner of a total and definitive reconciliation, to vanish.

Two and a half years later, in an important speech, "Better Fewer, but Better," published in *Pravda* on March 4, 1923, we hear a completely different tone: "Improving our state apparatus," "we must strive to build up a state," "create a republic that is really worthy of the name Soviet, socialist." It was a long-term task that would require "many, very many years," and to solve it, Soviet Russia must not hesitate to study the most advanced capitalist countries.[70] Beyond the question of the state (and the nation), a rethinking and a learning process also had to occur in the economy. Lenin had branded Taylorism a "scientific system" for squeezing sweat out of the "wage slave,"[71] but after the October Revolution, he stressed that "the Soviet power" must know how to increase the productivity of labor, teaching the Russian worker, traditionally "a bad worker," how to work better, and promoting the critical assimilation of the "Taylor system" and "the more recent advances in capitalism."[72]

The distinction between Western and Eastern Marxism was temporal in the Bolshevik leadership group. Before the turning point of 1917, many of them had lived in the West, and they had lived not like the Chinese Communists, staying for a brief time in France or Germany to learn science and technology to bring back to their homeland as soon as possible. Not a few among the future leaders of Soviet Russia had spent a considerable part of their lives in the West without any certainty of returning home and remaining largely isolated in the countries where they had found refuge but where they could not obtain work in government or administration even at the most modest level. Even more than in the French Revolution, a group or class of "abstract" intellectuals was called upon, so to speak, from one day to the next, to transform themselves into a governing class.

Beginning with the exemplary case of Lenin, we can understand the learning process through which the Bolshevik leaders had to pass: Before the conquest of power, they tended to think of postcapitalist society as the total and immediate negation of the previous sociopolitical order, with the first experience of exercising power the growing awareness that the revolutionary transformation would not be an instantaneous and painless creation *ex nihilo*, but a complex and tormented *Aufhebung* (to use a central category of Hegelian philosophy) to simultaneously inherit the highest points of the sociopolitical order that was being negated and overthrown.

It goes without saying that not all achieved or were disposed to achieve at the same time and in the same way the learning process imposed on them by the objective situation. In other words, as far as Soviet Russia is concerned, the border between Western Marxism and Eastern Marxism was of a temporal character on the one hand, and on the other, it ran through that very leadership group. The contradictions and conflicts that ended up tearing it apart prefigured in the final analysis the conflict between the two Marxisms. Trotsky, who saw the power achieved by the Bolsheviks as a trampoline to launch the revolution in the West, eminently represented Western Marxism. Accused by his antagonist of national and provincial sentiments, Stalin was instead the incarnation of Eastern Marxism: He never left Russia, and already between February and October 1917 he presented the proletarian revolution as a necessary instrument for building a new social order but also for reaffirming Russian national independence, which was threatened by the Entente that wanted to force it to provide cannon fodder for the imperialist war and which treated it like a country in "central Africa." It was the vague presentiment that, far from being able to "export" the revolution to the West, Soviet Russia would have to work to not become a colony or semicolony of the more advanced capitalist West.

9. The Difficult Reciprocal Recognition Between Two Struggles for Recognition

From the start, Western Marxism and Eastern Marxism tended to follow different paths. Nor were polemical motives lacking, sometimes directly, often indirectly. In accepting the ideology of U.S. president Woodrow Wilson, for whom the defeat of despotism, represented primarily by Germany's Wilhelm II, would have smoothed the way for "definitive peace," Bloch distanced himself from Lenin, whom he criticized for having treated the two war coalitions as the same, and for not taking seriously the democratic character of Great Britain and its allies. In the eyes of the German philosopher, the Russian Revolution "evidently reveled in the sovereign skepticism that sees nothing but the interests of capital, and nothing else, and scolds the English over their protectorate in faraway Egypt."[73]

Bloch rolled his eyes over the trifling colonial question: the greatest empire of all time was thereby absolved with the argument that it would be misleading to condemn it because of a single colony, indeed a single "protectorate," and one that is "faraway" from Europe and so not worthy of any particular attention. The German philosopher gave not even a nod to the ferocious repression that gunned down the Irish people, who had rebelled against the war and colonial domination just a little earlier. What a difference from Ho Chi Minh, who followed that revolt with impassioned attention, and for the national liberation of a people not in the "faraway" Middle East but in Europe![74] More generally, if Bloch scolded Lenin for giving excessive importance to the colonial question, Ho Chi Minh in 1923 criticized Marx for the opposite reason: "Marx built his doctrine on a certain philosophy of history. What history? That of Europe. But what is Europe? It is not humanity in its entirety."[75]

The minimizing of the colonial question is a direct form of Eurocentric chauvinism. For another thing, aside from the horrors of the carnage of war, officially unleashed on each side in the name of the defense of the fatherland, in large sectors of Western Marxism an exalted and abstract internationalism spread that considered the national question transcended and consequently to delegitimize the movements for national liberation of the colonized peoples (this was an indirect form of Eurocentric chauvinism). It is against this tendency that Ho Chi Minh polemicized in his speech at the Congress of Tours in December 1920: "Today, instead of contributing, together with you, to world revolution, I come here with deep sadness to speak as a member of the Socialist Party, against the imperialists who have committed abhorrent crimes on my native land."[76]

The world revolution risked losing sight of the most modest yet most concrete task of political support for the people struggling to throw off colonial subjection and constitute themselves as independent national states. Bloch never tired of criticizing militarism; he criticized Marx for having directed his attack almost "only against capitalism" rather than concentrating his fire on "militarism, " whose embodiment would be represented by Prussia.[77] Again, Ho Chi Minh, whose argument was quite different, called attention to "colonialist militarism," which had unleashed in the colonies the hunt for "human material," for "black or yellow meat" that the great capitalist powers arrogated to themselves the right to calmly immolate in a war for world hegemony.

We see the Communist International launch, a year after its founding, a call to become protagonists in the revolution not only to the "proletarians" but also "the oppressed peoples" of the entire world and that expressed a clear awareness of the centrality of the colonial question. However, in 1924, on the occasion of the Fifth Congress of the Communist International, Ho Chi Minh still felt obligated to intervene in the debate with a brief but eloquent declaration that criticized the persistent underestimation of the colonial question: "I feel that the comrades have not yet sufficiently grasped the idea that the destiny of the proletariat of the whole world . . . is closely tied to the destiny of the oppressed nations in the colonies."[78]

Along with Great Britain, Bloch tended to glorify the United States. These are the years in which, without renouncing its own colonies (the Philippines) or the Monroe Doctrine and its neocolonial control of Latin America, the North American republic, under Woodrow Wilson, sought to give itself an "anticolonialist" image, waving the banner of the self-determination of peoples. Bloch joined this campaign enthusiastically, so he took no account of the colonies, the semi-colonies, or the treatment reserved for the peoples of colonial origin by the persistent regime of white supremacy (particularly Black people).

Now let's look at Ho Chi Minh: Seeking work after having arrived in the United States in 1924, he was a horrified witness to a lynching; the slow, interminable torture of a black man was attended by a festive and cheerful crowd of whites. Let's look at some of the particulars to better focus on the political conclusion: "While on the ground, stinking of fat and smoke, a black head, mutilated, roasted, deformed, grins horribly and seems to ask the setting sun, 'Is this civilization?'"[79] And so, beyond the colonial peoples, likewise suffering oppression, humiliation, and dehumanization, are those, despite being citizens of the country that celebrates itself as the oldest democracy in the world, whose skin color betrayed their outsiderhood with respect to the self-styled superior race. The young Indochinese, whose choice of being a revolutionary and a Communist had matured, denounced the infamy of the white supremacist regime and the Ku Klux Klan in *International Correspondence* (the French version of the organ of the Communist International).[80] Reflections on the treatment reserved for African Americans must have played a role in the development of Mao Zedong as well. According to an authoritative witness, "He knew something about the Negro question in America and unfavorably compared the treatment of Negroes and American Indians with policies in the Soviet Union toward national minorities. He was interested when I pointed out certain great differences in the historical background of the Negro in America and that of minorities in Russia."[81]

In the West and in the development of Western Marxism, Lenin's writings denouncing the carnage of the war and the total mobilization and regimentation resonated particularly strongly. In the East and in the development of Eastern Marxism, it was his targeting of imperialism and the pretensions of the presumed "elect nations" or "model nations" that dominated and robbed the rest of the world. We are in the presence of two struggles for recognition. As far as the colonies are concerned, this is evident from Ho Chi Minh's analysis of their dehumanization: The colonial peoples were reduced to "human material" or to "black and yellow meat" to be sacrificed in more or less enslaved labor or by being immolated in a war in which they face, thousands of kilometers away from home, people whose rulers were in mortal competition among themselves.

A more careful analysis of the demand for recognition emerges from the struggle by the popular masses in the West against the First World War. Italy was dragged into the conflict, notwithstanding the opposition of the great mass of Catholics and Socialists, and when by that point it was clear to all the enormous price of human life that was to be paid. We can understand, therefore, Gramsci's conclusion: Treated throughout history as the equivalent of a multitude of children and therefore considered incapable of understanding and making demands at the level of politics, the popular masses could be calmly sacrificed by the dominant class on the altar of its imperial projects. And so, as it happens, the "working people" didn't remain in the condition of a "good prey for all" and of simple "human material" available to the elites, of "raw material for the history of the privileged classes."[82]

There should not be any contradictions between Western Marxism and Eastern Marxism. We are dealing with two different perspectives on the same social system, each taking off from Lenin's analyses. In other words, two struggles for recognition called into question imperialism-capitalism. In the first, the protagonists were entire nations seeking to free themselves from the yoke of oppression, humiliation, and the dehumanization inherent in colonial domination; in the second, the protagonists were the working class and the popular masses who refused to be "raw material" available to the elites. However, unity and reciprocal recognition between these two struggles could not be taken for granted from the start.

PART II

Socialism versus Capitalism, or Anticolonialism versus Colonialism?

1. FROM THE ONLY PROLETARIAN REVOLUTION TO THE ANTICOLONIAL REVOLUTION

We have seen how different socioeconomic contexts and varying cultural traditions contributed to bifurcating the Marxisms in the West and the East. Now we must analyze the influence on this process exercised by the international situation's rapid transformation and the ever-greater discrepancy between the initial hopes raised by the October Revolution and successive historical developments. The indignation over the First World War spread a firm conviction among European communists: on the order of the day was the overthrow of the sociopolitical system responsible for the horrendous carnage, and there were no intermediate objectives to pursue; everything turned on the contradiction between capitalism and socialism or between bourgeoisie and proletariat. This was also Lenin's view. He repeatedly stated, "Imperialism is the eve of the socialist revolution." It was "the highest stage of capitalism" because, with its infamies and the mass upheavals it provoked, imperialism signaled the "transition from capitalism to a higher socioeconomic order."[1]

The qualitative leap that loomed just over the horizon would be of an immeasurable magnitude compared to the upheavals of past events. In January 1917, to commemorate the twelfth anniversary of the Russian Revolution of 1905, Lenin concluded that the imminent Russian Revolution would be "the *prologue* to the coming European revolution" and could "only be a proletarian revolution, and in an even more profound sense of the word: a proletarian, socialist revolution also in its content" beyond merely the participation of the masses of the proletariat and the popular classes.[2] (The 1905 revolution was "a *bourgeois-democratic* revolution in its social content, but a *proletarian* revolution in its methods of struggle"—it aimed to overturn the Czarist autocracy and the feudal nobility, but not yet the capitalist bourgeoisie; however, its shock troops were constituted by the workers, the anti-capitalist class *par excellence*.) On the immediate eve of the overthrow of the "government of the imperialist carnage" and of the conquest of power by the Bolshevik Party, the revolutionary leader reiterated that the "great turning point" of the time went well beyond Russia: it brought ever closer the "world proletarian revolution," the "international socialist revolution," and the victory of "internationalism."

But, in his more reflective moments regarding the gigantic flaring up in Europe and worldwide, Lenin began to nurture doubts about this theoretical and political program. In the summer of 1915, he characterized the world war that had broken out the year before as a "war between slave owners for fortifying and strengthening (colonial) slavery." "The peculiarity of the situation lies in that in this war the fate of the colonies is being decided by war on the Continent."[3] This formulation suggests that the "original" situation in which the "slave owners," the great colonial and imperialist powers, held the initiative would not last long. The slaves of the colonies would not be long in revolting. Indeed, as Lenin noted a year later, the revolt had already begun: "In Singapore the British brutally suppressed a mutiny among their Indian troops." Something similar had happened in "French Annam" (Vietnam) and in "the German Cameroons." It was a process that reached Europe itself: Ireland rose against colonial domination, a domination that London restored by firing squads.[4] This analysis reached a conclusion of startling foresight. Before the war had even broken out, Lenin indicated with precision the two epicenters of the gigantic revolutionary and national storm growing on the horizon that would mark the entire twentieth century: "Western Europe," "Asia," and "Eastern Europe" on the one hand, and "the colonies and semi-colonies" on the other.[5] Essentially, the first would see the unleashing of Hitler's project to construct a continental colonial empire for Germany; the second would contribute decisively to the fall (at least in its classical form) of the world colonial system. (One thinks of the national liberation movements in China, India, and Vietnam.) We are far from the prospect of the "only proletarian" revolution and of the "world *proletarian* revolution," or of the "international socialist revolution."

Lenin himself had already become difficult to follow in his oscillations, having become conscious of the permanent and growing importance of the colonial question. Notwithstanding the victory of the October Revolution and its socialist and internationalist pathos, he encountered strong resistance among the ranks of the Marxist and communist left in Europe. Legitimate as they were, did the protests of colonial peoples and their struggles for national liberation still make sense? Didn't the gigantic conflict for world hegemony that broke out in 1914 between the opposed imperialist coalitions demonstrate the quixotic character of the oppressed nations' attempts to win their national independence? What could David do against Goliath? If, even by some miracle, they managed to win political independence, they would remain deprived of economic independence and would have continued to submit to one form or another of oppression by this or that great power. And so, the real problem was to put an end once and for all, and on a world scale, to the capitalist-imperialist system. So argued, on the wave of indignation over the First World War and of enthusiasm for the October Revolution, an important strain of Western Marxists and communists, a strain that was highly active across Europe.

Lenin referred to it, writing between August and October 1916, when he reported on a position held by "*one* Left group," namely, the German "*International* group" whose members included Mehring, Liebknecht, and Luxemburg. According to them, "national wars *are no longer possible* in the era of this unbridled imperialism."[6] Given this assumption, one can understand the disdain with which a Swiss newspaper, the *Berner Tagwacht*, though firmly against the war, spoke of the insurrection of 1916 in Ireland, whose protagonists were a people seeking to liberate themselves from English domination and to constitute themselves as an independent national state. It was a "putsch" that caused a "sensation" but was politically insignificant.[7] In the era of imperialism, it made no sense to linger over obsolete intermediate and provincial objectives, losing sight of and weakening the only struggle that mattered, overthrowing the entire world system of imperialist capitalism.

Lenin objected strongly to this thesis, which had circulated widely among the extreme left in Germany, Switzerland, and around the West:

> To imagine that social revolution is *conceivable* without revolts by small nations in the colonies and in Europe . . . is to *repudiate social revolution*. . . . So one army lines up in one place and says, "We are for socialism," and another, somewhere else, says, "We are for imperialism," and that will be a social revolution! Only those who hold such a ridiculously pedantic view could vilify the Irish rebellion by calling it a "putsch." Whoever expects a "pure" social revolution will *never* live to see it. Such a person pays lip service to revolution without understanding what revolution is.[8]

Does this last critical observation not end by also bashing the "only proletarian" revolution we have seen Lenin call for during a moment of hopefulness? It is clear that the principal aspect of his thought for a long time was that the anticolonial revolutions were an integral part of the era of imperialism (and of the struggle against capitalism). The persistence of national oppression internationally and within countries that boasted of their democracy (for example, the oppression of African Americans) demonstrated the "immense significance of the national question."[9] We understand well that this vision emerged in the first place in a country, Czarist Russia, that had traditionally been known as a "prison house of peoples," where national oppression could not be ignored, and which was moreover located close to the colonial world properly speaking. On the national (and colonial) question in the imperialist era, a differentiation was developing between Western Marxism and Eastern Marxism.

The demarcation line between the two is not to be understood as merely geographic since, as we know, not a few of the Bolshevik leaders came from the West. And it is in polemics against two of them, Parabellum (Radek) and Kievski (Platakov), that Lenin made clear his position: "The division of nations into oppressor and oppressed . . . forms the *essence* of imperialism" and the struggle for overcoming it must constitute the "principal question" of the revolutionary program. "This division . . . is most significant from the angle of the revolutionary struggle against imperialism."[10]

To reiterate and make official this point of view, in the summer of 1920, the Congress of the Peoples of the East took place in Baku immediately after the Second Congress of the Communist International. It felt the need to modify the slogan that concludes the *Manifesto of the Communist Party* and the *Inaugural Address of the Workingmen's International*. The new slogan went, "Proletarians of all countries and oppressed peoples of the entire world, unite!" Now, alongside "proletarians" were also the "oppressed peoples" emerging as a revolutionary subject in their own right. Awareness grew that the class struggle was not only the proletarian struggle in the capitalist metropolises but also that waged by the oppressed peoples of the colonies and semicolonies. And it would be, above all, this latter type of class struggle that would define the twentieth century. The October Revolution had come to power launching an appeal to the West to make the socialist revolution and one to the East to make the anticolonial revolution. The latter, therefore, was never lost sight of and, within a short time, assumed an unexpected centrality, one looked on with suspicion by Western Marxism.

2. The National and Colonial Question in the Heart of Europe

For all intents and purposes, the colonial and national question emerged with a force reaching beyond the colonial world. On this point also Lenin showed himself to be extraordinarily lucid. We have already seen him hinting at the gathering storm over Eastern Europe. There is more. In July 1916, after having seen the armies of Wilhelm II advance to the gates of Paris, the great revolutionary reiterated the imperialist nature of the First World War then underway and called attention to a possible overturning. If the gigantic conflict were to end "in victories similar to those achieved by Napoleon, in the subjugation of a whole series of nation-states capable of independent life ... then a great national war in Europe would be possible."[11]

In this context, it is useful to reread an important passage in Lenin's essay analyzing imperialism, whose character was such that it "strives to annex *not only* agrarian territories but even most highly industrialized regions," if only to weaken its "adversary."[12] The imperialist competition for world hegemony knew no boundaries. However industrialized or ancient its civilization, no country was sheltered from the risk of seeing itself transformed into a colony or semi-colony; not even the colonialist and imperialist powers could consider themselves safe. After the victories "similar to those achieved by Napoleon" won by Hitler in the spring of 1940, France became a colony or semi-colony of the Third Reich. It is interesting to note that even before coming to power, Hitler proposed a racialization of the French people, relegating them among the colonial peoples and inferior races: France did not truly belong to the world's white community; it was on the road to "negro-ization" (*Vernegerung*). France did not protect itself in any way from interracial marriages and sexual relationships and so shamelessly "negro-ized its blood." So advanced was this ruinous process that "France is racially becoming more and more negroid. So much so that now one can actually speak of the creation of an African State on European soil," indeed a "Euro-African mulatto state."[13] Driven from the colonial world, the French were forced to carry out a national and anticolonial revolution to recover their independence and national dignity.

What was happening in Italy was perhaps more significant. Mussolini entered the Second World War voicing explicitly imperialist slogans: conquering a place in the sun, the return of the Empire "on the fatal hills of Rome," etc. When he fell, Mussolini left the country not only prostrate and broken but also in large part controlled by an army that acted like an army of occupation and that considered and treated the local population as a colonial people, members of an inferior race. The diary entries of Goebbels for September 11, 1943, are revealing: "The Italians, by their infidelity and treachery, have lost every claim to a national state of the modern type. They had to be punished most severely, as the laws of history demand."[14] In effect, in the eyes of the Nazis' bosses, the Italians were by now "negroid," and so it was important to avoid sexual contamination. After the war, they were to be utilized as a more or less servile labor force, "workers at the service of the Germans."[15] Having participated in the unleashing of an imperialist war for the conquest of colonies in Africa and the Balkans, Italy found itself having to conduct a national liberation war to throw off the colonial yoke imposed by their ex-ally and recover their own national independence and national dignity.

In conclusion, as in part foreseen by Lenin, in the heart of Europe, far from being "only proletarian," the revolution ended up being anticolonial and national.

3. The Socialist Countries in the Epoch of the Napoleonic Wars

At least as far as Soviet Russia was concerned, was the contradiction socialism/capitalism or proletariat/bourgeoisie unequivocally the principal one? While Lenin tried to convince his party comrades of the need to sign the Treaty of Brest-Litovsk, regardless of how humiliating it was, between February and March 1918, he observed, "Another epoch may—like the epoch of the Napoleonic Wars—be an epoch of liberation *wars* (not one war, but wars) imposed by aggressors upon Soviet Russia."[16] If this scenario were to be realized, the Bolsheviks would first have had to struggle for national independence. In that case, for the country of the socialist October Revolution, neither socialism/capitalism nor proletariat/bourgeoisie would have been the principal contradiction, and such a situation would have lasted for an entire "epoch."

What concrete form would the struggle between Napoleonism and anti-Napoleonism have taken? At the end of the Second World War it was clear that the Third Reich had conducted its campaign in the East in a different frame of mind than it did in the West. The advance in the East had racial and colonial overtones. At least for the most ultra-Nazi circles, it was about driving Russia back within borders before those established by Peter the Great and opening an enormous area for German colonial and semi-colonial domination. Did the threat of colonial domination come from only one direction? Between the February and October revolutions, Stalin denounced the Entente, which sought to force Russia to continue fighting and furnish resources and cannon fodder for the great Western powers. The latter sought to transform the great European and Asian country through "the conversion of Russia into a colony of Britain, America and France." Not by chance did they behave in Russia as if they were in "Central Africa."[17]

In effect, compared with the country born of the October Revolution, a frankly racist attitude was widespread among the dominant classes in the West: could the country governed by those barbarians and savages that were the Bolsheviks still be considered an integral part of the community of civilized peoples and of the white race? In denouncing the "rising tide of colored people" in a book that was extraordinarily successful on both sides of the Atlantic, a U.S. writer handed down an irrevocable judgment: by inciting the revolt of the colonial peoples, Bolshevism must be considered and treated as "the renegade, the traitor within the gates, who would betray the citadel," as "the mortal enemy of civilization and the white race."[18] Oswald Spengler in Germany took up this thesis: by becoming Soviet, Russia had thrown away its "white mask" to "once again become Asiatic," indeed "Mongolian." It has "instilled into the whole of the earth's colored population" a hatred toward "the white nations."[19]

On January 27, 1932, addressing the industrialists of Düsseldorf (and all of Germany) and gaining their definitive support for his rise to power, Hitler made clear his vision of history and politics. During the nineteenth century, the "white peoples" had conquered an unprecedented dominion, concluding a process that had begun with the conquest of America and developing further under the banner of "absolute, innate sovereign sentiment of the white race." By questioning the colonial system and provoking or aggravating "the confusion of European white thought," Bolshevism was a mortal danger to civilization. If one wanted to confront that threat, it was necessary to reiterate in theory and practice "the conviction of the superiority and therefore of the superior right of the white race." It was necessary to defend "this economic superiority over the rest of the world."[20] So with clarity a program of colonialist and pro-slavery counterrevolution was announced. The necessary reaffirmation of the planetary dominance of the white race presupposes the assimilation of the fundamental lesson that arises from the history of colonial expansionism of the West: one must not hesitate to have recourse to the "brutal ruthlessness" required by the "right to organize the rest of the world" (*Herrenrecht*).

These were the assumptions of barbaric aggression on which Nazi Germany sought to build in Western Europe its colonial empire enslaving the "indigenous," that is, the Slavs, seen as an inferior race, good only for servile labor. Checkmating this project was the Great Patriotic War of the Soviet Union, born of industrialization conducted as a forced march and at a terrible human and social cost. If this is how things were, was Soviet Russia's priority to build a new social order, or was it defending itself from the dangers of colonial subjection? Was it necessary to profoundly rethink and redesign social relations or to undertake the development of the productive forces and the growth of industrial (and military) production in particular? In the workplaces and the battlefields, did an appeal have to be made to a specific class (the proletariat) or the nation as a whole, given that what was at stake was the defense of national independence?

Other countries that underwent socialist revolutions faced analogous considerations. In China, the liberated areas governed by the Communist Party, which had sprung up from the retreat to the countryside made necessary by the disastrous defeat of the workers' revolution of 1927 in Shanghai, were forced to take note of the colonial expansionism of the Empire of the Rising Sun. Beginning in 1937, with the large-scale invasion by the Tokyo government, the struggle against colonialism ended up overwhelming every aspect of political life, to the point that Mao Zedong, under these circumstances, theorized "the identity between the national struggle and the class struggle." This identity governed the war of resistance against Japanese imperialism, a war of direct resistance led by the Communist Party to save the entire Chinese nation from the enslavement that the Empire of the Rising Sun sought to impose upon it.

In conclusion, the historical chapter that began with the October Revolution saw the emergence of socialist countries grappling with aggression or the threat of aggression and with "an epoch of Napoleonic Wars" imposed by imperialist powers. It was an objective situation that made secondary the problem of building a socialist or communist society. There took place what we might call a turning point in the turning point of the twentieth century.

The epochal importance of the October Revolution must be clear to all. Yet, while the public debate and the political struggle seemed entirely to regard the dilemma between capitalism and socialism, there intervened, unnoticed by many, an entirely unexpected phenomenon: it became progressively clearer that the colonial question would play an essential role even in the socialist countries born of the October Revolution. We can now better understand why the hopes initially aroused by the revolution were not realized. The development of the objective contradictions placed as the order of the day and, on a worldwide scale, the conflict between imperialism and anti-imperialism, and between colonialism and anticolonialism. And this conflict continued to take priority even if it was communist forces sustaining the cause of anti-imperialism and anticolonialism, that held firm to this political orientation.

The great historical crisis of the first half of the twentieth century ended with the defeat inflicted on Hitler's plan to build his colonial empire in Eastern Europe. So ended what has been called "the greatest colonial war in history."[21] This definition is one hundred percent correct if we add a small amendment. It is one of the two greatest colonial wars in history, the other being that which ended with the defeat of the Empire of the Rising Sun, which had sought to emulate in Asia what Hitler was doing in Eastern Europe.

Therefore, the revolutionary cycle that began in October 1917 ended with two gigantic national wars, the Great Patriotic War of the Soviet Union and the War of National Resistance against Japanese imperialism fought by China. Not only was a barbaric colonialist and pro-slavery counter-revolution defeated, but the world anticolonialist revolution was born, which marked the twentieth century and would put an end to a world system that had lasted for more than a century under the banner of the most illiberal and oppressive forces. All this counted for little in the eyes of those who, above all in the West, awaited the abolition of the state or the coming of the "new man" to use an expression from *The Spirit of Utopia* by Ernst Bloch.[22]

4. Danielson's Dilemma and the Two Marxisms

We are concerned with an old problem that predates the October Revolution. Not long before his death, Engels observed that "warfare" became "a branch of the *grande industrie*" so that large-scale industry "became a political necessity" for a country that did not want to suffer subjugation, and it could have this *grande industrie* in "one form only: the capitalist form."[23] His reflections were expressed in a letter to Nikolai F. Danielson, editor of the Russian-language edition of *Capital*. Do they not make explicit the dilemma in which socialists in Russia would find themselves once they had achieved power, forced to undergo the process of industrialization (leaving a more or less ample space open for capitalism) to make up for their backwardness compared to the more advanced countries? The collateral effect would be to aggravate the social polarization within the country. To bet instead on a slow and gradual socialist development starting with the *mir*, the village community traditionally characterized more or less by egalitarian relations? That would have perhaps avoided the inequality and the tragedy intrinsic to capitalist industrialization but would have exacerbated the backwardness of the country and "might leave

Russia vulnerable to colonial domination by one or another of the world's great powers."[24] Therefore, which of the two inequalities had to be taken up first, the one internal to Russian society or global and planetary inequality?

Danielson's dilemma became much more urgent as the revolution led by a Communist Party spread to countries even more backward than Czarist Russia had been. The priority of the struggle against global inequality and rapid modernization mattered not only to consolidate independence but also to foil once and for all the danger of recurring famine and to make concrete the ideal of equality at every level. The case of China is exemplary here. Once assured of victory against Japanese imperialism, Mao hurried to make clear that the struggle against colonialism and neocolonialism was far from over. "Genuine and actual equality" required incisive transformations meant to overtake at every level the gap between China and the more advanced countries; "otherwise there will be only nominal and not actual independence and equality."[25] Announced while China was going through the most tragic period of its history, the goal of "modernization" assumed an ever more central role as liberation came closer. Mao clearly defined his government program: "Only modernization could save China."[26] Modernization meant a commitment to overcoming backwardness compared to the more advanced countries in a way that established a relationship of substantial equality with them, economically and technologically.

Not even the conquest of power changed this political agenda. On the eve of the official Proclamation of the People's Republic, the Communist leader sounded the alarm: Washington sought to reduce China to having "to live on U.S. flour" to "turn China into a U.S. colony."[27] And again, rather than building a new social order, the struggle against colonialism and neocolonialism became a priority. This struggle had an essential economic dimension. Only the development of productive forces could make national independence real and end the threat of neocolonial dependence.

Mao took his own measure of Danielson's dilemma theoretically. He emphasized the necessity for his country to precede socialist transformation with a phase of "new democracy."

Although such a revolution in a colonial and semi-colonial country is still fundamentally bourgeois-democratic in its social character during its first stage or first step, and although its objective mission is to clear the path for the development of capitalism, it is no longer a revolution of the old type led by the bourgeoisie to establish a capitalist society and a state under bourgeois dictatorship. It belongs to the new type of revolution led by the proletariat, aiming to establish a new-democratic society and a state under the joint dictatorship of all the revolutionary classes in the first stage. Thus this revolution actually serves the purpose of clearing a still wider path for the development of socialism. In the course of its progress, there may be some further sub-stages because of changes on the enemy's side and within the ranks of our allies, but the fundamental character of the revolution remains unchanged.[28]

In the Marxian sense of the term, socialism is a transitional phase; the Chinese Communist leader theorized a sort of transition within the transition. Far from being replaced or lost sight of, socialism became a goal spread over a much longer period than had been foreseen. On the other hand, it was also called for and pursued in the name of the conquest and defense of national independence. We have seen that Mao in 1949 identified Marxism-Leninism as the only scientific theory capable of leading the Chinese people to national redemption. The Chinese leader added, eight years later, "Only socialism can save China. The socialist regime has stimulated the rapid development of our productive forces."[29] Later, Deng Xiaoping said, "Only socialism can save China, and only socialism can develop China." Thus, socialism was evoked to ensure the economic and technological development that was the precondition for real national independence. He firmly stated the essential point: "Deviate from socialism, and China will inevitably regress to semi-feudalism and semi-colonialism."[30]

Even more than his predecessor, Deng Xiaoping insisted that "to achieve genuine political independence, a country must lift itself out of poverty."[31] And together with poverty, technological backwardness must be eliminated: "The gap between us and the countries with the most advanced science and technology" was distressing also in international relations. But, just as the new leader was promoting policies of reform and openness to gain access to the technologies of the most advanced capitalist countries to bridge a gap that might endanger China's national independence, others in the West cultivated a different dream and counter-position:

> Some analysts even predicted that the Special Economic Zones would become like American colonies in East Asia. . . . The Americans believed that China would become a gigantic economic branch of the United States thanks to a revival of the Open Door system of the early twentieth century, and today they find themselves, instead, facing a new economic rival.[32]

As we have seen, the struggle between colonialism and anticolonialism has characterized the history of the People's Republic of China throughout its existence. The same considerations apply to other, much smaller countries with a socialist orientation and, therefore, all the more exposed to the danger of losing independence. In the 1960s, Che Guevara called for vigilance against "economic aggression" and called on Cuba and the newly independent countries to "liberate themselves not only from the political yoke but also from the economic imperialist yoke."[33] In the small island threatened by the U.S. superpower and the Monroe Doctrine, the new power born of the revolution embraced the cause of socialism and communism and continued to identify its principal task as the struggle against colonialism and neocolonialism.

Western Marxism largely ignored Danielson's dilemma. At the end of the First World War, Ernst Bloch called attention to the colonial aims of the Germany of Wilhelm II, which not by chance treated "the country of Tolstoy as if it were part of the Black Continent" and had recourse to brutality typical of colonial wars. Beyond annexing vast territories, Germany had "destroyed the liberty and let drown ten million Ukrainian Bolsheviks near the city of Taganrog." That did not prevent the German philosopher from accusing the Soviet government of postponing the building of socialism and achieving socioeconomic relations of freedom and equality to a time that would never arrive. There was no justification for the policy followed by Lenin, "the Red Czar," because "there still exists in the Russian countryside the old institution of the *mir* or the semi-communist village communities." "In accordance with that and the will of the majority of the Russian people, the agro-proletarian policy he wants can be achieved."[34]

Max Horkheimer later expressed a similar attitude. While the German army was at the gates of Moscow, he denounced the Soviet government's lack of attention to the problem of the abolition of the state. Later, in a not dissimilar way, Perry Anderson celebrated the absolute superiority of Western Marxism over the Eastern version. The year before, the Vietnam War had concluded with the precipitous escape of the U.S. Army from Saigon. It was a defeat inflicted on an apparently invincible superpower by a small people in a little country; one led, however, by a Communist party and supported by a Communist movement that had contributed to making the war unleashed by Washington unpopular even in the West.

However, just as the desperate resistance of the Soviet people and the Red Army was for Horkheimer, so the victorious People's Army of Vietnam was without philosophical relevance for Anderson. These thinkers developed a fine and interesting analysis of the varying configurations of the relationship between nature and history and between object and subject in the two Marxisms but avoided posing any questions that today would seem ineluctable: what philosophical theory and what political line had made possible this great new victory of the anticolonial revolution, which followed that in China in 1949 and that in Cuba ten years later? Why did this revolution continue to be guided by the communist movement, and what relationship was there between this revolution and the cause of building a post-capitalist world? Was the struggle for national independence definitely over in China, Cuba, and Vietnam, or did a new phase open under the banner of economic and technological development? On what, then, should the relations of production be modeled? Without such questions, the failure to realize the initial expectations and hopes of the October Revolution ended as

5. The Two Marxisms at the Beginning and End of the Second Thirty Years' War

Along with the unexpected ramping up of the national and colonial question, the spread of Marxism worldwide deepened the differences between the West and East that had already emerged in the years that saw the birth of the international communist movement. Let's see what happened on the eve and at the start of the Second World War. In 1935, facing the ever-increasing threat of the Third Reich, the Communist International launched the antifascist Popular Front policy and promoted an alliance of the Soviet Union, Great Britain, France, and the United States. This turning point did not meet with a chorus of agreement among Black emancipation activists. Didn't allying with the traditional colonial powers and with the countries that incarnated the principle of white and Western supremacy both internally and internationally mean turning one's back on the struggle for the emancipation of the colonial peoples? This was the opinion of the great Black historian from Trinidad, the fervid admirer of Trotsky, C.L.R. James, who in 1962 described the evolution of another great activist in the cause of Black emancipation, also from Trinidad, George Padmore:

> Once in America, he [George Padmore] became an active Communist. He moved to Moscow to head their Negro department of propaganda and organization. In that post, he became the best-known and most trusted of agitators for African independence. In 1935, seeking alliances, the Kremlin separated Britain and France as "democratic imperialisms" from Germany and Japan, making the "Fascist imperialisms" the main target of Russian and Communist propaganda. This reduced activity for African emancipation to a farce: Germany and Japan had no colonies in Africa. Padmore broke instantly with the Kremlin.[35]

Something analogous happened in South Africa, at that time a "dominion" of the British Empire. Suspected also in this case of undermining the struggle against the regime of white supremacy, the United Front anti-fascist policy was often criticized and rejected by the Black communist militants, who called attention to Great Britain's role in the racist regime that exploited and oppressed them.[36]

The position of Eastern Marxism was: you can't correctly evaluate the nature of a country by erasing that country's behavior toward the colonial peoples and those of colonial origins. It is necessary, however, to add that this was a provincial and short-sighted Eastern Marxism. Germany and Japan "had no colonies in Africa," but they were preparing to impose an enormous colonial empire on Eastern Europe and Asia. Certainly, Germany and Japan did not count among the principal colonial powers, but they explicitly planned to establish slavery and to swallow whole peoples hitherto sheltered from colonial rule. In other words, the policy of the antifascist Popular Front was not in contradiction with the anticolonial struggle.

Four years later, the international scene changed radically: in August 1939, the Non-Aggression Pact between the Soviet Union and Germany was signed. It did not arouse any particular disturbance among the colonial peoples or those of colonial origin. We find W. E. B. Du Bois, the great historian and African-American activist who was already moving toward the communist movement, continuing to compare the Third Reich to the United States since both sought to defend white supremacy domestically and internationally. Even a person as far from the communist movement as Gandhi, in an interview while the Soviet-Nazi pact was still in effect, compared Great Britain to Germany. He saw them as two great powers committed to defending or achieving colonial empires.

The storm broke instead in the West and hit Marxists and communists hard, particularly in the North American Republic, where there was perhaps the most important section of the Fourth International, founded recently by Trotsky, and in this section, among the white activists, indignation knew no limits. The two countries that had signed the villainous pact must be put on the same level. They had come to an understanding because they both personified the horror of "totalitarianism." Now, this category, totally separated from the colonial question, included in its condemnation, on the one hand, the country that from the moment of its founding (in the October Revolution) had called on the "slaves of the colonies" to break their chains, and on the other the country that intended to take over and radicalize the colonialist tradition, making it work in Eastern Europe as well, and even reestablishing slavery. Influenced by this climate, Trotsky resorted to using the category "totalitarian dictatorship" and put into the genus of this category the species "Stalinist" and "Fascist" (and "Hitlerian"), a usage that would become the common sense of the Cold War and the dominant ideology of today. And yet, this was not enough to avoid a devastating rift in the U.S. Trotskyist party.

The dissidents demanded that the Soviet Union be condemned as imperialist and co-responsible for the outbreak of the war on a par with Nazi Germany. On this point as well the conflict between Western and Eastern Marxism emerged. Did the Second World War start on September 1, 1939, with Germany's invasion of Poland? Even if we want to remain focused only on Europe, why not add the dismemberment of Czechoslovakia and the Italian-German intervention against the Spanish Republic, which had been supported by the Soviet Union but not by Great Britain and France? Above all, why ignore what was happening in Asia? In May 1938, Mao took stock of the situation:

> By now, one-third of the world's population has entered the war. Look! Italy, then Japan; Abyssinia, then Spain, then China. The population of the countries at war now amounts to almost 600 million, or nearly a third of the world's total population. . . . After attacking Abyssinia, Italy attacked Spain and Germany joined in; then Japan attacked China. What will come next? Undoubtedly, Hitler will fight the great powers.[37]

Instead, the war had already begun and was aimed above all at the colonial peoples. Stalin shared this vision: "A new imperialist war is already in its second year, a war waged over a huge territory stretching from Shanghai to Gibraltar and involving over five hundred million people. The map of Europe, Africa, and Asia is being forcibly redrawn."[38]

From China's point of view, it was difficult to consider 1937, a year that brought the "rape of Nanking" by Japanese imperialism, with the massacre of 200,000 to 300,000 people, a period of peace. Far from sharing in the indignation of American Trotskyists (and Western Marxists in general), the Chinese Communist leader expressed satisfaction over the Non-Aggression Pact. It "constitutes a great blow to Japan and a great help to China" since it "will enable the Soviet Union to increase rather than decrease its aid to China" by freeing it for some time from the threat of the Third Reich and from the danger of fighting on two fronts, to support China's "resistance to Japanese aggression."[39] The Chinese Communist leader was focused on the pro-slavery war of colonial subjection against his country unleashed by the Empire of the Rising Sun, a war largely ignored by Western Marxism.

To conclude, the great historical crisis of the first half of the twentieth century, which we have defined as the Second Thirty Years' War, caused both at its start and at its end a bifurcation between Western Marxism and Eastern Marxism. At its start, Ho Chi Minh emphasized that the tragedy and horror had already begun to rage well before 1914 for the colonial peoples. Lenin called attention to the fact that the First World War was, in reality, the intersection of two wars—one raging in Europe among the slave owners and another unleashed by the slave owners to round up slaves and cannon fodder in their colonies. The final stage of the Second Thirty Years' War saw Western Marxism date the Second World War from its start in Europe rather than in the colonies (particularly in China). In any case, the defeat inflicted on Germany, Japan, and Italy flowed into the world anticolonialist revolution, which would spread worldwide in the second half of the twentieth century.

PART III

Western Marxism and the Anticolonial Revolution: A Meeting That Didn't Happen

1. THE BOBBIO-TOGLIATTI DEBATE IN THE YEAR OF DIEN BIEN PHU

For some time, thanks to the enormous prestige gained by the Soviet Union in the wake of Stalingrad and the powerful echo sounding through Asia and around the world from the victory of the anticolonialist revolution and of the Communist Party in China, the latent tensions between the two Marxisms seemed to be a chapter in a history now concluded. But this was only in appearance, as is demonstrated by the debate in Italy in 1954 among Norberto Bobbio, who was on the verge of becoming a world-famous philosopher, Galvano Della Volpe, at the time the most illustrious philosopher of Marxism and Italian communism, and Palmiro Togliatti, General Secretary of the Communist Party and one of the principal leaders of the international communist movement.

It was the first who initiated the debate. Bobbio recalls that in the years of the Resistance and in those immediately following, he was "one of those who believed in the by-now irresistible force of the Communist Party." And, he adds, in the irresistible force of the revolutionary wave that continued to grow:

We left decadentism behind us; it was the ideological expression of a class in decline. We had abandoned it because we participate in the birth and the hopes of a new class. I am convinced that if we have not learned from Marxism to see history from the point of view of the oppressed, gaining a new and immense perspective on the human world, we will not be saved. Either we will have sought refuge on the island of interiority, or we will have put ourselves at the service of the old masters.[1]

As a higher and more mature expression of modernity, Marxism here is not the thought of a single author so much as "the starting point of a movement of social revolution that is still ongoing," and which seems unstoppable. It is not possible to "turn history back" toward the past. Whoever wants to reject Marxism wholesale knows they are preparing a quixotic effort: "They must retrace the journey of four centuries and hurl themselves back into the Middle Ages."[2]

Beyond Marxism itself, Bobbio's judgment on the revolution it has inspired is positive. The October Revolution led to a radical "transformation of the economically and socially backward feudal world." It brought forth "a tumultuous and subversive wave" that sooner or later would be uncorked and channeled into a more regular course.[3] Indeed, we are in the presence of "totalitarian regimes," but that was not cause for shock because these were a "hard historical necessity," serious in the present but fated to be superseded.[4]

The praise of Marxism and communism was not addressed exclusively to the unresolved social question in the capitalist metropoles. "Western Civilization" itself is put into question. Thanks to its "technological success," it "arrogates to itself the right to be the only possible form of civilization, and to consider therefore the course of human history as its exclusive prerogative."[5] It was time to put an end to the philosophy of history that had overseen the colonial expansion of the capitalist West:

> History has only one direction, that is, the direction followed by the white civilization, on the margins of which lie only petrification,

arrested development, barbarism.... That there is not only one civilization worthy of the name, and that this one is the only one called on to exercise exclusive dominion, is the implicit assumption and the explicit consequence of the colonial expansion of the last four centuries that has not known any other form of contact with the other civilizations than to exterminate them (in America), to enslave them (in Africa), and to exploit them economically (in Asia).[6]

We come to the debate of 1954. On the socialist states, the philosopher from Turin was somewhat more reserved. To their credit was having "initiated a new phase of civil progress in politically backward countries, introducing traditionally democratic institutions, of formal democracy such as universal suffrage, and elective offices, and of substantial democracy such as the collectivization of the forces of production."[7] The new "socialist state" had to take to heart the mechanisms of liberal guarantees, pouring "a drop of oil in the machine of the revolution already accomplished."[8]

So far, this was a position that, with good reason, insisted on the essential character of "formal" freedom and its juridical-institutional embodiment. Unfortunately, the Turin philosopher identified the cause of "formal" freedom with the liberal-capitalist West, separating it from the colonial question. On May 7, 1954, at Dien Bien Phu, a popular army led by the Communist Party put an end to French colonial domination of Indochina and to the terror and infamy connected to it, which had already been forcefully denounced, as we have seen, by Ho Chi Minh. On the eve of the battle, the U.S. secretary of state, John Foster Dulles, asked the French prime minister Georges Bidault, "And if we gave you two atomic bombs?" (to use immediately, he meant).[9] In this same period, just to give another example, Great Britain responded to the challenge to its colonial dominion in Kenya by enclosing the civilian population in this country in terrible concentration camps in which the mass death of women and children was the norm.

One understands, therefore, the position of Palmiro Togliatti, the secretary of the Italian Communist Party: "When were these liberal principles, on which the British State of the nineteenth century is said to have been based, a model, I believe for those who think like Bobbio, ever applied to the colonial peoples?" The truth is that the "liberal doctrine . . . is founded on a barbaric discrimination between human creatures." Beyond that of the colonies such discrimination rages in the very capitalist metropoles themselves, as is demonstrated by the case of American Blacks "for the most part deprived of elementary rights, discriminated against and persecuted."[10]

The Communist Party leader did not show any disdain for "formal" freedom. Of course, its realization cannot be heedless of the international situation, geopolitical context, or the terrible threats that weigh on the Soviet Union and the other socialist countries. But, notwithstanding the need to take into account the Cold War that, as the conversation between Dulles and Bidault demonstrates, was always on the verge of transforming itself into a nuclear holocaust, there was no doubt that freedom, mistakenly considered "formal" only by vulgar Marxism, was in fact essential in and of itself: "The liberal and democratic upheavals have made clear a progressive tendency, of which the declarations of the rights of liberty are a part as much as are those of the new social rights. Rights of liberty and social rights have become and are the patrimony of this movement."[11]

Together with "social rights," it is also and especially the demand for "rights of liberty" for the colonial peoples and those of colonial origin that constitutes the dividing line between the socialist and the communist movements on the one hand and Western liberalism on the other.

2. MARX, CUT IN HALF BY DELLA VOLPE AND COLLETTI

Della Volpe, considered the most illustrious Italian Marxist philosopher of the time, intervened in the debate opened by Bobbio before Togliatti. One thing leaps out immediately: the difference in the positions of the great intellectual and those of the secretary of his party! Unlike the latter, the former made no mention of the colonial question (nor of the permanent state of exception imposed on the agents of revolutions looked on with hostility by the liberal West). Della Volpe instead followed a different strategy, concentrating on the celebration of *libertas maior* (the concrete development of individuality guaranteed by the material conditions of life and made possible by socialism). By doing so, on the one hand, he devalued the juridical guarantees of freedom by the liberal state, which he now happily demoted to *libertas minor*; on the other hand, he ended up confirming the transfiguration by which Bobbio made the liberal tradition into the champion of the cause of universal enjoyment of civil rights, formal freedoms, of the *libertas minor*, of limitations on state power.

Bobbio had called for studying and "understanding liberalism" by going to the school of "Locke and Montesquieu" and the "Federalist Papers."[12] Colonial questions and histories were eliminated. Beyond being a shareholder in the Royal African Company, the society that organized the African slave trade, Locke was, as noted by the illustrious historian of the institution of slavery, David Brion Davis, "the last great philosopher who sought to justify absolute and perpetual slavery." As for Montesquieu, he had called for taking note of the "uselessness of slavery among us . . . in our climes," and therefore wanted "to limit natural servitude [*servitude naturelle*] to certain countries."[13] Finally, one of the authors of the Federalist Papers, Madison, was himself a slave owner.

The authors Bobbio regarded as teachers were the embodiment of the "barbaric discrimination between human creatures" that Togliatti charged liberalism with. John Stuart Mill's hymn to liberty in his most celebrated text, *On Liberty*, was particularly important to the philosopher from Turin.[14] And yet, in this essay, the English liberal justifies the "despotism" of the West over the still "juvenile races" kept in a state of "implicit obedience" so that they can be set on the path of progress.[15] In the 1950s, the "despotism" and the "implicit obedience" imposed by the West were felt in Indochina, in Africa, and throughout the colonial world; in the United States itself (at least in the South), Blacks were exposed to the violence of both the local police and of racist and fascist bands (encouraged and tolerated by the authorities). And, overwhelmed by the celebration of *libertas maior*, Della Volpe remained unconcerned or was unable to highlight Bobbio's glaring injuries.

Unfortunately, Della Volpe was giving lessons: his disciples also distinguished themselves by their scarce attention to the colonial question. One thinks of Lucio Colletti. In his Marxist period, he demonstrated the underlying limits of the freedom so dear to the liberal-capitalist world, referring to the "workhouses" or "houses of correction," where, often on the simple word of the police, the unemployed and the poor, all those considered suspect of being "idle vagabonds," were incarcerated, and defining them as "concentration camps of the 'enlightened bourgeoisie.'"[16] The argument was fitting; a shame that it was partially undermined by the actual concentration camps of the "enlightened bourgeoisie" reserved for the barbarians in the colonies!

Consistent with this silence, at the moment of his break with Marxism and communism, Colletti outlined a disastrous account of the historical events initiated by the October Revolution without saying a word about the inspiration this event had given to the worldwide anticolonial revolution. The crisis of Marxism, he observed in 1980, "dates from many decades ago," but to be exact, "a revolutionary Marxist like Karl Korsch had already identified it in 1931."[17] He had identified it when the world colonialist system was still quite vigorous, so much so that Hitler proposed extending it to Eastern Europe to build the "German Indies." Did the anticolonial revolution that subsequently exploded on a planetary scale have something to do with Marxism and communism? It was a question completely absent in the work of the philosopher happily ensconced in the liberal-capitalist world.

Indeed, he mocked the interest that obstinate, incorrigible Marxists showed toward the "underdeveloped" countries and the "peasants," the "rural plebes," "a subject not only extraneous to the Marxist tradition but to which at least 'classical' Marxism had often shown itself to be hostile."[18] As if Marx had not dedicated a considerable part of his work to the struggle for the liberation of the Irish and Polish peoples (each consisting in large part of peasants), and as if (together with Engels) he had not bitterly and repeatedly criticized the English working class for its substantial subordination to British colonialism! Ignored in particular was Marx's great thesis: "The profound hypocrisy and inherent barbarism of bourgeois civilization lies unveiled before our eyes, moving from its home, where it assumes respectable form, to the colonies, where it goes naked."[19]

By reducing Marx to a critic of the "respectable forms" assumed by capitalist dominion and by erasing the colonial question, Colletti had no difficulty in developing a Manichean evaluation of the chapter of history that began with the October Revolution, a revolution, as Lenin noted, that had exploded on the scene to put an end to the "war between slave owners for the consolidation and strengthening of (colonial) slavery." In the view of the philosopher finally converted to the ideals of the liberal and capitalist West, these ideals permanently embodied the cause of freedom and tolerance. Indeed, he does not fail to mention "the massacre of more than one million communists in Indonesia," nor the "bloodbath" that followed the "military coup in Chile" and the "assassination of Allende" in September 1973.[20] In both cases, however, no reference was made to the role of the United States, which had decided to destroy Third Worldism (of which the Indonesia of Sukarno, whom they took aim at in 1965, was a leading example), and to uphold the Monroe Doctrine (in Latin America). No, the "massacre" and the "bloodbath" were evoked only to reiterate the failure of communism and Marxism, which cut a poor figure compared to the West, champion of the cause of freedom!

3. Workerism and the Condemnation of Third Worldism

Disinterest in the colonial question can also be asserted and practiced in the name of a rigorous revolutionary theory and practice that, without letting itself be distracted by the countries of the periphery and by classes that, for the most part, are still linked to the preindustrial world, instead concentrate on the capitalist metropoles and on the antagonist of class struggle *par excellence*, the working class. This is what happens in Italian *operaismo* (workerism), and in particular in the work of Mario Tronti: "Our workerism should be given credit for not falling into the trap of Third Worldism, of the countryside against the city, of the farmers' long marches. We were never Chinese."[21]

The founding text of Italian workerism made clear, in unequivocal terms in the title *Workers and Capital*, who the social subjects that interested Tronti were. We are in 1966. In Vietnam, the struggle for national liberation dared to challenge the mastodon-size military apparatus of the United States, which the year before had played a not-to-be-forgotten role in the repression in Indonesia, in the massacre of hundreds of thousands of communists, during the defeat inflicted on the Third World militants of that country. In Latin America, the struggle against the Monroe Doctrine was fierce, and in the name of that doctrine, in 1961, the Kennedy administration attempted to invade and subjugate Cuba. In summary, the struggle between colonialism and anticolonialism had exploded, and this contributed to feeding a crisis that, starting with installing Soviet missiles on the rebel island, pushed the world to the verge of a nuclear catastrophe.

Without letting himself be distracted by all this, Tronti imagined "Lenin in England" (as the title of a central chapter of his book has it). Leaving behind a still scarcely developed Russia, the great revolutionary relocated himself to the center of the capitalist metropole, but not to analyze from within the British Empire, which was involved in one colonial war after another and was ready to battle for world hegemony, as "the country that exploits the whole world" (Engels) and because of which, according to Marx's denunciation, the very same working class, infected by the dominant ideology, considered and treated the Irish, inhabitants of a colony barbarically exploited and oppressed, as "niggers."[22] No, instead, in England, Lenin was exclusively concerned with the factories and working conditions. In other words, the great revolutionary is here read as the kind of trade unionist he bitterly criticized.

Instead of England in the nineteenth and twentieth centuries, let's try to imagine Lenin in the United States in the 1960s. He would have found in the most developed capitalist country and leader of imperial and colonial oppression around the world, in the country where not a few times the workers and their unions threatened, and not only with words, students (often of bourgeois origins) protesting the draft and the war in Vietnam. However, from the theoretical point of view of workerism, Lenin should have only concerned himself with the working class!

Tronti did not give up his search for a pure state of class struggle, and, in a recent essay, four decades after the publication of *Workers and Capital*, he felt he could finally state that "1969 was the true *annus mirabilis*. In 1969, the issue wasn't anti-authoritarianism but anti-capitalism. Workers and capital found themselves physically face to face with one another."[23] Here, he refers not to England or the United States but to Italy. It is worth noting that, to find a class struggle in a pure state, Tronti was forced to have recourse to a country where the Communist Party exercised an enormous influence, thanks to the same political line of grand alliances that the theoretician of workerism did not in any way share.

However, there is no doubt that the autumn of 1969 saw great developments in workers' struggles. The workers were encouraged by and joined with a mass presence of students. Not a few of these were of bourgeois origin and arrived at militant political activity starting precisely from the struggle against "authoritarianism" identified and denounced first and foremost in the family and at school. Others underwent a process of political radicalization on the wave of protest against the barbaric war waged against Vietnam and also from their enthusiasm for the effective resistance of an intrepid people against the gigantic military apparatus of their invaders. These were the years when, in Asia, Latin America, and the Middle East, the anticolonial revolution (supported by the socialist countries) achieved brilliant success, and U.S. imperialism was in serious difficulty. It was a climate that made itself felt in Italy, where there was a Communist Party, stronger than ever, to which a large part of the militants and leaders that organized the great popular and workers struggles belonged.

With a more attentive look, the class struggle, which in the eyes of Tronti seemed to have finally achieved its pure form, reveals itself to have been nurtured from the start by the most diverse set of contradictions, including that of an anticolonial revolution. The polemic against the possible contaminations of the class struggle assumed militant tones. We have already seen the mockery of the campaign "of the countryside against the city, of the farmers' long marches." Here, the greatest anticolonial revolution in history (which in China achieved success through the victory of the countryside) is the target of workerist sarcasm, along with one of its high points, which saw the revolutionaries led by the Communist Party march for thousands of kilometers, under fire from reactionaries, to fight the Japanese invasion that sought to enslave the Chinese people.

This type of more or less workerist sarcasm is not new. Proudhon was likewise concerned with safeguarding the purity of the struggle between the poor and the rich or between victims and beneficiaries of the "theft" that he considered "property" to be. He made fun of the struggles for national liberation of the Polish people oppressed by the Czarist autocracy. Marx, who had founded the International Workingmen's Association in 1865, dubbed this kind of mockery "moronic cynicism."[24]

Tronti does not seem to have reflected on this page of the history of the workers' movement. Instead, he doubles down on the question:

> The workers always had—they had to have!—a "mission" to complete, and it was always saving something—it had to be!—this mission: Save the factory, save the country, save peace, save the people of the Third World from imperialist aggression.[25]

It is not explained here what, for example, the Chinese workers should have done while their country was being invaded: continue to make wage demands without worrying about the enslavement that loomed over them and their fellow citizens? The binary reading of social conflict, which sees only one contradiction (between workers and capital), transforms this same contradiction into a prison marked by the most narrow-minded corporatism. And this corporatism distorts the reading of history. The twentieth century is "the age of worldwide civil war."[26] In this frame, the world anticolonial revolution has vanished, and it has vanished both as armed struggle and as economic struggle. While the countries that have achieved national independence sought to make that independence concrete and solid through the hard work of economic and technological development, workerism called for the "workers' suppression of work"!

4. Althusser, Anti-Humanism and Anticolonialism

However, even when it was cheered on and supported, the anticolonialist revolution could be approached using categories that made it difficult to comprehend. Let's return to the "barbaric discrimination between human creatures" that Togliatti charged the capitalist-colonialist system with. It was a denunciation that rang with humanism, and the humanism, as we shall see, was celebrated by Gramsci but later on would be demonized by Louis Althusser. This thinker, unlike Tronti, could not pretend to never having been "Chinese."

The French philosopher referred repeatedly and positively to Mao Zedong, appreciating him most of all as a theoretician of contradictions and dialectics.[27] It was a homage rendered to thought that had matured, starting from what can be considered the greatest anticolonialist revolution in history, one that saw the most populous country in the world and one with a millennia-old civilization confront theoretically and practically, and in a long struggle, multiple contradictions and enemies of diverse natures.

However, Althusser undermines the homage to the world anticolonialist revolution then occurring with anti-humanist theorizing. This precludes comprehension of those class struggles that, far from being merely economic, are struggles for recognition. This is true especially for the struggles of colonial peoples and those of colonial origin, to the detriment of whom the de-humanization imposed by the capitalist-imperialist system manifested in a particularly brutal way. This is why, throughout contemporary history, the great tests of strength between abolitionism and slavery, between anticolonialism and colonialism, saw, ideologically, the pathos of the universal concept of humanity on the one side and its negation and denigration on the other. These struggles saw, in other words, the confrontation between humanism and anti-humanism.

At the end of the eighteenth century, Toussaint Louverture led the great revolution of Black slaves, invoking "the absolute adoption of the principle for which no man, red [that is, mulatto], black or white may he be, can be the property of his kind." No matter how humble his condition, men cannot be "confused with animals," as was the case under the system of slavery. On the other side, Napoleon, determined to reintroduce colonial domination and Black slavery to Saint-Domingue/Haiti, proclaimed, "I am for the whites because I am white; there is no other reason beyond this, but this is good enough."[28]

Let's move on to the English-speaking world now. A celebrated abolitionist poster showed a Black slave in chains exclaiming, "Am I Not a Man and a Brother?" A few decades later, while the colonial system was at its apogee, at the entrance to certain public parks in the U.S. South, signs said, "Entrance Forbidden to Dogs and Negroes," while in Shanghai, the French Concession defended its purity by making quite visible signs reading "Entrance Forbdden to Dogs and Chinese." It was a phenomenon of worldwide dimensions. Fully used to being considered "niggers" after the great revolt of the Sepoys in 1857, the inhabitants of India in the spring of 1919 found themselves the subjects of a terrible humiliation. After making an essential contribution to Great Britain's victory in the First World War, they protested to demand, if not independence, some form of self-government. At Amritsar, the repression by the colonial power was distinguished by its brutality; it not only cost the lives of hundreds of unarmed protesters; it also required the inhabitants of the rebellious city to crawl on all fours to return home or to go out from their homes.

The dehumanization of the colonial peoples is manifested in a way that is simultaneously flexible and repugnant. We can therefore understand the view of a nineteenth-century author who would become dear to Nazism. Houston S. Chamberlain, while celebrating the dawn of the twentieth century as "the century of race" and "the century of colonies," mocked the "so-called unity of the human race," which, in his view, science and history refuted and which remained pathetically embraced only by "the socialists." Later, the most illustrious ideologue of Nazis, Alfred Rosenberg, intoned against the dogma of a presumed "general development of humanity" and ironically commented on the persistent influence of religion and Jewish mythology: the old Jehovah "is now called 'humanity.'"[29]

It was a chapter of history that went well beyond Germany and

Europe. The universalist pathos that resounded from the October Revolution and its appeal to the colonial slaves to break their chains was met with the theory of the *underman/Untermensch*, the "subhuman." It is a category that the American author Lothrop Stoddard would later formulate in a book (soon translated into German) that prescribes Hitler's campaign to colonize Eastern Europe, enslave the Slavs, and exterminate the Jews, along with the Bolsheviks, who were seen as ideologues and instigators of the revolt of the "inferior races."

For Italian fascism, likewise committed to colonialist and racist counterrevolution, the abyss separating one "race" or nation from another was unbridgeable, to the point that, in Mussolini's eyes, expressions such as "the human race" were "too evanescent" or even without meaning.[30] Finally, in Asia, Japan continued its colonial expansion together with the dehumanization of the Chinese, who, from the late nineteenth century, had been represented as similar to beasts, often compared to apes or pigs.[31]

Certainly, under pressure from denunciations that brought to light its inhuman character, colonialism was sometimes forced to assume a universalist guise. Historically, how did the protagonists of the movements for emancipation react? Du Bois has no difficulty in noting that the (universalist) keywords "Peace, Christianity, Commerce," used so often by the "British Empire" and the "American Republic," coexisted with "raging hatred for the darker races" that they accused each other of. The fact was that colonialism and imperialism were "built on the inhuman exploitation of human beings," considered to be "outside of humanity."[32] The struggle for universalism led to a confrontation with a sociopolitical system whose practice of dehumanization was intrinsic.

The communist movement's position was no different. Lenin called attention to the fact that, in the eyes of the West, the victims of the war and of colonial expansionism "don't even deserve the appellation of peoples (perhaps the Asians and Africans are peoples?)"; they were excluded from the human community.[33] Gramsci was even more explicit. Writing in the 1930s, he observed that even for a philosopher such as Henri Bergson, "In reality, 'humanity' means West"; this is how the champions of the "defense of the West" argue and is the dominant culture in the West. Communism, instead, was synonymous with "integral humanism," a humanism that challenged the prejudices and the arrogance of the "white supermen."[34] In other words, pseudo-universality, which consists of the arbitrary upgrading to a universal of a particular and often vicious determinate, is frequently masked by recourse to a truer and richer meta-universality.

5. Althusser's Idealist and Eurocentric Regression

While politically compromising understanding of the great sociopolitical struggles of contemporary history, theoretically, anti-humanism leads to two relevant and quite negative consequences. Marx more than once insisted that his theory was the theoretical expression of real processes and movements, of a real class struggle. With Althusser, instead, historical materialism and the real movement that it contributed to and promoted were the result of an "epistemological break" (just as for Della Volpe, they are the result of a scientific method that is the fruit of the teachings of Galileo, and before him, Aristotle, the critic of Plato). And so we encounter an idealist distortion of historical materialism, which came to us thanks to the work of one individual who discovered a new continent. Following the discovery of "the continent of mathematics by the Greeks," Marx launched the discovery of "continent history."[35] After having repeatedly accused humanism of obscuring the class struggle, Althusser (together with Della Volpe) would make the class struggle vanish from historical materialism.

This idealistic regression was, at the same time, a Eurocentric regression. In Marx and Engels, historical materialism presupposed, on the one hand, the Industrial Revolution, and, on the other, political revolution, starting with the French Revolution. Neither of these revolutions is exclusively European. The former led to the formation of the world market, to colonial expansion, to the original accumulation of capital; the latter saw one of its highest points in the rising of the Black slaves of Saint-Domingue and in the abolition of colonial slavery decreed in Paris by the Jacobin Convention.

With Althusser (as with Della Volpe), the development of historical materialism is a chapter of intellectual history conducted exclusively in Europe. We can well understand the reasons for the attitude taken by the French philosopher. These were the years when the banner of "humanism" was waved to mute the struggle against imperialism; it began the process that would later lead to Gorbachev's capitulation. Looking carefully, we see that the philosophical critique of humanism, which tended to obscure social conflict, was a way to distance oneself from "conceptions tainted with reformism and opportunism, or quite simply revisionist" that were widespread during these years.[36]

Unfortunately, this polemic took off from an erroneous position. In the first place, it is worth keeping in mind that the appeal to the human community (and to morality) and the call to science can lead to forgetting the class struggle. However, the French philosopher quite rightly took a position against the phrase that, condemning the inter-classist view of science, counterposed "proletarian science" to "bourgeois science." He recognized Stalin's merit in being opposed to the "zeal" of those "who were making strenuous efforts to prove language a(n ideological) superstructure." Thanks to these "few simple pages," concludes Althusser, "we could see that there were limits to the use of the class criterion that we had been made to treat science, a status claimed by every page of Marx."[37] And as far as morality is concerned? To put on the same plane positions that demanded the unity of the human race and positions that denied and mocked it, to argue in the name of a self-styled, purely proletarian class struggle meant losing sight of the real class struggle based on the dehumanization of large masses of human beings, degraded to *Untermenschen* and destined only to be oppressed, enslaved, or annihilated.

Arguing against a humanist reading of Marxism, Althusser never tired of repeating that Marx did not start from "man" or the "individual" but from the historical structures and social relations. However, it's clear that the concept of "man" or of the "individual" is taken for granted. In reality, the concept of the individual and of man as such, independent of sex, status. or skin color, is the result of the centuries-long struggle for recognition, conducted under the banner of humanism so disparaged by Althusser. That also goes for women (considered by nature incapable of being political actors and thinkers and of engaging in intellectually skilled work), for the waged workers of the metropoles (reduced to instruments of labor, to bipedal machines, and to pack animals), and in a particular way to the colonized peoples (de-humanized in every way). The French philosopher recognized that a "revolutionary humanism" could also be born from the October Revolution.[38] But on this point, he is somewhat hesitant, so he precludes understanding of the gigantic struggle conducted by the "slaves of the colonies" (to use a phrase dear to Lenin) and aimed at gaining recognition of their human dignity.

Althusser considered the category of man to be compromised by inter-classism and incapable of calling attention to the reality of exploitation and oppression. But here, he made his second theoretical error. There are no terms that in themselves can express in a pure state social and political antagonisms. There are no ideologically and politically "pure" terms that were always and only utilized by revolutionaries and only in a revolutionary way. In the United States in the nineteenth century, "democratic" referred to the party committed to defending the enslavement of Blacks and the regime of white supremacy. This is also true for the categories that seem to be inextricably intertwined with the history of the workers' movement. In France, after the 1848 revolution, the banner of "labor" and respect for the "dignity of labor" began to be waved by conservatives committed to denouncing as "idle" and as bums revolutionary agitators or workers on strike to improve their living and working conditions. Further along this road than anyone else is Hitler, who, in the name of the party he founded and led, sets himself up as the champion of "socialism" and the "German workers."

Notwithstanding their different starting points, Althusser comes to the same conclusions as Tronti. The Italian author never tires of restating that "universalism is the classical bourgeois vision of man." Fortunately, there are the workers: "With them, and only with them, we can finally leave behind universal values because, from their point of view, these are always ideologically bourgeois."[39] In place of universalism, Althusser takes aim at humanism. But we are in the presence of the same outlook: without being aware of it, he ends up embellishing his target with a critique that, nevertheless, seeks to be intransigent and to eschew all compromise.

In reality, stamping universalism or humanism as in itself "bourgeois" or inclined to compromise with the bourgeoisie means halting the critique of capitalist society halfway. It means reproaching the purely formal nature of civil and political rights, whose owner should be humanity as such, in its universality, but without mention of the frightening exclusion that deprives colonial peoples or peoples of colonial origin of civil and political rights (and economic and social rights). That is, it glosses over the colonial condition, which also, in Marx's view, reveals *par excellence* the barbarity of capitalist society. In that case, the dehumanizing character of the existing order was revealed in all its brutality and ended up manifesting itself explicitly, as was confirmed in a particularly sensational way in the United States, where theories of racial inferiority preceded the theory of the *underman Untermensch*. In other words, Togliatti was much more consequential and radical when he denounced the "barbaric discrimination between human creatures" on which capitalist society is founded.

6. Bloch's Legacy and the Transfiguration of Liberalism

Notwithstanding their passionate denunciation of universalism and of humanism, which substantially eliminates the colonial question, Tronti and Althusser end up paradoxically converging on the position of Bloch, who, from the start, credited without hesitation both universalism and humanism to the Western liberalism he loved to boast about. During the First World War, we have seen that the German philosopher endorsed the ideology of the Entente, which claimed it wanted to bring to the Central Powers and the entire world the very democracy that was obstinately denied to the colonial peoples.

The liberal West was counterposed positively by Bloch to not only the Germany of Wilhelm II but also the country born of the October Revolution. On the latter, the young philosopher expressed a severe judgment without waiting for the withdrawal from Russia of the German army or, even less, for the end of the civil war: "The proletarians of the world have not fought for four and a half years against Prussia in the name of worldwide democracy, to then abandon freedom and the democratic line (the pride of Western culture) in the name of the conquest of socioeconomic democracy," referring to Soviet Russia. As this last passage suggests, he made a comparison to the North American Republic: "With the admiration for Wilson, already one could think, as socialists, that it would have been possible that the sun of Washington would one day supersede the awaited sun of Moscow, that freedom and purity could come from capitalist America."[40]

There is a duplicitous erasure at work here. We pass over the fact that the war provoked a climate of terror and witch hunts in the countries where the liberal tradition was most firmly rooted and that, thanks to their geographic location, were a safe distance from the battlefields or from the threat of invasion. The most serious erasure, however, concerned the colonial question. Only a few years earlier, the United States that Bloch celebrated put down through merciless repression and genocidal practices the revolution for independence in the Philippines. On its own territory, between the nineteenth and twentieth centuries, a terrorist regime of white supremacy repeatedly subjected Black people to lynchings—to torture and slow and interminable execution staged as a mass spectacle for the festive white community.

The Second World War saw an eruption of the colonial question well beyond the colonial world. Hitler sought to build a "German Indies" in Eastern Europe, at times comparing it to a kind of Wild West: like the American "Indians," the "indigenous" in the Third Reich had to be deported and exterminated to conquer their territory for the white and German race. The survivors were destined to work like the Black slaves forever at the service of the master race. Not dissimilar was the practice of the Japanese Empire in Asia. However, the centrality assumed by the colonial question did not lead to any rethinking by Bloch.

In 1961, Bloch published *Natural Law and Human Dignity*. As the title indicates, this is far from the underrating so dear to the Della Volpe of *libertas minor*. On the contrary, the defense of the legacy of the liberal tradition is front and center. The criticism of this tradition continued to be that which we have already seen the young Bloch express with the words of Anatole France: in the liberal-capitalist world, "equality before the law: that it forbids rich and poor alike to steal firewood or to sleep under bridges."[41] In *Natural Law and Human Dignity*, the philosopher reiterated that liberalism is wrong to advocate for a "formal judicial equality" that remains "purely formal."[42]

This affirmation can be read in a book published in the same year that Paris police unleashed a merciless witch hunt against Algerians, drowning many in the Seine or killing them with their batons. And all this happened in the light of day, indeed in the presence of French citizens who, under the protection of the law, assisted while enjoying the spectacle: anything but "formal equality"! In the capital city of a liberal and capitalist country, we see at work the dual legislation that consigned to arbitrary will and to police terror a defined ethnic group.[43] If then we take into consideration the colonies and the semi-colonies, and we turn our attention to, for example, Algeria, Kenya, or Guatemala (a formally independent country but, in fact, a U.S. protectorate), we see that the dominant capitalist and liberal state has recourse on a large scale and in a systematic way to torture, concentration camps, and genocidal practices against the indigenous populations. There is not a trace of any of this in Bloch.

The colonial peoples and those of colonial origin continued to be absent when the author of *Natural Law and Human Dignity* reconstructed the history of modernity and liberalism. He appreciates Grotius's and Locke's natural law approach but does not mention their efforts to justify Black slavery. Referring to the American War of Independence, he paid homage to the struggle of the "newly liberated states" but passed over in silence the weight of slavery in the sociopolitical reality and the U.S. Constitution itself.[44]

Even more striking is his silence over the fact that it was in precisely these years that the African American struggle to definitively abolish the regime of white supremacy developed in the Republic on the other side of the Atlantic. It was a development that caught Mao Zedong's attention in Beijing. And it is interesting to compare the positions of two such different personalities. The German philosopher denounced the merely "formal" character of liberal and capitalist equality. The communist leader instead emphasized the intersection of social and racial inequality: the Blacks suffered from a higher unemployment rate than whites, were confined to inferior segments of the labor market, and were forced to accept reduced wages. Mao did not stop here. He also called attention to the racist violence unleashed by the authorities of the South and by bands tolerated and encouraged by them, and he celebrated "the struggle of the American Black people against racial discrimination and for freedom and equal rights."[45]

Bloch instead criticized the bourgeois revolution for limiting "equality to political equality."[46] Regarding African Americans, Mao noted, "Most of them are deprived of the right to vote."[47] Reduced to commodities and dehumanized by their oppressors, the colonial peoples for centuries have conducted memorable battles for recognition, but in Bloch we read that "the idea that men are born free and equal can already be found in Roman law; now it should also be found in reality."[48] Now, let's look at the conclusion of the article by the Chinese Communist leader devoted to the struggle of African Americans for emancipation: "The evil colonialist-imperialist system rose with the enslaving and trafficking of the black people, and it will certainly come to an end with the complete liberation of the black people."[49]

As we see in the citations from Mao, as in those we have noted by Ho Chi Minh, there is none of the undervaluation dear to Della Volpe and his *libertas minor*, nor the illusion, common in different ways to Della Volpe, Bloch, and Bobbio, that capitalism and liberalism would guarantee in any case "formal equality" or even "political equality."

7. Horkheimer: From Anti-Authoritarianism to Philo-Colonialism

The incomprehension of the colonial question culminated in a current of thought to which we are indebted for its brilliant and acute analyses of the social, political, and moral problems peculiar to capitalist society. I refer to the Frankfurt School. In his 1942 work *The Authoritarian State*, Max Horkheimer summed up the history that began with the October Revolution. The condemnation was unconditional: in Russia, there was not socialism but "state capitalism." Of course, we need to recognize that it "increases production" in an extraordinary way, and this was of great benefit to the "economically retarded territories of the world" so that they could make up in rapid time their backwardness with respect to the more advanced countries.[50] At least this could be considered a positive result, right? In reality, it is true that the Russia the Bolsheviks governed with an iron fist succeeded in bringing about industrial and economic development and had become a model, but who feels its appeal?

> Instead of dissolving in the end into the democracy of the councils, the group [the Communist Party] can maintain itself as a leadership. Work, discipline and order can save the republic and tidy up the revolution. Even when the abolition of the state is written on its banner, that party transfigured its industrially backward fatherland into the secret vision of those industrial powers who were suffering from their parliamentarism and could no longer live without fascism.[51]

While these lines were being written, the Nazi army, after having subjugated the better part of Europe, was at the gates of Moscow and Leningrad. Their entire populations faced the threat of death at the hands of a terrifying war machine or through a merciless siege and the starvation stemming from it. In these circumstances, what sense did the evocation of the "democracy of the councils" or even less the utopian idea of the abolition of the state have? At that moment, the accomplishment of Hitler's project seemed to be at hand, a project that explicitly aimed at enslaving the peoples of Eastern Europe to build a great colonial empire on a continental scale.

If subjected to the formidable pressure of a gigantic military apparatus and of an experiment in brutal efficiency, the Soviet Union could resist because of the forced march to industrial development to which Horkheimer refers. But he paid no attention to all this and saw as irrelevant the fact that in this conflict, there was, on one side, colonialism and slavery, and on the other, anticolonialism and antislavery. In the eyes of the prestigious exponent of critical theory, it was, if anything, the country of the October Revolution that was on the verge of being enslaved (after its population was decimated) that deserved the most severe judgment:

> Integral statism, or state socialism, is the most consequential form of the authoritarian state, which has freed itself from dependence on private capital.... In integral statism, socialization is simply decreed. Private capitalists are eliminated. Integral statism is not a retreat but an advance of power. It can exist without racism.[52]

And so the crisis of critical theory emerged again. To Horkheimer, it seemed irrelevant that there were differences between a country committed to imposing a racist state and to decimating and enslaving "the inferior races" and exterminating the political and ethnic groups (Bolsheviks and Jews) seen as instigators of the revolt of the "inferior races," and a country that knew it was one of the intended victims of this racist state, and which desperately defended itself against it.

Even with an eye to the past and on the level of the philosophy of history in general, Horkheimer pays little or no attention to the colonial (or racial) question: "The French Revolution tended toward totalitarianism."[53] So he targeted the revolution that, at the dawn of the contemporary age, spurred the great uprising of enslaved Blacks in Saint-Domingue and pushed the Jacobin Convention in Paris to decree the abolition of slavery in the colonies. Two other revolutions—in seventeenth-century England and in Britain's North American colonies in the eighteenth century—were immune from the suspicion of totalitarianism and authoritarianism. Both revolutions furthered the institution of slavery. In the North American Republic, revolution brought about the first emergence of the racial state (not by coincidence, slave owners presided over it in its first decades).

Horkheimer's condemnation of the French Revolution knew no limits: "The 'sans-culottes Jesus' heralded the coming of the Nordic Christ."[54] Robespierre, the figure stirred by the most radical currents of the French Revolution with a view to breaking down once and for all the quasi-naturalistic barrier that in the *ancien régime* separated the working classes from the elites, is likened to the figure cultivated by the reactionary culture that resulted in Nazism and who was committed to reestablishing the natural barrier between peoples and "races" swept away by the epic uprising of the Black Jacobins of Saint-Domingue and by the abolition of Black slavery in Paris achieved by Robespierre.

Once the French Revolution and the October Revolution had been disposed of, all that remained was to genuflect before a liberalism mythically transfigured and identified with the slogan and the defense of "the autonomy of the individual."[55] It is a transfiguration that also affected Locke, whom Horkheimer read as a champion of the principle that all people are "free, equal and independent."[56] And, again, as if by magic, slavery and the defense of Black slavery disappeared from the work of a philosopher who benefited materially from it, being a stockholder in the Royal African Company, which managed the traffic in human beings.

Given these presuppositions, the lack of attention, the diffidence, and even the hostility with which Horkheimer views the worldwide anticolonial revolution is not surprising. He read the history of his time as a struggle between "civilized states" and "totalitarian states." This also went for the Cold War: "I must say that if the civilized states didn't spend enormous sums on armaments, we would find ourselves already under the domination of those totalitarian powers. If one criticizes, one must also know that those criticized cannot act differently."[57] It was 1970. The war against Vietnam raged greater than ever, and its colonial character and genocidal practices were evident to all. And yet, the most authoritative exponent of critical theory had no doubts: The "civilized" West must defend itself from the barbarians of the East!

Nor did the African-American struggle against the persistent regime of white supremacy in the U.S. South trouble Horkheimer's certainty. Yes, he discussed "the current difficult situation of race relations beyond the Atlantic," but he emphasized the "terrorism of the Negro activists over other Negroes that is much stronger than one thinks." "The average Negro is more afraid of other Negroes" than of whites, he wrote.[58] All in all, the worldwide anticolonial revolution was pretty useless: "The Negro American issue" could be rapidly resolved "if the conflict between East and West did not exist" and if the same were true of "the backward parts of the world."[59] The discrimination that African Americans were fighting against was put on the bill of the Cold War and the anticolonial revolution, as reflected in the critical reference to the "terrorism of Negro activists" in the United States and to the role of the Third World.

In reality, things were exactly the opposite. In December 1952, the Supreme Court declared racial segregation unconstitutional in public schools, but only after the Justice Department informed it that a different decision would have radicalized the "colored races" and promoted the communist movement in the Third World and in the United States itself.[60] The passage from diffidence to hostility is smooth:

> Our most recent critical theory has not fought for the revolution because after the fall of Nazism in the Western countries, the revolution would bring about a new terrorism, a terrible situation. It is instead a question of preserving that which has positive value, for example, autonomy, the importance of the individual, his differentiated psychology, some moments of culture, without arresting progress.[61]

This declaration does not seem to distinguish between the West and the Third World, so even the anticolonial revolution then occurring in Vietnam or that which had been victorious some years earlier in Algeria was compared to a "new terrorism."

Of a more general character is this additional declaration:

> Critical theory has the function of expressing that which, in general, is not expressed. It must, therefore, emphasize the costs of progress, the dangers that follow it and that end up dissolving even the idea of an autonomous subject, the idea of the soul, because it appears irrelevant in the presence of the universe.... Now we want the world to be unified; we want the Third World to no longer suffer from hunger or be forced to live on the brink of hunger anymore. But to achieve this goal, we must pay the price of a society that takes the form of a

world administration.... That which Marx imagined to be socialism, in reality, is the administered world.[62]

We see the condemnation of socialism, the anticolonial revolution, and the economic development of the peoples liberated or seeking to liberate themselves from the colonial yoke. We face a terrible alternative: resign ourselves to the poverty of the masses prevailing outside the West or fall into the horror of an administered world. And, at least for the critical theorist, the second option is much worse than the first.

8. Adorno's Imperial Universalism

It is possible to ascertain an element of regression in Horkheimer and Theodor Adorno. Regarding "fascism," *Dialectic of Enlightenment* (the book they jointly published in the 1940s) observes that, before its spread and triumph in the heart of Europe itself, "totalitarian capitalism" and "the totalitarian order" had involved only "the poor and savages."[63] The preparatory stages of fascism were identified with the violence perpetrated by the great Western powers against the colonial peoples and consummated in the heart of the capitalist metropole against the poor and marginalized trapped in a sort of concentration camp, the workhouse. It was acknowledged, to some extent, that Nazi fascism had made its first attempts at expansionism and colonial rule. It is true the victims were "savages" rather than peoples with their own history and culture who sought to build an independent national state. However, it was still a condemnation of colonialism and the nexus between Nazism and colonialism.

All this disappears without leaving a trace a few years later, with the coming of the Cold War, when the anticolonialist revolution merged with the international communist movement and, reaching the Middle East, put into question the policies and even the existence of the state of Israel. At this point, the polemic against the revolutionary agitation of the Third World became a constant theme and was developed in the name of universalism. In *Negative Dialectics*, Adorno rejected the Hegelian category of the "spirit of the people," that is, the attention to the national question, as "reactionary" and regressive compared to the Kantian universal of his time, humanity now seen "as affected by 'nationalism' and 'provincialism' in the era of world conflicts and of the potential for a global organization of the world."[64] Even worse, it was devotion to a "fetish," a "collective subject" (the nation), in which "individuals disappear without a trace."[65]

It was a stance that, in retrospect, delegitimized the revolution promoted and directed by the National Liberation Front of Algeria, a people and a country undoubtedly more provincial, more backward, and less cosmopolitan than the France against which they were waging an insurgency. It also delegitimized the anticolonial revolutions taking place under Adorno's eyes, beginning with the one led by the National Liberation Front of Vietnam. In the latter case, the philosopher's negative judgment was unequivocal and without nuance: "In the security of America, an emigrant could endure the news of Auschwitz; it would be difficult to believe that Vietnam is robbing anyone of sleep, especially since every opponent of colonial wars must know that the Vietcong for their part use Chinese methods of torture."[66]

Adorno made this declaration in 1969. The year before, the My Lai massacre had occurred. A brigade, at the orders of Lieutenant William Calley, did not hesitate to kill 347 civilians, including the old, women, children, and newborns. It was the irrefutable confirmation of the genocidal practices by which Washington's army disgraced itself. Still today, forty years after the end of that war, no count exists of the Vietnamese killed by dioxin sprayed without concern on the civilian population by U.S. aircraft. All this was compared to Auschwitz and reduced to a trifle, and such trifles did not make Adorno lose sleep. On the contrary, he mocked those who did lose sleep because of it rather than because of the "Chinese methods of torture" attributed to the Vietcong, who were, after all, the victims!

It is a page that dishonors philosophy. But it is a page that does not constitute an isolated incident en route. Even as historical reconstruction and philosophy of history, Adorno did not pay any attention nor show any sympathy for the victims of the West and its expansionist march:

Even the assaults of the conquistadors on ancient Mexico and Peru, which must have been experienced therein like invasions from another planet, murderously advanced the expansion of rational bourgeois society— irrationally for the Aztecs and Incas—all the way to the conception of "one world" teleologically inherent in the principle of that society.[67]

Albeit in an objective and "irrational" way, did colonial expansion contribute to bringing the human race closer together, to realizing a world finally united? One world is the "collective subject" in which the individual subject and even individual peoples "disappear without a trace," to pick up the critique by Adorno directed at Hegel. In any case, we have to ask: did colonial expansion not dig an unbridgeable gulf between the world's peoples, conferring on the superior race of the masters the right to enslave and sacrifice en masse the *undermen* and the *Untermenschen*?

If we move from the discovery-conquest of America to the French Revolution, the framework doesn't change: "The specific privation at least of the Parisian masses might have ignited the movement, while in other countries, where it was not so acute, the bourgeois process of emancipation succeeded without a revolution and at first did not touch the more or less absolutist form of domination."[68]

On the theme of the rise of modernity, different countries are compared without considering the colonial question. "The more or less absolutist form of domination" is denounced with reference to the Bourbon monarchy and Jacobinism in France, but never the power exercised over the Black slaves by the white masters (the latter regularly held the office of president in the United States' early years).[69]

Polemically turning on its head Hegel's great dictum "the truth is the whole,"[70] Adorno instead claimed, "the whole is the false."[71] Except when he idealized the West's dominant country and the West itself, Adorno confirmed the validity of the aphorism in the *Phenomenology of Mind*, not the one he proclaimed in *Minima Moralia*. Hegel makes clear that, in attenuating the social conflict beyond the Atlantic, the "outlet of colonization" had played a large role.[72] The view of the whole allowed the great philosopher of the dialectic to grasp the nexus between the freedom of the white community and the total unfreedom of the native population, which suffered a merciless process of expropriation, deportation, and decimation. This escaped a vision that, infantilizing and absolutizing a particular aspect of the reality investigated, ended up losing sight of the whole.

A final consideration. The return to Kant by Adorno was anything but convincing. In the essay "Toward Perpetual Peace," which *Negative Dialectics* alludes to, there is a memorable denunciation not only of colonial slavery and of colonialism but also of "universal monarchy" as synonymous with a "soulless despotism" founded on the oppression of nations and therefore destined to fail: "Nature has wisely divided the peoples from one another" and this allows for "differences in languages and religions." The attempt to unite the world under the banner of international despotism would clash with the resistance of the peoples and would result, if anything, in "anarchy."[73]

On another occasion, tracing the historical and philosophical results of the French Revolution, Kant observed that if patriotism runs the risk of sliding into exclusivity and of losing sight of the universal, an abstract love of humanity "cannot fail to dissipate this inclination through its excessive generality" and risks in this way reducing itself to an empty declaration. It is a question, then, of reconciling "global patriotism" with "local patriotism" or with "love of country"; whoever is authentically universalist "in fealty to his country must have an inclination to promote the well-being of the entire world."[74] Looking closely, Adorno laid claim to a philosopher who had already criticized and refuted his argument.

9. Whoever Is Unwilling to Talk about Colonialism Should Also Keep Quiet About Capitalism and Fascism

With the anticolonial revolution in full swing, the two leading exponents of critical theory did not limit themselves to counterposing their imperial universalism. Let's read this eloquent declaration from the 1960s:

Joy makes men better. It is impossible for happy men, capable of enjoyment and who see many possibilities for being happy, to be particularly evil.... Of Kant and Goethe it is said that they were great connoisseurs of wines, which means that when they were alone they were certainly not tormented by jealousy, and they had instead the possibility of enjoyment, they were enriched by experiences.[75]

So this is how things stood: nothing good could come from the "wretched of the earth" so dear to Frantz Fanon or from the anticolonial movement. And yet, this is the same Horkheimer who recognized that "the industrialists approved of Hitler's program." Men who were presumably "happy," perhaps because they were "great connoisseurs of wines" (no less than were Kant and Goethe), but who had shown themselves to be "particularly evil" in giving the green light to a program of war, colonial expansionism, and annihilation.[76]

However, the motivation in question is also present in Adorno. For him, too, the source of evil is "resentment" (of classes and of peoples in subaltern conditions) and the rancor that "*ressentiment* strikes every happiness, even its own, and so a consequence is that "satiety has become a term of rebuke a priori, even though the only thing bad about it would be that there are those who have *nothing* to eat." This last issue was a problem that could be solved "technically," that is, not through political action by the disinherited but by the beneficent intervention of the classes and countries that possess a superior culture (and wealth and power).[77] In his time, Nietzsche had rejected any objectivity on the social question, putting it in the category of the *ressentiment* of failures. Analogously, the two principal exponents of critical theory likewise deal with the social question at the international level.

We can, therefore, understand that the main target of Adorno's polemic is the revolutionary agitation of the Third World:

Today, the fascist fantasy undeniably blends with the nationalism of the so-called underdeveloped countries, which already are no longer called that but rather "developing countries." So also, during the war, in slogans about Western plutocracies and proletarian nations, sympathy was expressed with those who felt that they had come up short in the imperialist competition and wanted to find a seat at the table. It's hard to say if and to what extent this tendency is already embedded in the anti-civilizational, anti-Western current of the German tradition: whether in Germany too, there is a convergence of fascist and communist nationalism.[78]

After having psychologically delegitimized them as an expression of *ressentiment*, using Nietzsche's polemic against the socialist movement, the critical theorist condemns the anticolonialist and Third World movement also ethically and politically. Behind the agitation is not the desire for justice in international relations but the aspiration to participate in the imperialist banquet. In this framework, there is no place for the anticolonialist revolution. The contenders are merely satisfied and now peaceful imperialists and potential imperialists, who are more aggressive and dangerous.

But to what political reality does Adorno allude when he denounces the substantially fascist character of the "nationalism of the so-called underdeveloped countries" or the "convergence of fascist and communist nationalism"?[79] We are in 1959. At that time, only two countries were nurturing a "fascist fantasy" in a strict sense: Portugal and Spain. Neither of these two was part of the Third World; they were colonial powers, and both considered themselves integral to the West. The first was a founding member of NATO; the second was already on the way to joining this political-military organization and would join in 1982.

How can we explain, then, Adorno's discourse? Three years earlier, there had been the colonial expedition by Great Britain, France, and Israel against the Egypt of Nasser, which had nationalized the Suez Canal, and which, enjoying the support of the "socialist camp," had called on the Arab world to throw off the colonial and semi-colonial yoke. On that occasion, Anthony Eden, the prime minister of Great Britain (which until that moment had controlled the Suez Canal) and a loyal supporter of the empire, portrayed Nasser as "a sort of Islamic

Mussolini" and as a "paranoid" with "the same mental structure as Hitler."[80] At this point, we find a perfect coincidence in the ideology of (colonial) war and in the (philo-colonialist) false consciousness of Adorno. The nationalism of Egypt—"underdeveloped," but determined to recover its national sovereignty and territorial integrity—was fascist, and the support of it by Moscow and Beijing constituted the confirmation of the "convergence of fascist and communist nationalism."

What is most striking in the declarations we have just seen is that they were made in an essay dedicated to "coming to terms with the past" (*Aufarbeitung der Vergangenheit*). To take account of Nazism and the horror of the "Final Solution" meant taking one's distance from the anticolonial revolution. It is the viewpoint of Horkheimer as well, who, as demonstrated by a well-informed scholar and admirer of his in our own time, should be recognized for the merit of having promptly identified "the inhuman essence of imperialism" and the line of continuity (under the banner of "anti-Western anti-imperialism") that supposedly runs from the Third Reich through the national and revolutionary movements of the Third World and Third Worldism.[81]

Horkheimer and Adorno began from the assumption that recognizing national differences and demanding respect for them is synonymous with "nationalism," chauvinism, and perhaps even racism, so the discourse on the nation should be situated in an ominous political tradition leading to the Third Reich. In reality, the principal Nazi theorist explicitly condemned "enthusiasm for nationalism in itself," for "the slogan of the right of peoples to self-determination" serves "all the elements of the inferior races that are on the earth to help them demand freedom for themselves" as did "the negroes of Haiti and Saint-Domingue."[82]

We hear, stronger than ever here, hatred of the national revolutions of the colonial peoples. The particularly barbaric character of Nazism lay, among other things, in its attempt to construct a colonial empire in the heart of Europe itself, with the intention thereby of abolishing the right to self-determination and of autonomous national existence for even those peoples who had until now been recognized by the international community as a whole. The line of continuity that Adorno fantastically declared, erased from history the vaunted pathos of the West to defend at all costs against the rise of the colonial peoples of color who had been incited by the Jewish and Bolshevik agitators, as stated in the discourses of Hitler.

Horkheimer is the author of a great saying: "Whoever is not willing to talk about capitalism should also keep quiet about fascism."[83] It is a saying that, in a polemic against critical theory itself, could also be reformulated as "whoever is not willing to talk about colonialism should also keep quiet about capitalism and fascism." As we will better see below, the removal of colonialism also made any authentic coming to terms with the past impossible.

10. Marcuse and the Difficult Rediscovery of Imperialism

Contrary to Adorno, Marcuse supports the Hegelian thesis that the truth is the whole. Given this theoretical assumption, he, in retracing the framework of the liberal West, cannot erase the relations it instituted with the Third World and with the colonial and ex-colonial countries: "The War in Vietnam has revealed for the first time the nature of the existing society" and "the necessity for it is innate in expansion and aggression. . . . Vietnam is in no way just one more foreign policy event but rather connected with the essence of the system."[84] Beyond the "inhuman and unnecessary" violence unleashed on that country, what reveals the oppressive nature of the North American Republic (considered as a whole) is the treatment reserved for the population of colonial origin in the South: "Murders and lynchings of blacks go unpunished though the criminals are well known."[85] The whole must not lose sight of this either when it examines the problem of wealth and poverty: "The conquest of scarcity is still confined to small areas of advanced industrial society. Their prosperity covers up the Inferno inside and outside their borders."[86] It thus hides the areas of poverty in the capitalist metropoles and, above all, the desperate poverty of the colonies and semi-colonies.

Therefore, it is essential to recover the categories usually left out of the dominant ideology: indignation for the "neo-colonial massacres"[87] must push us to end colonialism and "abandonment of neo-colonialism in all its forms."[88] Above all, "the world is experimenting with an imperialism of a reach and a power unexampled until now in history."[89] It is an aggressiveness that threatens not only small countries: "Faced with the immense aggressive force of the system of late capitalism (and of the United States in particular), Eastern totalitarianism in reality was on the defensive, and indeed it was defending itself desperately."[90]

Even if rediscovered with difficulty, in an uncertain and oscillating way, the category of "imperialism" tended to put in crisis that of "totalitarianism." Marcuse well understood the problems facing the countries weighed down by the colonial yoke. They were inclined toward "a widespread presumption that remaining independent would require rapid industrialization and attainment of a level of productivity."[91] But "industrialization in these backward areas does not take place in a vacuum. . . . The transformation of underdeveloped into industrial societies must as quickly as possible discard the pre-technological forms." And here is the greatest difficulty: "In these same countries, the dead weight of pre-technological and even pre-'bourgeois' customs and conditions offers a strong resistance to such a superimposed development." Therefore, Marcuse asked, "Can one reasonably assume that, under the impact of the two great systems of total technological administration, the dissolution of this resistance will proceed in liberal and democratic forms?" This would be an unrealistic expectation:

> On the contrary, it rather seems that the superimposed development of these countries will bring about a period of total administration more violent and more rigid than that traversed by the advanced societies, which can build on the achievements of the liberalistic era. To sum up, the backward areas are likely to succumb either to one of the various forms of neo-colonialism or to a more or less terroristic system of primary accumulation.[92]

The Soviet Union had found itself in a position not very different from the newly independent countries. We know the dangers from the "immense aggressive force" of the capitalist and imperialist West weighed upon it. In what way could the USSR have confronted the threat? "By the power of total administration, automation in the Soviet system can proceed more rapidly once a certain technical level has been attained."[93] As for the newly independent countries, for the Soviet Union the choice was between capitulation to colonialism and imperialism and accelerated economic and technological development, which could be accomplished only by sacrificing, to a greater or lesser degree, the exigencies of democracy.

But, as if faced with this conclusion, which emerged from his own analysis, Marcuse retreated, shocked. And not from lack of intellectual courage but because he did not fully grasp the progressive and emancipatory reach of the world anticolonialist revolution. He warmly welcomed the struggle for national liberation of the Vietnamese people, who "with the poorest weapons can keep in check the most efficient system of destruction of all times, representing "a world-historical novelty."[94] More generally, "the national liberation fronts" can make a precious contribution to the "crisis of the system" of capitalism. And yet, causes for doubt were not far behind. Yes, the victory of the Vietnamese resistance "is an immensely positive and constructive step," but "this has nothing to do with the construction of a socialist society."[95] For the newly independent countries, rapid economic and technological development was a question of life and death. However, "is there any evidence that the former colonial or semi-colonial areas might adopt a way of industrialization essentially different" from the model of "capitalism" and substantially copied by the Soviet Union?[96]

The philosopher who argued in this way was not touched by doubt. Didn't the transcendence of an international division of labor that saw a handful of countries hold a monopoly on technology and on technologically advanced industry to exercise a (not purely economic) power over the rest of the world have something to do with the realization of a "way of industrialization essentially different" from the past?

After speaking about the persistent scarcity outside the "advanced industrial societies" as an "Inferno," Marcuse seemed to consider the reduction of this infernal area irrelevant. He called attention to the scandal of extreme polarization between the comfort of "advanced industrial society" and the desperate misery of the Third World but then argued as if its development was not in any substantial way a novelty or alternative to the existing order. Why should reducing planetary social polarization be less important than reducing it within a single country? We think of the proverbial situation of not seeing the forest for the trees. The result was paradoxical: after having called attention to the conflict between the anticolonial revolution and colonialist and imperialist reaction, unsatisfied by the insufficiently "different" and new character of the political and social reality that was emerging, Marcuse invites us to take note that the "world system" is by now united for life and death![97]

11. The August 4th of Critical Theory and of the Concrete Utopia

If Vietnam was the reason for the rift between the philosophers of critical theory and concrete utopia (their condemnations of the United States intersect and conflict with the declarations of support), unity was reestablished on the occasion of the Six-Day War (June 5–10, 1967) that saw Israel triumph over Egypt, Syria, and Jordan. Certainly, this unity I refer to was far from being set in stone. Horkheimer and Adorno identified so completely with Israel that they did not even worry about defending it from the accusation of colonialism or imperialism that was leveled at that moment by anticolonialist and Third Worldist forces. On the contrary, for the two exponents of critical theory, it was a question of putting these very forces on trial as the accused.

Although on the most immediate political level, Bloch took a very similar position to Horkheimer and Adorno, on a different note, he also defended Israel from the accusation of colonialism or imperialism. It is true, he argued, that it was a country that enjoyed the support of the U.S. president, "the Johnson of the Vietnam War" (itself a colonial and imperialist war); however, we must not confuse different things. In conformity with his style of thought, the philosopher of the "concrete utopia" evoked a bright future under the banner of peaceful co-existence and "symbiosis" between Jews and Arabs. He declared further that he did not recognize himself in Zionism, and he regretted that the founding of Israel happened under the ideology of Herzl, the follower of "nationalism" who was in no way inclined to the "symbiosis with the other peoples residing in the territory." And so he explained the injustice that the new state imposes on "Arab refugees" and the "Arab minority remaining in Israel." Things would have gone very differently if the political line and legacy of the internationalist and "socialist Moses Hess," worthy heir to the great tradition of the Hebrew prophets, had prevailed instead. However, updating a glorious past, one can hope for a "new symbiosis" between Arabs and Jews and even "in case of necessity" in a symbiosis that sees "the autonomy of Israel" guaranteed in the context of an "infinitely larger Arab state space."[98]

Unfortunately, despite the evocation of a radiant future and perhaps corresponding utopia, things looked quite different as far as the present was concerned. Bloch did not limit himself to totally identifying with Israel. He was not content to merely support the war against Nasser's Egypt. He went further. He accused Nasser of following a "Nazi model," of being inspired by a "hatred against Jews up to the Final Solution," and all this with the complicity of the entire Arab world, from which come "mortal threats" against Israel. And so, the left that in some fashion supported the Arab cause itself emitted "sounds of a pogrom," whether it was aware of doing so.[99]

So arguing, the philosopher of the "concrete utopia" ended up accusing anticolonialism and Third Worldism in their entirety, in the same manner as the two exponents of critical theory. It is worth noting that, even if they wanted to erase the Palestinian tragedy in the Middle East in those years, colonialism was alive and well, even in its classical form and with racist connotations. Little over a decade earlier, in 1956, Egypt, for having nationalized the Suez Canal, was subjected to a joint attack by Israel, Great Britain (anything but inclined to renounce its Empire), and France (which decided to teach Nasser a lesson to consolidate its shaky dominion over Algeria). Notwithstanding the disagreement and the rivalry between Washington and London, if Churchill had called on the West to sustain the presence of England in the Suez Canal "to prevent a massacre of the whites," Eisenhower had lamented that with the nationalization of the Suez Canal Nasser sought to "overthrow the whites." Clearly, for these two Western statesmen the Arabs continued to be part of the negroid population.[100] We know that the pathos of the white race was anything but foreign to Hitler, but Bloch still had no trouble putting Nasser in the same camp.

On the occasion of the 1967 War, the most problematic seemed to be Marcuse. His recommended attitude "does not imply a complete acceptance of the arguments of Israel nor of those of its adversaries." On the one hand:

> The founding of Israel as an autonomous state can be defined as illegitimate to the extent that it happened thanks to an international accord, on foreign soil and without considering the local population. ... I admit that to the initial injustice, others have been added on the part of Israel. The treatment of the Arab population was reprehensible, if not worse. Israel's policy has revealed racist and nationalist traits that we Jews should be the first to reject. ... A third injustice ... is the fact, I believe incontrovertible, that from the founding of the state, Israeli policy has followed too passively American foreign policy. Never, on any occasion, have the representatives or the representative of Israel in the United Nations taken a position in favor of the struggle for liberation of the Third World against imperialism.[101]

On the other hand:

> The initial injustice cannot be repaired by a second injustice. The State of Israel exists, and a place of meeting and understanding must be found with the hostile world surrounding it. ... In the second place, we must also consider the repeated attempts at accord made by Israel and always rejected by the representatives of the Arab world. And in the third place of the declarations, not generic but clear and strong, by Arab spokesmen on wanting to conduct a war of annihilation against Israel.[102]

Such a tortured calculus of the wrongs and rights seems like it must go hand in hand with doubts and uncertainties. Instead, the conclusion was peremptory: "In these circumstances, the preventive war (as, in fact, was the war against Egypt, Jordan and Syria) could and must be understood and justified."[103] It was a conclusion entirely based on the assumption of a "war of annihilation" that the Arab states are scolded for.

That assumption had behind it the terrible memory of the Final Solution; yet not only was it not demonstrated to be true, its meaning was not even made clear or precise. Historically, the annihilation of a state or a country has not been a rare phenomenon. One thinks of Poland at the end of the eighteenth century divided between Russia, Austria, and Prussia; of the states or statelets absorbed into a larger entity in the course of the national unification process in Italy or Germany; of the disappearance of the Confederate States of America at the end of the American Civil War; of the dissolving of the Soviet Union (or the Evil Empire in the words of its implacable foe Ronald Reagan). Or one thinks of the transformation of the old South Africa, founded on white supremacy, into a completely new South Africa. In all these cases, the political annihilation of a state, however arbitrary and unjust it may be, did not bring about the physical annihilation of its inhabitants. Marcuse flew above all this; his certainty, however, was fragile:

> On the left [in the United States] there is a quite strong and entirely understandable tendency to identify with Israel. On the other hand, the left, particularly the Marxist left, cannot pretend to ignore that the Arab world coincides in part with the anti-imperialist camp. In this case, emotional and conceptual solidarity are objectively separate, indeed even split.[104]

Why does "emotional solidarity" win out over "conceptual solidarity"? At least for a philosopher, it should be the opposite. Marcuse justifies himself by recourse to his Jewish ancestry: "You understand how I feel solidarity with, and I identify with Israel for very personal and not only personal reasons."[105] But wasn't letting oneself give in to "emotional solidarity" from national and ethnic connections the viewpoint of German Social Democracy of the era of Wilhelm II? And so, June 1967 was the August 4th of critical theory and of the concrete utopia (and, in fact, of Marcuse himself).

12. 1968 AND THE MASS EQUIVOCATION OF WESTERN MARXISM

During the 1960s and 1970s, mass equivocation characterized the Marxist left in Europe and the United States. The great demonstrations in favor of Vietnam connected happily with the homage paid to Adorno and Horkheimer, who considered the movements of national liberation backward and reactionary and who watched from a distance or (in the case of the latter) did not fail to support the war the United States unleashed in Vietnam. In those years, together with Vietnam, China also enjoyed mass support, but we find here another comedy of equivocation, and not only because the People's Republic, born of a centuries-old struggle for national and anticolonial liberation, aspired to put itself at the head of the movements of national and anticolonial liberation disdained by critical theory.

There is another reason. In 1966, Mao launched the Cultural Revolution. In Italy, the communist daily *Il Manifesto* saluted him in its first issue (April 18, 1971) with an article by K. S. Karol that expressed pleasure that "during the Cultural Revolution, the party and state apparatuses were strongly reduced." It was the start of the realization of utopia and the beginning of the withering away of the state! In reality, Mao had publicly distanced himself from that ideal some years before in exercising power on a national scale. By now, it was clear that the "organs of our state" would endure indefinitely. "Let's take the courts . . . we'll still need courts ten thousand years from now, even after the elimination of classes." The contradictions, even if no longer antagonistic, will have continued and survived under communism and require a juridical and state order to regulate them.[106]

Regarding the Cultural Revolution, in 1969, on the occasion of the Ninth Congress of the Chinese Communist Party, Lin Biao, at that moment the designated heir to Mao Zedong, had made the objectives pursued by the leaders of Beijing unequivocally clear:

> As the Sixteen-Point Decision indicates, the Great Proletarian Cultural Revolution is a powerful force for developing the social productive forces in our country. Our country has seen good harvests in agricultural production for years running and there is also a thriving situation in industrial production and science and technology. The enthusiasm of the broad masses of the working people both in revolution and production has soared to unprecedented heights. Many factories, mines and other enterprises have time and again topped their production records, creating all-time highs in production. The technical revolution is making constant progress.... "Grasp revolution, promote production"—this principle is absolutely correct.[107]

This was a point Lin Biao insisted on forcefully:

> We must . . . firmly grasp revolution and energetically promote production and fulfill and over-fulfill our plans for developing the national economy. It is certain that the great victory in the Great Proletarian Cultural Revolution will continue to bring about new leaps forward on the economic front and in our cause of socialist construction as a whole.[108]

Not by accident, one of the principal indictments made against the deposed president of the People's Republic of China, Liu Shaoqi, was "the doctrine of trailing behind at a snail's pace," namely incomprehension of the fact that the Cultural Revolution would, in the eyes of its advocates, accelerate prodigiously the development of the productive forces, bringing the country rapidly up to the level of the more advanced capitalist countries.[109] The Cultural Revolution relaunched the Great Leap Forward that had been going on since 1958, through which China adventurously hoped to make record time in economic and industrial development thanks to the mass mobilization and enthusiasm for work and production.

What did Western Marxism understand of all this? In Italy, the same people enthusiastic over the new course adopted by Beijing also welcomed the book whose central thesis was that the socialist revolution would "suppress work. And in so doing, it will abolish class domination. Suppression of work by the working class and the violent destruction of capital are one and the same."[110]

At this point, the comedy of equivocations reached its culmination. Already in 1937, in the essay "On Practice," Mao had made clear the centrality of "activity in material production" to the growth not only of social wealth but also of "human consciousness." Indeed, "the small scale of production limited man's outlook." Thanks to its pedagogical function, activity in material production was not destined to disappear even "in the classless society."[111] In the West, instead, celebrating the leader of the Chinese Revolution could be connected to the expectation of the end of work; the essay "On Practice" was cited often, but only to discuss the class struggle, removing both the struggle for production and the struggle for "scientific experimentation." With the principal slogan launched by the Cultural Revolution, "make revolution, increase production," Western Marxism forgot Mao's thought, to which it paid homage. Moreover, the slogan "worker suppression of work" also broke with Marx and the post-capitalist scenario he had sketched. According to the *Communist Manifesto*, "the proletariat will use its political supremacy" and control of the means of production "to increase the total productive forces as rapidly as possible."[112]

These general theses assumed a particular importance in the East. After shaking off the colonial yoke, the countries and peoples of the newly independent states were committed to consolidating this independence economically. They did not want to depend on their ex-masters' alms and arbitrary will. They considered it essential to break the monopoly that the most powerful countries held (and in part, and to a declining degree, they still hold) over the most advanced technology.

Mao, who in 1949 had already sought to guard against the danger for the Chinese People's Republic of economically "becoming an American colony," felt a strong commitment to abolish two types of inequality: that existing inside of China, but also and perhaps even more so, that which separated China from the more advanced countries. Powerfully accelerating the development of the productive forces, overcoming the former contradiction would have facilitated the overcoming of the latter. In this way, the Chinese nation would rise steadily, and the long struggle for recognition made necessary by oppression and the humiliation imposed by imperialism would be crowned with complete success. Thanks to a political revolution to promote equality both domestically and internationally, and thanks at the same time to the powerful development of the productive forces, the Asian country would become an irresistible model for the world anticolonialist revolution (and for building socialism).

The Vietnamese Communists expressed a similar view. While completely immersed in the war for independence and national unity, the then-First Secretary of the Workers Party of North Vietnam declared that once power had been achieved, the most important task would be the "technical revolution." Starting from that moment, it was "the productive forces that played the decisive role." It was, therefore, a matter of working hard to "achieve a higher level of productivity, stimulating the construction of the economy and the development of production."[113]

Of the great conflicts going on in Asia (and throughout the Third World), Western Marxism perceived only one aspect, that of the revolt against capitalism more than that against imperialism (scarce attention was reserved for the struggles for national liberation), and above all that of the revolt against power as such. It was in this sense that the West read the slogan, "It is right to rebel!" with which Mao sought to rid himself of the adversaries who still occupied important positions of power in the Communist Party. If in China rebellion was invoked to free the enthusiastic commitment of the masses at work and in the development of social wealth, in the West rebellion against power as such made impossible the building of an alternative social order and reduced Marxism to an (impotent) critical theory or, in the best of hypotheses, to messianic expectations.

Anarchy was the objective and unforeseen result of the Cultural Revolution, remedied by the army's intervention. In the West, instead, the appeal to rebellion against power as such, in society and at work, served to reboot anarchism theoretically as well. Defeated with effort by Marxism during the Second International, anarchism was to see a spectacular revenge in the movement of 1968 and in important sectors of Western Marxism in those years.

13. Sartre's Populist and Idealist Anticolonialism

Even authors strongly committed to the struggle against colonialism could not resist it. Let's take Jean-Paul Sartre. As is made clear in a key chapter of *The Critique of Dialectical Reason*, various human conflicts ultimately derive from "scarcity" (*rareté*), to which a decisive role is attributed: "Scarcity, whatever form it takes, dominates all praxis.... In reciprocity modified by scarcity, the same person appears to us as the counter-human insofar as this same person appears to us as radically Other (i.e., the bearer of a death threat to us)."[114]

The result of this assumption is devastating. To the extent that it appears to make a struggle of life and death necessary, the condition of scarcity ends up justifying the oppressors themselves, who are in some fashion also victims of a tragic struggle for survival that, in the present, imposes itself and which in the future could be eliminated only by the development of the productive forces. On the opposite side, the oppressors appear moved first and foremost or even exclusively by the desire to escape from the intolerable conditions of life. But then, given that language, culture, identity, and national dignity play no role in this situation, it becomes impossible for the part of the social strata that enjoys a comfortable life or more or less considerable ease to understand participation in struggles against national oppression. *The Wretched of the Earth*, by the Algerian revolutionary Fanon, refutes Sartre. The French philosopher contributed a passionate preface to Fanon's book:

> Today, we know that in the first phase of the national struggle, colonialism tries to disarm national demands by putting forward economic doctrines. As soon as the first demands are set out, colonialism pretends to consider them, recognizing with ostentatious

humility that the territory suffers from serious underdevelopment, which necessitates a great economic and social effort.[115]

The rejection of "economic doctrines" is, in fact, the critique of the thesis that would make the colonial question derive exclusively from "scarcity." In Sartre himself there was a contradiction. If *The Critique of Dialectical Reason* relies on "scarcity," in the preface to *The Wretched of the Earth* the heavy lifting is done by the paradigm of recognition: the "enemies of mankind" obstinately deny recognition to "the race of less-than-humans" such as the Algerians and the colonial peoples in general.[116] As we see, indignation over the crimes of colonialism and empathy and solidarity with the colonial peoples in their struggle against oppression did not guarantee an adequate understanding of the national question.

For Sartre, the protagonists of the anticolonial revolution were always "the wretched of the earth" engaged in a desperate struggle to liberate themselves from colonial domination. Missing, however, was any reference to the second stage of the anticolonial revolution, which focused on economic construction. Fanon insisted forcefully on this: to make concrete and solid the independence won thanks to the armed struggle, the newly independent country must leave behind underdevelopment. The commitment to work and production thus took the place of courage in battle; the figure of the more or less skilled worker took over from that of the guerilla fighter. When it is forced to surrender, the colonial power seems to say to the revolutionaries, "since you want independence, take it and starve." And so, in this way, "the apotheosis of independence is transformed into the curse of independence." This new challenge of a non-military character required knowing how to reply: "now, to do all this, other things are needed over and above human output—capital of all kinds, technicians, engineers, skilled mechanics, and so on." What was needed was a "gigantic effort" by an entire people.[117]

The impasse in many African countries that failed to move from the military phase to the economic phase of the revolution was somewhat to be expected. On the other hand, this turning point was achieved by anticolonial revolutions such as the Chinese, Vietnamese, and Algerian. We are in 1961. In that year, another eminent theoretician of the anticolonialist revolution dedicated a book to Toussaint Louverture that also was a summing up of the revolution of which the great Black Jacobin was a central protagonist. After the military victory, he posed the problem of economic construction. To this end, he fostered a culture of work and productivity and even sought to utilize white technicians and experts from the defeated enemy. This was exactly what Lenin would do in the years of the NEP, introducing into workplaces the end of "indolence" and "the most rigorous discipline" and turning to "bourgeois specialists."[118]

It is a point that was difficult for Sartre to understand and accept. The theory of revolution formulated in *The Critique of Dialectical Reason* expressed disappointment that the "fused group,"[119] the protagonist of the overthrow of the *ancien régime* filled with revolutionary enthusiasm, tends to transform itself after the assumption of power into a "practico-inert" structure, with new hierarchies that take the place of those overthrown. But it is not the fused group that can achieve economic and technological development in a newly independent country.

An anticolonial revolution—or one in a country at the margins of the more advanced capitalist world and therefore exposed to the dangers of aggression and colonial or neocolonial subjection—is truly victorious only if it can boost economic construction. Given Sartre's philosophical assumptions, he showed little interest in understanding this problem. The pathos of the subject—"our point of departure is, indeed, the subjectivity of the individual"—and the polemic against "the myth of objectivity" flowed from a subjective idealism: "what is needed is, in a word, a philosophical theory that shows that human reality is action and that action upon the universe is identical with the understanding of that universe as it is, or, in other words, that action is the unmasking of reality, and, at the same time, a modification of that reality."[120] We are led to think of Fichte, for whom the French Revolution found its theoretical expression in the philosophy of Fichte himself, which liberated the subject "from the constraints of things in themselves, from external influences," and, in the final analysis, from material objectivity. It is a vision that can perhaps stimulate the overthrow of the *ancien régime* of colonial domination, but that is of little help as soon as economic construction (necessary for establishing real independence) is called upon to take account of material objectivity, with "things in themselves."[121]

We have seen Sartre stress "action" as an instrument for understanding and transforming political reality. The action he speaks of is exclusively political. Quite different is the argument of the leaders of the anticolonial revolution. In 1937, Mao Zedong insisted that the truth comes not from solitary speculation but "from the process of social practice."[122] But Mao quickly added that beyond the "class struggle" (or political action), "material production" and "scientific experimentation" were both integral parts of "social practice."[123] Engaged in governing the liberated areas during the anticolonial revolution, the Chinese leader could certainly not ignore the challenge of material objectivity inherent in fulfilling the unavoidable task of economic and technological development.

Concentrating his attention only on the desperate efforts of the "wretched of the earth" to break the chains of their colonial enslavement and reserving his empathy exclusively for the fused group, the subject of a magical but brief moment of the revolution, that of the collective enthusiasm that accompanies the overthrow of the universally hated *ancien régime*, Sartre championed an anticolonialism that was passionate and praiseworthy, but that remained populist and idealist. It was an anticolonialism that could not understand the phases of the revolution involving the construction of a new order. So, as Fanon explained, technical competence became the slogan of the day. To cite the Algerian revolutionary again, the "grandiose effort" of an entire people is needed, or, to use this time Césaire's phrase, the end of "indolence" and "the most rigorous discipline" at work.

14. Timpanaro, Anticolonialism, and Anarchism

Sebastiano Timpanaro also demonstrates an understanding of the colonial question, and he harshly criticizes the Marxism developed in the capitalist metropoles for being incapable of seeing beyond itself. Between the nineteenth and twentieth centuries, "the Marxism of the Second International" was in the grips of "a schematic and tenaciously Eurocentric 'philosophy of history'" that paid little attention to the "militarist and reactionary adventures" of the bourgeoisie and the "imperialist phase of capitalism."[124] Was there a turning point with the October Revolution? Unfortunately, only a partial one. Eurocentrism and the scarce attention paid to the tragedies inflicted by Europe and the West on the colonial peoples were anything but transcended by "Western Marxism," which was inclined to "anti-Leninism."[125] It was a ruinous tendency both theoretically and politically, and it became accentuated, although necessarily so, in 1956: "De-Stalinization, because of the confused way in which it was prosecuted and the potentially social-democratic character which it all too soon acquired, led to a reflorescence of 'Westernizing' tendencies."[126]

But, as with Sartre, even in the case of this Italian philologist-philosopher, though in a different way, we find a mismatch between the political platform and the theoretical categories. It is true, referring to Lenin, that Timpanaro recognized "the continued existence ... of national questions,"[127] which were legitimate given the oppression by imperialism and that he unhesitatingly supported the struggle of the Vietnamese people against U.S. imperialism. However, he cast a heavy shadow of suspicion on national liberation movements when they assimilated "racial hatreds and national conflicts."[128] Indeed, the individual "may feel, because of mystifying ideologies, national, religious, or racial solidarity above class solidarity."[129] But it is precisely, in each case, "mystifying ideologies" that seek to conceal "the inconsistency of race and nation as biological-cultural categories."[130] We have seen that an oppressed people's desire for national redemption can be well combined with a universalistic pathos that puts into question the arrogance and the racist intrigues that the colonial powers exemplified.

Timpanaro's impassioned anticolonialist commitment contradicts his theoretical platform on many levels. He takes the Marxist thesis of the withering away of the state and further radicalizes it with an explicit reference to the anarchism of Bakunin.[131] Already unrealistic, the expectation of the vanishing of every norm directly contradicts the military struggle or the economic one and the building or defense of independent national states.

The urgency of economic and technological development, an unavoidable precondition for real independence, brings about (in China, Vietnam, and Cuba) an opening to the market and concessions to the national bourgeoisie (whose entrepreneurial and managerial competence is needed) and the international bourgeoisie (whose assent is needed for access to the most advanced technology). Yet Timpanaro formulated a critical judgment on the policies that in Soviet Russia ended so-called war communism: "the NEP, in Lenin's intention, was to be only a transitory 'catching of breath,' whereas after his death it became an enduring reality."[132] Together with the nation and the state, the philologist-philosopher seemed to dream of the withering away of the market, a messianic and anarchist vision of post-capitalist society.

15. The Isolation of Lukács

When he analyzed nation and race, Timpanaro found himself in a dilemma without an escape: Either the nation is biological (as theorists of biological racism maintain), or, once we have put aside this ominous vision, there is only the "inconsistency" of the nation itself. In either case, there was no place for the national or colonial question. With the later Lukács, we can say, "either social being is not distinct from being in general, or else it is seen as something radically different without having any longer at all the character of being."[133]

We have arrived at the Western philosopher who, together with Gramsci, most intensely identified with Lenin. His early great text, *History and Class Consciousness*, did not pay much attention to the colonial and national questions. And, even in his more mature works, it is curious that the historical account of the period from 1789 to 1814, from the overthrow of the ancien régime to the Restoration, lacks any reference to the abolition of Black slavery in the colonies (the work of Toussaint Louverture and Robespierre) or of its reintroduction (by Napoleon).

However, it is a great relief that, in his 1924 book dedicated to Lenin, he analyzes with precision the revolutionary role of "the nations oppressed and exploited by capitalism."[134] Their struggle was an integral part of the world revolutionary process: he harshly criticizes those who, searching for a "purely proletarian revolution, neglect the colonial and national question and end up losing sight of the concrete revolutionary process."[135]

Thanks to the attention paid to colonialism and its intrinsic barbarism, the Hungarian philosopher was far from the idealist transfiguration of the liberal West, of which Bloch, Horkheimer, and Adorno repeatedly wrote. He called attention to Marx's denunciation of the "enslavement of Ireland"[136] by the British Empire and lamented that this denunciation had found little echo in "the contemporary English labor movement" and the Second International.[137] Unfortunately, we must add that even the thesis (that Lukács derives from Lenin) of the centrality of the colonial and national question in the context of the world revolutionary process found little echo in Western Marxism.

Despite being characterized by various positions, ranging from a committed anticolonialism but an often fragile theoretical platform to a declared pro-colonialism, on the whole Western Marxism missed the meeting with the world anticolonialist revolution.

PART IV

The Triumph and Death of Western Marxism

1. *Ex Occidente lux et salus!*
(Light and Salvation from the West!)

We can now better understand the manifesto with which Perry Anderson, in 1976, proclaimed the excellence of a Western Marxism that had finally rid itself of every connection to the Eastern version. It was the year of Mao's death. Following this event came a test of strength between aspirants or potential heirs, with the rise to power of a leadership group that quickly ended the "Cultural Revolution." However, the tension between China and the Soviet Union remained high. Not only the socialist camp but also the anticolonialist camp was filled with contradictions and an air of crisis. In Europe, "Eurocommunism" affirmed itself by distancing itself from actually existing socialism (which was entirely located in the East), gathering up the most important communist parties of Western Europe, those of Italy, France, and Spain. Even on the left, the religion of the West proliferated: *Ex Occidente lux et salus!*

And so a tendency that had manifested itself immediately after the October Revolution reached maturity. While the civil war still raged in Russia, the Italian reformist leader Filippo Turati scolded the followers of Bolshevism for having lost sight of "our great superiority of civil evolution from a historical point of view" and of having abandoned themselves therefore to "infatuation" for the "Eastern world, ahead of the Western world and Europe";[1] they forgot that the Russian "Soviets" were to the Western "parliaments" as the barbaric "horde" was to the "city."[2]

The first of the two essays by the reformist leader I cited was contrasted in its title, "Leninism and Marxism." Leninism was synonymous with Eastern Marxism (crude and barbaric by definition), while Marxism was synonymous with Western Marxism (civil, fine, and authentic, again, by definition). This Orientalist reading of the social, political, and cultural reality of Soviet Russia was widespread in the West. Even before Turati, while the war was still ongoing, Bloch declared of Soviet Russia: "nothing comes of it but stink and barbarism, or in other words, a new Genghis Khan, which poses as the liberator of the people and abusively waves the emblems of socialism."[3]

And yet this was the same philosopher who called attention to the dramatic nature of the situation in the country of the October Revolution, criticizing the Bolsheviks for being guilty (in Bloch's eyes) of having refused to continue to fight alongside or at the service of France, Great Britain, and the United States. One important point remained: the Germany of Wilhelm II had invaded Russia, annexed vast areas, and was responsible for colonial-style massacres. Recognition of the tragic state of exception did not affect Orientalist readings of the revolution and Bolshevik power. A decade later, Kautsky lamented, "Russia's cities are still saturated with Oriental essence."[4]

There was some truth to these arguments. The country of the October Revolution did not have a history of constitutionalism. Ignored or erased, however, was the support provided by the liberal West, first for the Czarist autocracy and then for the bands of "Whites" that sought to bring this autocracy back or to install a military dictatorship. Nor was any reference made to the highly precarious geopolitical situation that the country of the October Revolution found itself in, nor to the permanent state of exception imposed on it by this condition and by the power of the liberal West. Bloch did not consider a basic contradiction. He demanded liberal and parliamentary development of the regime born of the October Revolution. But he supported the continuation of the war that, because of its intrinsic brutality and barbarism and because the great majority of the population opposed it, could be conducted only by merciless dictatorial methods. As far as Kautsky was concerned, it was no accident that he turned to "Oriental essence" rather than history and geography.

It was an essentialist approach that persisted over time. Still, in 1968, while the war unleashed in Vietnam by the United States revealed itself in all its horror, rather than indignation over U.S. and Western cruelty, Horkheimer explained Stalin and Mao and the "totalitarian apparatus" they put in place as the result of the "collective cruelty practiced in the East."[5] In that same year, despite recognizing (as we know) "the immense aggressive force" of capitalism-imperialism that forced the countries targeted by it to "desperately" defend themselves, Marcuse spoke of "Eastern totalitarianism," with recourse to a category that tended toward essentialism. Without making any reference to the difficult geopolitical situation of the Soviet Union or of China, and ignoring the theoretical limits of Marx—a *Western* philosopher little interested in the problem of the limitation of power because, at times, he was prone to the messianic expectation of the extinction of the state and power as such—the category of "Eastern totalitarianism" attributed the lack of democratic development of those countries entirely to a mythic Orient.

Western Marxism continued to the end to show the influence of the ideology of the Cold War. George F. Kennan, the great U.S. theorist of the policy of "containment," also argued that it was necessary to keep under control the "Oriental mind."[6] Indeed, in Western Marxism, the Orientalist approach survived the Cold War. We have seen Žižek paint Mao Zedong as a despot so ferocious and capriciously bloody as to make us think of the most grotesque Orientalist stereotypes.

Situated in this context, the success of Anderson's book was anything but surprising. Abandoning to their fate Eastern Marxism and the countries inspired by it, Western Marxism would be rid of something that had clipped its wings and prevented it from flying high. In reality, the success and even the triumph that Western Marxism and

Eurocommunism enjoyed would be revealed to be short-lived. The times rapidly brought about the death of both.

2. The Cult of Arendt and the Erasure of the Colonialism-Nazism Nexus

For some time, the disdainful refusal to understand what was happening in the East with the anticolonial revolution and post-capitalism had prepared the terrain for ideological capitulation. This brings to mind the cult devoted at a certain point to a philosopher who, having moved away from positions of the extreme left, ended up defining Marx as an enemy of freedom who inspired totalitarian communism. I refer to Hannah Arendt, who in our own times has been somewhat adventurously compared to Rosa Luxemburg[7] and is one of the authors cited in *Empire*, a book that has been a major media success of Western Marxism. Already faint, the bonds linking Western Marxism to the world anticolonialist revolution here break apart.

The colonial peoples and those of colonial origin in the struggle for emancipation had long been aware of the close relationship between Nazism and the colonialist tradition. One year after the rise of the Third Reich, W. E. B. Du Bois compared the racial state that Hitler was building in Germany to the one that had long been in effect in the U.S. South and to the regime of white supremacy and colonial and racial domination that the entire West had created across the entire world.[8] Writing his autobiography some years later, the African American author repeated the essential point: "Hitler is the late crude but logical exponent of white world race philosophy. Therefore, the democratic United States and the West, in general, had no credibility, founded as they were on the exclusion of the 'inferior classes' and, above all, the 'colored peoples of Asia and Africa.'"[9]

Significantly, the nexus between the Third Reich and the colonialist tradition was sometimes made evident by using the category "totalitarianism." In 1942–43, while distancing himself from the violent methods that the communist movement was criticized for, an African American militant of the extreme left, A. Philip Randolph, made clear an essential point: in speaking about Nazi Germany, the colonialist and racial empire that Japan sought to impose on China, that which Great Britain maintained in India, and about the white supremacist regime of the U.S. South, one could speak of "Hitlerism," of "racism," but also of "totalitarian tyranny." The international situation was characterized by the struggle of the "colored races" against the various "imperialisms" and the different forms of "racism" and "totalitarian tyranny."[10] "Totalitarianism" was the power exercised by the so-called superior races over the peoples of color of the colonial world.

In taking this position, Randolph referred to Gandhi, leader of the independence movement, who, in an April 1941 interview, declared, "I assert that in India we have Hitlerian rule however disguised it may be in softer terms."[11] This method of argument was wrong to not provide the needed nuance regarding the existing differences between the political realities being compared but was right to make clear their common traits: the idea of racial hierarchy, the idea that the "racially inferior" peoples were destined by nature and by Providence to undergo the domination of the white or Aryan race. This set of ideas led Hitler to build the "German Indies" on the model of the British Indies or seek in Eastern Europe the Wild West or frontier to subject and colonize following the U.S. model.

After the end of the Second World War, the view that linked the regime of white supremacy still in power in the U.S. South to the Third Reich was widespread among African Americans. One episode that happened in those years in New York speaks eloquently to this, an episode that, though she did not understand its full meaning, Hannah Arendt referred to in a January 1960 letter to Karl Jaspers: "The high schools of New York gave all the students of the senior classes the assignment of thinking up an appropriate punishment for Hitler. A Negro girl wrote: 'He should have a black skin put on him and be forced to live in the United States.'"[12] In a fresh and ingenuous way, the candid Black girl imagined a sort of law of retaliation, in which those responsible for the racist violence of Nazi Germany would be forced to undergo as Blacks the humiliations and bullying of the regime of white supremacy that they had untiringly propagandized for, and carried out mercilessly.

In these same years, the activists of the Algerian Revolution and their theoretician (Fanon) once again compared the French colonial empire to the Third Reich. And that was not only because of the ferocious repression they faced from it. What was the Nazi state "if not colonialism when rooted in a traditionally colonialist country"?[13] And "not long ago Nazism transformed the whole of Europe into a veritable colony."[14] This view was not born of the character of a single personality but from the conclusions arrived at by the antifascist coalition. At Nuremberg, the leaders of the Third Reich were condemned for having carried out a program of colonial conquest in the name of the superior right of the "master race" and for having developed, throughout the Second World War, a gigantic system for draining and exploiting forced labor on a mass scale as "in the darkest times of the slave trade."[15]

Hannah Arendt was also conscious of the nexus between colonialism and Nazism, and during the war she defined Nazism as "the most dreadful imperialism the world has ever known."[16] In those years Arendt described imperialism with an eye ever to racist ideology and to the Third Reich, to the pretense of dividing humanity into "superior and inferior races," "into master and slave races, into higher and lower breeds, into colored people and white men." Imperialism's "cult of race" had led the British to define themselves as "whites" and then led the Germans to call themselves "Aryans"; this explained "the crimes of modern imperialism."[17]

The philosopher was thus very far from the theory of two more or less twin totalitarianisms when she hailed the Soviet Union (at the time led by Stalin) for "the Soviet attempt to liquidate anti-Semitism" in the context of a "just and very modern solution to the nationality question."[18] It was an appreciation that was repeated three years later: "what every political and national movement in our times should give its utmost attention to concerning Russia, namely, its entirely new and successful approach to nationality conflicts, its new form of organizing different peoples based on national equality, has been neglected by friends and foes alike."[19] Equally eloquent was her comment of January 1946: "in the country that made Disraeli its prime minister, the Jew Karl Marx wrote *Das Kapital,* a book which, in its fanatical zeal for justice, carried on the Jewish tradition much more efficaciously than all the success of the 'chosen man of the chosen race.'"[20] The contrast between the two ideal-type figures of Judaism could not help but sound like a contrast between the Soviet Union, which never ceased to evoke Marx, and Great Britain, which under Disraeli had nurtured an ideology typical of imperialism and of Nazism itself.

In any case, on the agenda was the struggle to tear up the roots of fascism for good. It was necessary to confront the "unresolved colonial problem" and "white supremacy," not to mention the rivalry "between imperialist nations." Thus, "This time, fascism has been defeated, but we are still far from annihilating evil entirely in our times. Its roots are still strong and carry the names of anti-Semitism, racism, imperialism."[21] The defeat inflicted on the Third Reich was not yet a definitive solution to the problem:

> That at the end of an "imperialistic age" we should find ourselves in a stage that would make the Nazis look like crude precursors of future political methods. Following a non-imperialistic policy and maintaining a non-racist faith becomes more difficult daily because it becomes clearer how much of a burden mankind is for man.[22]

It was a point that she repeated powerfully the following year:

> Imperialism, which first entered the scene toward the end of the last century, has today become the dominant political phenomenon. A war fought on an apocalyptic scale has revealed the suicidal tendencies inherent in every consistently imperialist policy. Yet imperialism's three main drives—power for power's sake, expansion for the sake of expansion, and racism—continue to rule the globe.[23]

Finally, in December 1948, on the occasion of Menachem Begin (the future prime minister of Israel) visiting the United States, in an open letter to the *New York Times*, also signed by Albert Einstein, Arendt called for protests against the man responsible for the massacre of the Palestinian village of Deir Yassin, noting that the party led by Begin, with its "admixture of ultranationalism, religious mysticism, and racial superiority," and of terrorist violence against the civilian Arab population, was "closely akin in its organization, methods, political philosophy, and social appeal to the Nazi and Fascist parties."[24] Promoting the merciless colonialist expansionism of a so-called superior race, Begin retraced the steps of Nazism and fascism.

The nexus between Nazism and colonialism at times emerges also in the first two parts of *The Origins of Totalitarianism*, those devoted to anti-Semitism and to imperialism. First published in 1951, the book gave ample space to the ideological and political history of the British Empire. Edmund Burke's reaction against the French Revolution elevated "the whole English people, establishing them as a kind of nobility among nations."[25] Later taking form was racism, "the main ideological weapon of imperialistic politics,"[26] along with eugenics,[27] the new pseudo-science dedicated to improving the race through forced sterilization (or even more radical measures) of the losers. Along these lines, we find Disraeli, who proudly contrasted the "rights of Englishmen" to "the rights of man," which he scoffed at, together with Arthur de Gobineau, who was one of the most "devoted supporters of the 'race.'"[28]

Given these ideological assumptions in the colonies, a power without the limitations it faced in the capitalist metropoles began to be theorized and experimented with. It was a power that tended to assume ever more troubling forms. Already in the context of the British Empire there emerged the temptation to carry out "administrative massacres,"[29] an instrument for liquidating every challenge to the existing order. We are on the threshold of the ideology and practice of the Third Reich. Of Lord Cromer, the representative of the colonial power in Egypt, Arendt paints a portrait that does not lack analogies to the one she would subsequently paint of the notorious Nazi executioner Eichmann. The banality of evil seemed to find its first, weaker incarnation in the British "imperialist bureaucrat"[30] who "in their indifference and aloofness, in their genuine lack of interest in their subjects"[31] had developed a "philosophy of the bureaucrat" and a "government without precedent" that was "more dangerous than the unorganized impotence of all those who are ruled by the tyrannical and arbitrary will of a single man."[32]

And this form of government that went beyond traditional despotism reminds us of totalitarianism. From the first, Arendt tended to use the category of totalitarianism to define the nexus between Nazism and colonialism. The first model of totalitarian power was exercised over the colonized peoples, who were dehumanized through racist ideology, decimated and enslaved.

The frame changes radically, however, when we move to the third part of *The Origins of Totalitarianism*, which is clearly influenced by the ideological climate that arrived with the outbreak of the Cold War. Analysis of the Soviet Union didn't matter very much, since thanks to the category of totalitarianism, it was put on the same plane as Nazi Germany. What was decisive was the removal of the linkage of the Third Reich to the colonialist and imperialist tradition, of which it sought to be the more intransigent heir.

A turning point was reached. While still in France, and before crossing the Atlantic in 1941, Arendt, according to her biographer, saw the piece she was writing "as an exhaustive work on anti-Semitism and imperialism, and a historical study of that phenomenon then called 'racial imperialism.'"[33] The essay on imperialism she published in *Commentary* in February 1946 had been preceded by a note in which the reader was informed that the author was "writing a book on imperialism." The Third Reich as "racial imperialism," as imperialism that brought to their extremes the racial components of colonial dominion and the subjection imposed on peoples and "races" considered inferior or stopped at a primitive stage of social development—the Third Reich as the highest stage of imperialism! This vision inspired Arendt in the years after the struggle against Nazism and was still apparent in the first two parts of the *Origins of Totalitarianism*. It was imperialism and colonialism; it was processes that involved the British Empire and other Western powers that had played key roles in the genesis and development of Nazism.

Read closely, the third part of *The Origins of Totalitarianism* was entirely different from the two preceding parts on "racial imperialism."

In the book as originally planned, still emotionally committed to the struggle against Nazism, the category of imperialism was at the center. The *genus* that subsumed various *species*, first of all, was the British Empire and the Third Reich (the most accomplished of the barbarisms of imperialism); and in this framework, the positive role of the Soviet Union was made clear, as the main protagonist of the struggle against Nazi imperialism and inspiration to the anticolonial movements of national liberation. In the third part of the book, essentially written while the Cold War raged, the center instead jumped to the category of totalitarianism as the *genus* that subsumed the Stalinist USSR and Hitler's Germany. This new framework conferred a positive role on the entire anti-totalitarian West, including countries like Great Britain and France that, for all intents and purposes, still had colonial empires.

The heterogeneous character of *The Origins of Totalitarianism* was not lost on historians. Immediately after its publication, the book was harshly criticized by Golo Mann:

> The first two parts of the work treat the prehistory of the total state. But here, the reader will not find that which they are used to finding in similar studies, namely research on the peculiar history of Germany or Italy or Russia. . . . Rather, Hannah Arendt dedicates two-thirds of her efforts to anti-Semitism and imperialism, and above to the imperialism of the British matrix. I cannot follow her. Only in the third part, in sight of all that has been undertaken, does Hannah Arendt seem to be truly on message.[34]

Therefore, it would be substantially off-message to dedicate pages to anti-Semitism and imperialism, yet she is explaining the genesis of a regime that Hitler declaredly sought to build in Central and Eastern Europe, a great colonial empire founded on the dominion of a pure white and Aryan race.

Mann could not understand the calling to the bar of the British Empire. In his critique of Arendt, he sought to involve Karl Jaspers, who had heatedly asked, "Do you also think that English imperialism, in particular Lord Cromer in Egypt, has something to do with the totalitarian state?"[35] The German historian considered it an act of treason against the Free World to throw a shadow of suspicion on a country that, more than any other, incarnated the liberal tradition. He would have done well to read the description from the nineteenth century that an illustrious liberal British historian, Thomas Macaulay, had written of the regime imposed in India in crisis situations by the government in London. It was a "reign of terror," to which "all the injustices of the preceding oppressors, both Asian and European, appeared to be a blessing." And again, notwithstanding the philistine indignation of the Cold War ideologues, the government practices in the colonies of the liberal West led the way toward totalitarianism.

The heterogeneous character of *The Origins of Totalitarianism* was grasped by other historians, who called attention to the artificial effort needed to make "Soviet Communism the totalitarian equivalent of Nazism," for example, inventing a Bolshevik pan-Slavism that would have been the counterpart of Nazi pan-Germanism.[36] All in all, "regarding Stalinism, the book is less satisfying," and the lack of a "clear theory" of "totalitarian systems" becomes quite evident.[37] To be more precise: "in many passages, the analysis of the Soviet Union appeared to have been mechanically made similar to that of Germany, as if it had been later inserted for symmetry's sake."[38] Certainly, Arendt's book on totalitarianism "was actually, in the main, an explanation of the rise to power of Nazism and focused its first two sections on anti-Semitism and imperialism, themes with little relevance to the nature of Soviet power." It would be worthwhile to bid adieu to the category of "totalitarianism," which aims only to destroy the USSR through an artificial but "deadly comparison" with Hitler's Germany.[39]

More on the heterogeneity of the book: if for Golo Mann it is a question of eliminating as off-message the first two parts that, together with anti-Semitism, accused colonialism and imperialism, for the later historians cited what was problematic was the post-hoc and ideological character of the third part that, adapting itself to the ideological needs and practices of the Cold War, sought to breathlessly link the Soviet Union to the Third Reich. And now we read in *Empire*, a key text of Western Marxism, "it is a tragic irony that nationalist socialism in Europe came to resemble national socialism."[40] In retracing the history of the first half of the twentieth century, the two authors erase the struggle between colonialism and anticolonialism, or between the reaffirmation and the abolition of colonial slavery, ending up with the positions of the Western champions of the Cold War, determined to criminalize communism, absolving and reducing to trivia colonialism and imperialism.

3. The Third Reich from the History of Colonialism to the History of Madness

In the philosopher's original formulation, the nexus between imperialism and anti-Semitism, and anti-Semitism and anti-communism, had been clear. "Racial imperialists" came to see a foreign body of Jews, whom they accused of being "organized internationally and bound together by blood."[41] The Jews were accused of being "ethnic representatives of the Communist International" and considered at the same time an instrument of the "world Jewish conspiracy of the Elders of Zion."[42]

These were the years in which Arendt critically contrasted Herzl to another great figure of Jewish culture, Lazare.[43] Unlike the former, the latter had sought to promote the emancipation of the Jews not by accepting some colonial concession from the great powers of the time but by inserting the struggles of the Jews and other oppressed peoples into a comprehensive revolutionary anticolonialist and anti-imperialist project against anti-Semitism and colonial racism. On the other side, Hitler was the irreducible enemy simultaneously of the anticolonial revolution and of the emancipation of the Jews.

It was in this context that the most monstrous crime of the Third Reich needed to be seen: the Holocaust. Imperialism was characterized by the idea of "natural law" of the right of the powerful and the extermination of "inferior races unworthy of survival."[44] It is important to remember that "the extermination of the indigenous peoples" was "put on the agenda" to accomplish "new colonial settlements in America, Australia, and Africa."[45] Though unprecedented for the systematic way in which it was conducted, the Holocaust had its roots in the history of genocide, colonialism, and imperialism.

It is a history, we may add, in the context of which the extermination of peoples was not only carried out but explicitly theorized. At the end of the nineteenth century, with an eye to the unrest that had begun to be seen among the colonized peoples, important personalities and circles embraced the temptation of genocide. Theodore Roosevelt wrote that if "one of the inferior races" were to attack the "superior race," it would "mean something approaching a war of extermination," and the white soldiers would "begin to put to death man, woman, and child, exactly as if they were crusaders."[46] Of course, there would be protests, but these would quickly subside if "white control" was in danger.

In practice, a few years later, the movement for independence of the Philippines, which had become a colony of the United States after the U.S. victory in the Spanish-American War, was dealt with by a systematic destruction of the crops and livestock, the enclosing of the mass of the population in concentration camps with a high death rate, even with the killing of all the men above ten years old.[47] Roosevelt's statement raises a question: what fate awaited those who incited the "inferior races" to rebel against the power of "white control"?

The problem became real with the October Revolution and its appeal to the "slaves of the colonies" to break their chains. In 1923, sounding the alarm for the mortal danger posed by Bolshevik agitation and the revolt of the peoples of color to civilization and to white supremacy worldwide, an American author, celebrated on both sides of the Atlantic, Lothrop Stoddard, made clear the eminent position that Jews occupied in the "officer corps" of the Bolshevik and anticolonial revolt. Starting with Marx, they played a leading role in the "revolutionary movement"; their "destructive criticism" made them "excellent revolutionary leaders," as was confirmed by the October Revolution itself and the emergence of the "Jewish-Bolshevist regime of Soviet Russia." Thus, even before Hitler, the American theorist of white supremacy identified the enemy to liquidate once and for all as the "Jewish-Bolshevist regime of Soviet Russia."[48]

The agenda that guided the genocidal crusade of the Third Reich was launched in a book published in the first edition ten years before the rise of Hitler to power. The author [Lothrop Stoddard] became a celebrity in the West for a 1921 book whose title, *The Rising Tide of Color Against White World-Supremacy*, called for a struggle to defend "white supremacy" from the "rising tide of color." And he never tired of repeating that against the "subhuman" (the rebellious colonized peoples and their Bolshevik and Jewish inciters), recourse to the most radical measures was inevitable. One could not stop halfway: "Bolsheviks are mostly born and not made," he writes, clearly aiming also at the Jews; "it is impossible to transform the subhuman, nature herself having decreed him uncivilizable." Against the sworn enemies of civilization, one can proceed to "wholesale extirpation."[49]

The Third Reich's war against the "Jewish-Bolshevist regime of Soviet Russia" declared by Stoddard began the process of the Holocaust and the systematic liquidation of the Communist Party and the Soviet state and the reduction of millions of Russians to the condition of colonial slaves, fated to die of hardships, starvation, and disease. One conclusion follows: the Holocaust was an integral part of the crusade against Jewish-Bolshevism and of the colonialist counter-revolution, which saw the Third Reich as the principal protagonist but which had its beginnings beyond Germany and before the rise of Hitler to power.

Arendt, early on, was thinking about this chapter of history when she observed, at the end of the 1920s, "the National Socialist Party has become an international organization, whose leadership resides in Germany" and whose objective was to relaunch "white supremacy." This all disappears in the third part of *The Origins of Totalitarianism*, such that the passage from the category "racial imperialism" to that of "totalitarianism" comes with a methodological slip. Totalitarianism was now read as psychology or psychopathology. It was characterized by "madness," the "totalitarian contempt for reality and factuality."[50] When we go inside Hitler's Germany and the "totalitarian society," we have the impression of entering a world of madness. This is not only because "punishment is meted out without connection with crime."[51] There's more:

The world of the dying, in which men are taught they are superfluous through a way of life in which punishment is meted out without connection with crime, in which exploitation is practiced without profit, and where work is performed without product, is a place where senselessness is daily produced anew. . . . Common sense trained in utilitarian thinking is helpless against this ideological supersense, since totalitarian regimes establish a functioning world of no-sense.[52]

The Third Reich's foreign policy does not follow any logic or calculation. It unleashes war "not from lust for power, and if it feverishly seeks to expand, it does so neither for expansion's sake nor for profit, but only for ideological reasons: to demonstrate on a global scale that their ideology was correct, to build a coherent, fictional world undisturbed by reality."[53] In other words, totalitarianism is madness that seeks madness. The philosopher forgot the observation she had made a few years earlier, that in the history of colonialism, "the new colonial settlements in America, Australia, and in Africa" went hand in hand with the "extermination of the indigenous peoples" and that this had been the agenda likewise for the colonization of Eastern Europe by the Nazis. Certainly, the genocidal violence uniquely hit the Jews.

This issue brings to mind another of Arendt's observations, that to the Nazis the Jews were the "ethnic representatives of the Communist International" together with the Bolsheviks such that it was difficult to distinguish between them. They were the most dangerous enemies of "white supremacy," which needed to be defended and maintained at any cost. Starting with the third part of *The Origins of Totalitarianism*, if everything is madness and madness in which it is useless to search for a method, it makes no sense to link the Third Reich to the colonial tradition, which was incontestably characterized by the "lust for power," the search for "profit," and relied on utilitarian calculation.

It is necessary to immediately point out that Arendt's method, or lack thereof, finds little confirmation in historiography. We refer not only to those historians that, explicitly critical, have made clear the "utilitarian ends" pursued by the Third Reich.[54] Perhaps even more significant are the authors who, without mentioning Arendt, have called attention to some essential points. With his war of decimation and enslavement in the East, Hitler set in motion a gigantic slave trade, which served admirably to feed the production of goods and arms for Germany at war. The Führer had unleashed the greatest colonial war in history to build his continental empire in Eastern Europe. A war conducted not only by armies but also by a wave of settlers from Germany and other countries following in the footsteps of the whites who had emigrated from Europe to North America and who, once there, then led the colonization of the West.[55] The policies of the Third Reich were not an expression of pure madness, just as the slave trade was not, nor the expansion of the North American Republic from one ocean to the other, nor were colonial wars in general.

The later Arendt placed herself in an intellectual tradition that explicitly spoke of madhouses in referring to the revolutions of 1848 (Tocqueville) or of the Paris Commune (Hippolyte Taine) and that read the great historical crises as explosions of madness that engaged in radical critiques of the existing order, as expressions of lack of common sense and of pathological breaks from reality.[56] In effect, the psychopathological paradigm allowed Arendt to lessen the role of colonialism and to embellish the liberal West, each considered extraneous to the horrors of the Final Solution. On the opposite side, after having made clear that Hitler's campaign against Jewish-Bolshevism identified and sought to destroy jointly, even if through differing methods, both Jews and communists, the third part of *The Origins of Totalitarianism* tends to treat twentieth-century communism as the twin brother of Nazism. The fact is that once set on the path of the psychopathological paradigm to explain totalitarianism, all that is left to her is recourse to "paranoia" and the cloying juxtaposition of one "paranoid" with another. All are seen as the same in a diagnosis detached from evidence and, indeed, by the sovereign and arbitrary decision of the interpreter herself.

Western Marxism did not know how to resist this ideological operation. In some ways, it represented a contrast with Eastern Marxism that we have seen in the decisive moments of twentieth-century history. With the outbreak of the First World War, the exponents of nascent Eastern Marxism insisted that the horrors of capitalism and imperialism did not wait for August 1914 to manifest themselves in the colonies. An analogous contrast emerged during the Second World War, which Western Marxism wrongly saw as starting in 1939 when imperialist expansionism broke out in Europe, an expansionism that already for years had raged to the detriment of the colonies. Finally, by adopting the positions of the later Arendt, Western Marxism—now moribund—lined up with the dominant ideology and developed a discourse on power and total institutions completely removed from the colonial world.

4. On Trial: Colonialism or Its Victims?

We must analyze in all its aspects the turning point in Arendt's work after the outbreak of the Cold War. By this point, the judgment she rendered on this or that country was made with a degree of abstraction from reality usually reserved for the colonial peoples: "Mussolini, who was so fond of the term 'totalitarian state,' did not attempt to establish a full-fledged totalitarian regime and contented himself with dictatorship and one-party rule."[57] Franco's Spain and Salazar's Portugal are seen as similar to the Italian Fascist state.[58] What type of power did the three countries exercise in the colonies they subjugated? As genocidal (and totalitarian) as they were, the three countries of the colonialist West were absolved of the charge of totalitarianism.

The preface to part three of the 1966 edition of *The Origins of Totalitarianism* asked if one should speak of "totalitarianism" regarding Mao Zedong's China, but the China enslaved by the Empire of the Rising Sun posed no such problems.[59] And yet, this was one of the most horrible pages of twentieth-century history. With the conquest of Nanking in 1937, massacres became a sort of athletic competition and, at the same time, entertainment. Who would be the quickest and most efficient at decapitating prisoners? The unleashing of power without limits and the dehumanization of the enemy had reached a rare degree of completion, perhaps with some unique elements. Instead of animals, vivisection experiments were conducted on the Chinese, who, in another episode, constituted the living targets for the Japanese soldiers to practice bayonet charges. Power without limits was also exercised on women, who faced brutal sexual slavery. However, only the regime that ended all this is suspected of totalitarianism.

Still more. We have seen Lord Cromer, of the top level of British colonial administration, as a sort of proto-Eichmann, but now read a passage that explains the genesis of "totalitarian" government:

> Conversely, the chances for totalitarian rule are frighteningly good in the lands of traditional Oriental despotism, in India and China, where there is almost inexhaustible material to feed the power-accumulating and man-destroying machinery of total domination, and where, moreover, the mass man's typical feeling of superfluousness—an entirely new phenomenon in Europe, the concomitant of mass unemployment and the population growth of the last 150 years—has been prevalent for centuries in the contempt for the value of human life.[60]

Far from accusing colonialism or imperialism, the discussion of totalitarianism's genesis ends up blaming the victims, the colonial peoples, independently of their political regime, as with India (a democracy, even if often allied with the Soviet Union during the Cold War). Constituting a precondition or a threat of totalitarianism was the "inexhaustible material"—the reserve army of human beings.

Paradoxically, Arendt ended up adopting a classic argument of colonialist ideology. The alarm over "racial suicide" that overwhelmed the white race (because of its low fertility and an inability to confront the human sea of colonial peoples of color) was a theme dear to Theodore Roosevelt, as it was to Oswald Spengler.[61] And it was not foreign to Winston Churchill either, who was committed to defending the British colonial dominion over a people, the Indians, who engaged in mass disobedience and rebellion because, according to him, they were an inconsiderate and uncontrollable "swarm."[62] In analogous terms, Hitler kept an eye on the danger that the proliferation of indigenous people in Ukraine and Eastern Europe constituted for the German

Indies.[63] From condemning colonial domination as the first manifestation of totalitarian power to making common cause with colonialist ideology to place blame on the colonial peoples who were inclined toward totalitarianism because of their limitless numbers, the bargain Arendt struck to pay homage to the ideological climate of the Cold War is evident in the pages of *The Origins of Totalitarianism* when read in its entirety.

Arendt's regression worsened over time, as made clear in *On Revolution*. Marx is the author of the "most pernicious doctrine of the modern age, namely that life is the highest good, and that the life process of society was the very center of human endeavor." The result is catastrophic:

> Politically, this development led Marx into an actual surrender of freedom to necessity. He did what his teacher in revolution, Robespierre, had done before him and what his greatest disciple, Lenin, was to do after him in the momentous revolution his teachings have yet inspired.[64]

The three greatest enemies of freedom, indirectly the most dangerous champions of totalitarianism, are now identified as Robespierre, Marx, and Lenin. These are, respectively, the Jacobin political leader who sealed the abolition of slavery in Saint-Domingue and the victory of the Black former slaves led by Toussaint Louverture (known, not by chance, as "the Black Jacobin" or as leader of the Black Jacobins, he could have easily been inserted by Arendt into her list of the enemies of freedom); the philosopher who before any other denounced the intrinsic barbarism of colonialism; and the political leader who, immediately after taking power had called on the "slaves of the colonies" to break their chains, thereby advocating for the world anticolonial revolution (the greatest accomplishment of the twentieth century). And so, it is no longer colonialism, the great antagonist, that stands accused. Rather, the two revolutions, the French (and Jacobin) and the October Revolution, which sought to dismantle the world colonialist-slavery system, were named as the enemies of freedom.

This conclusion is not reached by chance. Let's fly over the road accident that, for a moment, led Arendt to express a *topos* of colonialist ideology. One thing is clear. As is the case in the third part of *The Origins of Totalitarianism* and in her subsequent work, she erases the despotic power and totalitarian tendencies that colonialism and imperialism imposed on the colonial peoples and those of colonial origin, and she ignores the terrible difficulties that emancipation caused for subject peoples and those in danger of being subjected. If one concentrates exclusively on the present or only on the lack of liberal institutions capable of limiting power, it is clear that the suspicion of totalitarianism will not fall on those responsible for colonial wars but on their victims.

For example, the France of the July Monarchy that launched the conquest of Algeria at the start of the 1830s was more liberal than the Arab countries it subjugated. However, it was this liberal France that formulated and carried out a policy summarized by Tocqueville: "to destroy anything that resembles a permanent gathering of population or, in other words, a town: I believe it is of the utmost importance not to allow any town to survive, or arise, in the regions controlled by Abd el Kader" (the leader of the resistance).[65] So how useful is it to see the origins of totalitarianism only in the victims of such an openly declared policy of genocide?

However, perhaps also because of Arendt's past, when for a time she was influenced by Marx's thought and the communist movement, from the 1970s, *The Origins of Totalitarianism* did not encounter any resistance in the ranks of Western Marxism, which by now had reached its terminal stage.

5. With Arendt, from the Third World to the Western Hemisphere

The turning point in Arendt with the outbreak of the Cold War is not just an issue of the past. Let's jump two decades from when the first edition of *The Origins of Totalitarianism* was published. These were the years when the world anticolonial revolution manifested itself, even in the United States, through the African-American liberation struggle.⁶⁶ The Third World demanded the end of a centuries-long chapter of colonialism, neocolonialism, and white supremacy, politically, economically, and ideologically. It was against this tumultuous movement of colonies, semi-colonies, colonial peoples, and peoples of colonial origin that the philosopher took her position with a peremptory declaration: "the Third World is not a reality but an ideology."⁶⁷ In an interview, she repeated this declaration just a few years later: "I am truly of the opinion that the Third World is exactly what I said, an ideology or an illusion. Africa, Asia, South America—those are realities."⁶⁸

But if the Third World is an ideological abstraction, why should Asia constitute a "reality"? We are speaking here of political realities: it would be absurd to contrast Asia as a geographical category to the Third World, which is clearly a political category. Indeed, when Arendt made her declaration, Asia was embracing contrasting political realities. The income disparity that separated Japan from the less developed countries was enormous. And the horror with which the Empire of the Rising Sun had stained itself in attempting to colonize and enslave its Asian neighbors was still a living memory.

A few years before the declaration we have just seen, in condemning the revolutions that arose in the wake of Marx and Lenin, in her book *On Revolution*, the philosopher expressed with abandon another peremptory statement: "human life has been stricken with poverty since times immemorial, and mankind continues to labor under this curse in all countries outside the Western Hemisphere."⁶⁹ "Western Hemisphere!" Under a single category, the most disparate sociopolitical realities are mixed together: the most advanced industrial country and other countries that, at that moment, were more than ever afflicted by underdevelopment and mass misery. The superpower that, based on the Monroe Doctrine, arrogated to itself the right to sovereign intervention in Latin America, the countries that were forced to suffer such interventions and the semi-colonial condition that came with them. *On Revolution* cites James Monroe only once, and that citation unequivocally treats him as a champion of the cause of freedom.⁷⁰ No mention is made of the slaves that were his property, nor to the doctrine that goes by his name and that allows the neocolonial domination of the entire continent by the North American Republic over the "Western Hemisphere."

Justified in the name of rejecting "abstraction," the flight from the Third World landed Arendt on a much more abstract entity in sociopolitical terms. Yet this second abstraction hinted at a specific country, about which the philosopher again expressed herself peremptorily: "the colonialism and imperialism of European nations—that is, the one great crime in which America was never involved."[71] In this view, with an incredible lack of focus, there is no room for the war against Mexico and the dismemberment of that country, for the conquest of the Philippines and the merciless repression of its independence movement, and the often explicit celebration of the genocide against the American Indians.

And so, we encounter Arendt's most blatant erasure of history: the expropriation and decimation of the native population to steal their lands, which were to be cultivated in many cases by Black slaves transported from Africa in the course of a voyage with extremely high mortality rates. Not by accident did this chapter of history inspire Adolf Hitler, who identified the "indigenous" of Eastern Europe with the Indians of America, to be expropriated and decimated to make possible the Germanization of the conquered territories, while the survivors were destined to work as slaves in the service of the master race. And yet, this chapter of history, which coincided with the rise and period of the West's colonial expansion and all its horrors, had, according to Arendt, nothing to do (at least regarding the initial phase of American history) with the history of colonialism!

At the turn of the twentieth century, an illustrious British politician and historian observed that Tocqueville's *Democracy in America* "is not so much a political study as a work of edification."[72] In this latter category, we may also place Arendt's *On Revolution*. We have two texts that celebrate the founding of the United States as the greatest chapter in the history of freedom, without a word devoted to the fact that the newborn North American Republic sanctioned Black slavery in its constitution and for decades saw the slave owners exercise a decisive influence over its political institutions. "At a time when the movement for the abolition of slavery was already well underway on both sides of the Atlantic,"[73] the institution of slavery, politically and constitutionally triumphant, assumed its cruelest form. White slave owners could sell, like goods or cattle, the individual members of the Black families that were their property. Published shortly after the first great anticolonial revolution, that of Saint-Domingue/Haiti, which Arendt disparages, *Democracy in America* expresses admiration for the United States, which sought to reduce the country governed by former slaves to starvation and force it to capitulate. *On Revolution* saw the light of day at the height of the worldwide anticolonial revolution. Its author reacted in the same way as Tocqueville. She condemned the revolution and erected a monument to the superpower that sought to strangle it by any means.

Notwithstanding all this, Arendt continues to greatly influence Western Marxism. We will see that the thesis that colonialism and imperialism are foreign to the United States was uncritically reprised by Hardt and Negri. We can say that Arendt's path—flight from the anticolonial revolution and the Third World and ending up in the "Western Hemisphere" and its mythically transfigured leading country—was the same route taken by the two authors of *Empire*.

6. Foucault and the Removal of Colonial Peoples from History

Along with Arendt, another author made Western Marxism's break with the anticolonial revolution irreparable. In the 1960s, Althusser credited him with being the most prestigious Marxist philosopher of the times.[74] I refer to Michel Foucault. Thanks to his analysis of the pervasiveness or rather the omnipresence of power not only in institutions and social relations but also in the conceptual apparatus, he emanated an aura of fascinating radicalism that allowed for reckoning with the power and the ideocracy at the foundation of "actually existing socialism" as its crisis grew ever more serious.

Actually, his radicalism is not only merely ostensible; it becomes its opposite. The gesture of condemning every power relation, indeed every form of power in both society and in discourse about society, made problematic or even impossible the "determinate negation" (*bestimmte Negation*), that very negation of a "determinate content" that, for Hegel, is the precondition of a real transformation of society, the precondition of the revolution.[75] Further, this Foucauldian effort to identify and demystify domination in all its forms reveals surprising lacunae precisely where domination manifests itself in all its brutality: attention to colonial domination is scarce or nonexistent.

Foucault seems not to have been associated with the protest initiated by Sartre over the massacre of Algerians in Paris, a protest in which his friend Pierre Boulez participated. More generally, he does not play any role in the struggle against torture and the ferocious repression with which power sought to destroy the national liberation struggle in Algeria. It has been justly observed regarding Foucault that "his critique of power continues to look to Europe."[76]

In his work, the colonial peoples and those of colonial origin are historically absent. This explains his statement that at the end of the eighteenth century, "in Europe and in the United States, the entire economy of punishment was redistributed." This period saw "the disappearance of torture as a public spectacle"[77] and "the great public ritualization of death gradually began to disappear."[78] The periodization suggested references to the torture inflicted in 1757 on Robert-Francois Damiens (author of a failed assassination attempt on Louis XV) and described by Foucault with devotion to the gruesome details.[79] But if we insert African Americans into the picture, we must say that between the end of the eighteenth century and the early twentieth century, we find not the disappearance so much as the triumph of "torture as a public spectacle" and of "the ritualization of death." These methods are how white supremacy in the United States punished Blacks accused of making attempts on the sexual and racial purity of white women:

> Notices of lynchings were printed in local papers, and extra cars were added to trains for spectators from miles around, sometimes

thousands of them. Schoolchildren might get a day off to attend the lynching. The spectacle could include castration, skinning, roasting, hanging, and shooting. Souvenirs for purchasers might include fingers, toes, teeth and bones, even the genitals of the victim, as well as picture postcards of the event.[80]

We are far from Foucault's reconstruction of the history of the "economy of punishment" in "Europe and the United States" and from the "modern soul" that the French philosopher describes. He writes that "punishment had gradually ceased to be a spectacle in the first decades of the nineteenth century. And whatever theatrical elements it still retained were now downgraded."[81] In reality, as regarded African Americans, between the nineteenth and twentieth centuries, torture and death were made into spectacles to an unprecedented degree, and these practices, far from being exceptional (such as an attempt on the life of a head of state), became a nearly daily experience.

7. Foucault and the Esoteric History of Racism

All that is ignored by the French philosopher, and this is not by accident. He paints a bizarre picture of the history of racism, and indeed so bizarre as to be esoteric. In brief: "in the mid-nineteenth century," in contrast to all the traditional historiography that seeks to consecrate sovereignty, we find in France an entirely new discourse, anti-authoritarian and revolutionary, that divides society into races (or classes) in struggle and introduces "a principle of heterogeneity: the history of some is not the history of others."[82]

But, sometime later, we arrive at a watershed: "the idea of race, with its monistic, statist, and biological implications, will replace the idea of racial struggle."[83] It is a complete reversal: "racism represents, literally, revolutionary discourse, but in reverse."[84] However, rest assured that these new ideas "had their roots in the discourse of race struggle."[85] This is how Foucault would explain the tragedy and the horror of the twentieth century. The Third Reich "takes up the theme, established at the end of the nineteenth century, of a state racism that is responsible for the biological protection of the race."[86] Regarding the country founded by the October Revolution, "in Soviet state racism, what revolutionary discourse designated as the class enemy becomes a sort of biological threat."[87]

This reconstruction raises several problems. First, did "state racism" break out only in the twentieth century? Putting this periodization in doubt well before then, the nineteenth-century abolitionists burned the U.S. Constitution in the public square, calling it a pact with the devil for having consecrated racial slavery. Those abolitionists also violated the Fugitive Slave Law of 1850, which forced every U.S.-American citizen to become a hunter of human beings. The law made it a punishable offense not only to have hidden or otherwise aided Black people pursued by their legitimate owners but also to not assist with their capture.[88] To be fair to Foucault, we might say that he is ignorant of this history. But he had only to read the comment by Marx on the Fugitive Slave Law: "To play the part of slave-catchers for the Southern slaveholders appeared to be the constitutional calling of the North."[89] In any case, we are not discussing a form of racism that manifested itself only in civil society. Based on explicit constitutional and legal norms, race determined an individual's social status and fate, determined and sanctioned by law. We are clearly in the presence of "state racism."

If the thesis that "state racism" made its first appearance in the twentieth century is without any basis, it is at least indisputable that with the rise of the Third Reich, "we have an absolutely racist State."[90] The particular horror that marked Hitler's Germany, the horror of the Holocaust, is beyond question. But this is not really the main issue here. We read in an authoritative U.S.-American historian of racism that "the Nazi definition of a Jew was never as stringent as 'the one-drop rule' that prevailed in the categorization of Negroes in the racial purity laws of the American South."[91] The definition of a Jew, based on the Nuremberg laws, also was based on this or that ancestor being a member of the Jewish religion, while in the United States, religion played no role in the definition of who was Black. It was instead blood, even one drop of blood, that mattered.

If we then examine the antebellum United States, we are forced to reach a conclusion: state racism emerged there more clearly than even in the Third Reich. Hitler did not possess slaves, either Black or Jewish, while, as we know, for the first decades of the history of the North American Republic, almost all of the presidents owned Black slaves. But, in Foucault's version of the history of racism, there is no place for African Americans, nor for the colonial peoples or those of colonial origin who are left out entirely. In this way, our understanding of Nazism is compromised. We see Nazism's principal ideologue, Alfred Rosenberg, three years before Hitler's rise to power, refer to the "racial state" that was alive and well in the U.S. South as a model to keep in mind when building the racial state in Germany.

More generally, erasing colonialism from history makes understanding capitalism impossible. If we analyze the capitalist countries together with their colonies, we realize that we are looking at a double standard: one for the race of the conquerors and one for the race of the conquered. In this sense, the racial state, or "state racism," to use Foucault's term, accompanies the history of colonialism and capitalism like a shadow. Except that this phenomenon is most visibly present in the United States because of the spatial contiguity in which the different "races" live.

Unfortunately, in reconstructing the history of racism, the French philosopher erases not only the colonialist legacy but also sociopolitical history. He doesn't begin with the encounter-conflict between very different cultures and the relationship instituted by the West that, over time, became that of colonial and semi-colonial worlds. He focuses instead on a chapter of history that is entirely internal to the West and, indeed, to France. This is not about the country (metropolis and colonies) in which the revolution condemned and abolished racism and the slavery regime that had existed in Saint-Domingue that was based on the domination of the "aristocracy of skin" and sanctioned by law. It is not about the country in which the first epic test of power between champions of and opponents of Black slavery and of the racial state occurred.

No, it is another France that is at the center of the history of racism delineated by Foucault. In very vague terms, and without any mention of texts nor of specific authors, he refers to the discourse established at the turn of the revolution that read sociopolitical conflict in racial terms, not in the French Empire as a whole, but in metropolitan France (again, ignoring the colonies). If Boulainvilliers defended the privileges of the nobles as heirs of the victorious French, authors such as Sieyès and Thierry replied by demanding the Gallic-Roman right (or that of the Third Estate) to throw off the domination the Franks imposed on them.

Once again, the unique way Foucault proceeds stands out, as he starts not from Boulainvilliers but from his opponents: the revolutionaries would have been the first to read the sociopolitical conflict in racial terms. But let us also abstract from this: were Boulainvilliers' critics really suffering from racism? Did they intend to carve out a naturalistic and insuperable "heterogeneity" among the political-social subjects in struggle? Whether speaking of race itself or of peoples in struggle and war, Sieyès contested the position of absolute privilege demanded by champions of aristocracy: "the privileged actually come to see themselves as another species of man," a superior species.[92] As the reference to a common humanity demonstrates, we see here a critique of racism, not its theorization. Is it still true that "the history of some is not the history of others"?

When, in 1853, Thierry wrote the history of the Third Estate, he began with the struggle between the Franks and the Gauls but ended up celebrating the progressive "fusion of races."[93] This progress brought about the "end of the distinction of races" and of "all the legal consequences of diversity of origin," and all this happened thanks to a struggle that saw the serfs and others socially excluded polemicize against the feudal lords in the following terms: "*we are men as well as they*."[94] Is this a racist discourse or a critique of one?

Regarding Boulainvilliers, Thierry justified the privileges of the class he belonged to by referring to a conflict between different "races," but this always meant races that were internal to the West. He compared the Third Estate to the Gallic-Romans, who were, yes, defeated, but not outside of the area of civilization. They were not comparable to the Blacks of the colonies, that is, to a "race" considered inferior by nature and by nature capable only of servile labor. Boulainvilliers certainly did not propose to subject the bourgeoisie, which in France had experienced a remarkable social ascent, to slavery or colonial subjugation. He meant instead to strengthen the exclusive character of aristocratic privilege. The process of authentic racialization happened instead, first of all, to colonial peoples (and secondarily to the popular classes of the metropoles who were often compared to the savages of the colonies). The upper strata of the Third Estate participated in these processes, the same strata that claimed a common humanity only as part of the struggle against the privileges of the aristocracy.

All this has been omitted from Foucault's conceptual history. In his work, there is no space for the long-term processes of racialization and dehumanization that were imposed on the colonial peoples, just as there is no space for the great struggles of recognition, starting with that which, with the radicalization of the French Revolution, brought about the abolition of slavery in the colonies. We are led to ask ourselves: to explain the history of Western racism, is a handful of French intellectuals' debate over Franks and Gallic-Romans really more important than the wars of conquest against peoples considered a mass of homunculi bereft of human dignity and fated to be enslaved or annihilated, as happened during what has sometimes been defined, because of its immensity, "the greatest genocide in the history of humanity,"[95] the one committed in the wake of the discovery-conquest of the Americas? As far as France is concerned, is the small chapter of the history of ideas that Foucault focuses on more important than the French Revolution or the war fought in Saint Domingue over Black slavery? This was a gigantic conflict in which great masses of people were involved, and that constitutes a central chapter of world history. And yet, all that is too intrinsically tied to material things (the chains of real slavery, the profits made in the slave trade and from the sale of the products of slavery) and too well-known to gain any interest from Foucault, who is at work demonstrating that revolution and racism go hand in hand and pursuing an originality that borders on the esoteric.

His anti-revolutionary zeal and the cult of esotericism reach their culmination in the reading of the three decades of Stalinism as a regime of state and biological racism. The traditional theory of totalitarianism drags in and equates more or less radically Hitler's Germany and Stalin's Soviet Union. But a great distance and even an ideological antithesis remain between them. The former country openly proclaimed that it was building a colonial empire founded on white and Aryan supremacy. The latter, instead, was a champion of the struggle against colonialism and racism. Foucault carried out an operation that seemed too bold even to the theorists of totalitarianism: to make Hitler and Stalin seem similar, even ideologically, as champions of "biological racism." It was an undoubtedly novel thesis, but is it supported by some evidence or arguments resembling evidence?

As far as the relationship with the external enemy is concerned, it was Ernst Nolte, the leader of historical revisionism, who observed that, during the Second World War, the representation of Germany as "racist" was common in the West, "with a sort of replica" of the reading of the conflict "dear to National Socialism," but not in the Soviet Union, which instead adhered to a "historical representation."[96] Indeed, it was not Stalin but Roosevelt who considered a biological solution: "we either have to castrate the German people, or you have got to treat them in such a manner so they can't just go on reproducing people who want to continue the way they have in the past."[97] Not by accident, at the end of the Second World War, criticizing this attitude, Benedetto Croce stressed that invoking "sterilization" was to follow "the example of the very same Nazis." Indeed, in the years of the Third Reich, the Final Solution was preceded by repeated calls for "sterilization of the mass of the Jews." Moreover, Croce ignored that the Third Reich had taken much of its eugenics and racism from the United States, as evident in statements by Rosenberg and Hitler. Nevertheless, the fact remains that, with his pointed observation, the liberal philosopher refuted in advance the fantasy history of racism propounded by the French radical philosopher.

Regarding the internal enemy: we recall a statement by Stalin that "the son does not answer for the crimes of the father."[98] At the end of 1935, *Pravda* announced that children of the privileged classes would no longer be barred from going to college. It is eloquent testimony to a pedagogical obsession that, in the work of an anti-communist American historian, Anne Applebaum, we find the gulag characterized as follows: to the very end, while Hitler's war of annihilation raged, and the entire country found itself in an absolutely tragic situation, they managed to find and invest "time and money" for "propaganda, manifestos, and political indoctrination meetings" for those detained. The terroristic character of the dictatorship remains, as does the horror of the gulag, but where is the biology?

It is important to distinguish the political-moral despecification (exclusion from the human and civil community) of religious or ideological wars, which leaves the victim a way out through conversion, from racial despecification that is natural and insurmountable. We may be repulsed by the crusade against the Albigensians and the Night of Saint Bartholomew, but I know of no historians who contextualize these events as part of the history of biological racism!

A final consideration. When, in 1976, Foucault gave his lecture at the Collège de France that we have analyzed here, the racist regime of apartheid South Africa was still alive and well. Ten years earlier, Arendt called attention to the ban that still existed in Israel against interracial marriages and other laws of similar inspiration, making a paradoxical analogy to the "infamous Nuremberg Laws issued in the Fall of 1935."[99] But, when the French author searched for another reality comparable to the Third Reich as a form of "state racism," he was able to identify only the Soviet Union. This country, from its founding, had played a decisive role in promoting the emancipation of the colonial peoples, and, already in 1976, was on the front lines of denouncing the anti-Black and anti-Arab policies of South Africa and Israel.

8. On Biopolitics

No less esoteric and no less zealously anti-revolutionary is the history that Foucault reconstructs of "biopolitics," the category that owes its extraordinary success to the French philosopher and for whom it helped explain the horrors of the twentieth century. In an extremely brief summary, here is the history he explicated. Starting in the twentieth century, a new vision and a "new technology of power" arose. It was not a question, as in the past, of disciplining the bodies of individuals. Now, "power is applied not to man-as-body but to the living man, to man-as-living-being"[100] affected "by overall processes characteristic of birth, death, production, illness" and the "reproduction" of human life.[101] Indeed, with the rise of biopolitics, "power took possession of life in the nineteenth century,"[102] or at least, "power at least takes life under its care," and this "succeeded in covering the whole surface that lies between the organic and the biological, between body and population"[103] and "biological processes as a whole," to preserve "the security of the whole from internal dangers."[104]

The biopolitical turn was full of perils. Then racism intervened as well, or rather state and biological racism, which sought "a way of introducing a break into the domain of life that is under power's control: that between what must live and what must die," and this transformed biopolitics into a practice of death.[105] From this would come the catastrophic consequences that we know of in the Stalinist USSR and in Nazi Germany.

As with his history of racism, so with that of biopolitics, the silence on colonialism is deafening since colonialism was the site of the birth of the former (as we have seen) and the latter (as we shall see below). What happened in the Americas with the arrival of the conquistadors is enlightening. The indigenous peoples were often condemned to work themselves to death. There was an unlimited supply of potential slaves and no lack of those ready to increase their riches through the reproduction of the human animal they owned:

> Las Casas reports that the price of a female slave rises according to whether or not she is pregnant, exactly as in the case of cattle: "This godforsaken man . . . said that he worked as hard as he could to get the Indian women with child, for when he sold them as slaves he would be paid more if they were pregnant."[106]

The testimony of Las Casas referred to a period in which the indigenous peoples had not yet been replaced by Africans as the enslaved labor force. With this change, the indigenous were erased from the face of the Earth like some cumbersome ballast thrown overboard at sea, while the latter were made to work and reproduce themselves in slavery. Two practices reinforced and perpetuated the racial hierarchy in the English colonies of North America and then in the United States. First, a ban on miscegenation or "bastardization," that is, on sexual relations and marriage between the members of the "superior race" and the "inferior race." In this way, a rigid legal and biopolitical barrier separated the race of the masters from that of the slaves to guarantee that the latter would remain docile and obedient. This led to the second practice: death by horrifying torture awaited anyone who gave any sign that they had not understood the lesson. Once the undisturbed functioning of the institution of slavery had been assured, the human animal would be called upon to increase and multiply in numbers.

In 1832, Thomas R. Dew, an influential ideologue of the South, declared, without any embarrassment, indeed not without pride, that Virginia was a "Negro-raising state" and that it could export six thousand per year.[107] A planter boasted that his female slaves were "breeding animals of extraordinary quality." Among the slave owners, a widespread means of increasing their capital was the encouragement of frequent childbirth and promoting births in general. Girls often were mothers at age thirteen or fourteen and by twenty had already brought five children into the world. They might even be emancipated after enriching their master with ten or fifteen small slaves. It was a practice that did not escape the attention of Karl Marx, who analyzed the situation on the eve of secession. Some entire states specialized in the "breeding of slaves"; instead of traditional exports, these states raised slaves as goods for export.[108]

It was the triumph of biopolitics. If the conquistadores had recourse to a private biopolitics (but one always tolerated and encouraged by political power), now we instead find biopolitics in its second phase, practiced according to precise norms and regulations. We see here a state biopolitics (and a state racism). Here we find the state, "the power" concerned with "biological processes of the whole," "take possession of life," and in the most radical fashion, imposing a drastic "break between what must live and what must die," which transforms biopolitics into a practice of death. The breeding of Black people goes hand in hand with the deportation and decimation of the indigenous peoples. It is a break that is reproduced within the Blacks themselves: how many were suspected of putting in danger "the security of the whole" (to use Foucault's term) and so were considered unfit to live and were put to death, the others being thereby stimulated to increase and multiply themselves in slavery.

Later, at the start of the twentieth century, John A. Hobson, the honest English liberal whose work Lenin amply utilized in his writing on imperialism, summarized the biopolitics of the capitalist and colonialist West: the populations that survived (and indeed are even led to increase their numbers) were those that could be reduced to "the economic exploitation of white colonists," while the others "tend to disappear" (or to be more precise, were decimated and annihilated).[109]

There is no mention in Foucault of this central chapter of the history of biopolitics, the chapter on colonialism. Moreover, his silence does not stop here. Even in the capitalist metropoles, an excessive and unproductive population was present. This, too, was unneeded ballast, in the form of the "Indians." A similar fate awaited them as well. This was the viewpoint expressed clearly by Benjamin Franklin, who, regarding the indigenous peoples, observed

> and, indeed, if it be the design of Providence to extirpate these savages to make room for cultivators of the earth, it seems not improbable that rum may be the appointed means. It has already annihilated all the tribes who formerly inhabited the sea-coast.[110]

Six years earlier, Franklin had warned a physician in the following terms:

> Half the Lives you save are not worth saving, as being useless; and almost the other Half ought not to be sav'd, as being mischievous. Does your Conscience never hint to you the Impiety of being in constant Warfare against the Plans of Providence?[111]

Biopolitics reserved an analogous, radical treatment for the capitalist metropole's external and internal ballast. As we have seen stated for the Indians, it was also for the "Indians" of the metropoles that sovereign biopolitics separated that life "worth saving" from that of the others, or as Foucault puts it, "what must live and what must die." More than a century after Benjamin Franklin, Nietzsche pronounced the "annihilation of the decadent races" and "the annihilation of millions of failures."[112]

Biopolitical preoccupation pervades every aspect of capitalist society. How can it assure itself the docile and submissive workforce that capitalism requires? Sieyès dreamed of resolving social conflict by promoting the coupling of Black people and anthropomorphic apes. He hoped that from it could come forth a race of slaves by nature. More realistically, Jeremy Bentham proposed to enclose in "workhouses," together with their vagabond parents, children of tender age to have them couple and generate an "indigenous class" used to work and discipline. It would have been, assured the English liberal, "the most gentle of revolutions," a sexual one, or, to use the language common to our own days, a biopolitical one. From this ideological and politically backward terrain, we can understand the invention in England of "eugenics," a new science that in Europe saw mass diffusion and application.

Even this second chapter of the history of biopolitics, that which is strictly capitalist, is ignored by Foucault. He pays no attention to the third chapter either, which we can refer to by the term "geopolitics." Indeed, this term emerged after the First World War, coined by the Swede Rudolf Kjellén. We are in 1920. The climate was clearly affected by dismay over the dimensions of the carnage only recently terminated, so much so that the peace just concluded appeared to many as a mere armistice, a prelude to a gigantic new test of force and a new slaughter. On the other hand, after the appeal launched by the October Revolution and Lenin to the "slaves of the colonies" to break their chains, there was widespread distress in the West over the anticolonial revolution that loomed on the horizon, which had already begun.

In these circumstances, the prolific character of the colonial peoples, rather than growing the number of slaves or semi-slaves, risked multiplying the potential enemies of the West and the great colonialist powers. Hence, the widespread denunciation in the United States and Europe of those who tolerated abortion or the decline in birth rates. There was no lack of others who posed a terrible question: while total mobilization was underway in the economic sphere, was it worth wasting resources to treat incurably sick people who could only be a weight on society in the new war on the horizon? Or would it be better to round them up to increase their number and improve the conditions of the real and potential combatants? Clearly, politics had become "biopolitical."

The three chapters we have spoken of here can be distinguished conceptually but are not chronologically separate. Let's see what happened in England in the years before the First World War. One of the experts of the Royal Commission mandated to study the problem of the "weak-minded" warned that they "lower the general vigor of the nation" and even threaten it with "national destruction." Circulated widely by Churchill, the report recommended energetic measures: forced sterilization of the "weak-minded," of the misfits, of the presumed habitual delinquents. The "idle vagabonds" would be enclosed in work camps. Only in this way could the country adequately confront "a national and racial peril that it is impossible to exaggerate." Sometime earlier, Churchill had confided to one of his cousins, "the betterment of the British breed is the political objective of my life." The scholar who analyzed this chapter of history comments that as Home Secretary in 1911, "Churchill wanted a much more draconian scheme that would give him personally almost unlimited power over the lives of some individuals."[113]

Of these three chapters of the history of biopolitics, there is no trace in Foucault, who uses the term "biopolitics" as if he had invented it himself. In effect, he radically reinvented it. The category "biopolitics" now came to stand alongside that of "totalitarianism." The aim was to bring together Stalin's USSR and Hitler's Germany, at times adding to the list of the condemned even socialism as such, and the welfare state.[114] Hayek proceeded analogously, accusing the supporters of any form of socialism and those who supported the welfare state of "totalitarianism." Once again, notwithstanding his celebrity and radical posturing, Foucault largely ended up within the dominant ideology. It goes without saying that the more fully he ended up there, the more radical was his erasure of the history of colonialism.

9. From Foucault to Agamben (via Levinas)

Giorgio Agamben enters the ranks of the noted philosophers of Western Marxism, sometimes juxtaposed with Horkheimer and Adorno or Alain Badiou.[115] He is a co-author of collectively written books with some of the most prestigious exponents of Western Marxism.[116] Here I want to address only the important contribution that he has made to the destruction of the links between Western Marxism and the anticolonial revolution, and therefore I refer only to his Introduction to the Italian edition (2012) of *Some Reflections on the Philosophy of Hitlerism*, a 1934 work by Emmanuel Levinas. It consists of a few pages that directly address my work's central theme.

The elegy pronounced by Agamben is high and solemn praise: "this text by Levinas is perhaps the only successful attempt of twentieth-century philosophy to come to terms with the decisive political event of the century: Nazism."[117] What does it consist of? According to the author celebrated here, Hitlerism negates the foundation of "liberalism," of "Western civilization," of the "Western spirit," and "the structure of thought and the truths of the Western world." It rejects the thesis of the "unconditional freedom of man before the world," of the "sovereign freedom of reason."[118] Nazism instead counters with "the biological, with all the fatality that involves," "the mysterious voice of blood," and the idea of race. When did this perversion that seeks to question "the traditional thought of the West" begin? The answer: "Marxism, for the first time in Western history, contests this conception of man." Far from recognizing "absolute freedom, that which accomplishes miracles," Marx holds that "being determines consciousness" in such a way that he "catches European culture off guard, or, at least, he breaks the harmonious curve of its development."[119] It is the beginning of the catastrophe that culminates in Nazism. Historical materialism paved the way for biological racism.

Traditionally, Marx and the political movement that takes his name have been accused of the opposite motive, of abandoning themselves to the hubris of reason and praxis by engaging in adventurous experiments in social engineering to construct a society and a world that would be radically new. In this critique, there is a grain of truth. Every great revolutionary movement tends to underestimate the weight and the resistance of objective social conditions, to exalt, sometimes in extreme ways, the role of praxis, and to fall into what I have defined as "the idealism of practice."[120] This is not by accident. In prison, driven by the desire to mislead the fascist censors and needing synonyms for Marxism and historical materialism, Gramsci writes of the "philosophy of praxis," certainly not of the "philosophy of being."

But, to demonstrate his thesis of the continuity between historical materialism and biological racism, Levinas does not hesitate to force things. He attributes to Marx the thesis according to which "being determines consciousness" but does not waste time explaining which "being" is being referred to. So let's read *A Contribution to the Critique of Political Economy*: "it is not the consciousness of men that determines their being; on the contrary, their social being determines their consciousness."[121] Social being is history, and so what sense does it make to compare this to the incessant mutations of blood, of biological nature celebrated by the champions of racism as being synonymous with some eternal truth and so end up justifying the errors, deviations, fantasies, and ideological mystifications of which the historical process is so rich in examples?

The thesis of Levinas and Agamben is the reprisal of a common and outdated view, one already refuted in the late nineteenth century by an eminent representative of "European civilization" and the "Western spirit." I am referring to Emile Durkheim. The great sociologist distinguished historical materialism from "political and social Darwinism." Durkheim writes: "the latter merely explains the development of institutions by the principles and concepts sufficient for explaining zoological development."[122] Marx's theory is quite different:

It seeks the motivating causes for historical development, not in the cosmic circumstances which may have affected the organism, but in the *environment* which the *labor* of men in association has created from nothing and which has been added on to nature. It makes social phenomena depend not on hunger, thirst, sexual desire, etc., but on the state at which *human art* has arrived and the ways of living which have resulted from it—in short, on the collective *works* of men.[123]

I have highlighted in italics the terms in the passage above that constitute an earlier, direct refutation of the reading of Marx so dear to Levinas. Of course, from the latter's point of view, a philosophy that stresses the role of "social being" stands forever on a slippery slope. But Durkheim also has a reply to this objection: it is a central rule of the "sociological method" to not allow to enter into analysis the intentions and the conscious representations of individuals, but rather the situations, the relationships, the "social facts."[124] Indeed, "it even seems to us, on this condition, but only on this condition, that history may become a science and that sociology consequently may take on existence."[125] It is a point on which the convergence with historical materialism is so great that the French sociologist adds: "for our part, we arrived at this postulate before we had learned of Marx, whose influence we have not at all suffered from."[126] And thus, one of the greatest sociologists, an intellectual of Jewish origin in Third Republic France, would be co-responsible for the ruinous turn that resulted in Nazism.

The thesis that stresses the role of "material needs" is nonsense, according to Levinas, both historically and philosophically. Marx placed himself on a slippery slope that led to the triumph of biological and racial materialism. The "system of needs" is a section of Hegel's *Elements of the Philosophy of Right (*section 189) that begins by paying homage to this concept in political economy and to Smith, Say, and Ricardo.[127] Levinas and Agamben risk pointing out as precursors to the Third Reich a considerable part of the pantheon of Western intellectuals!

Lacking any philosophical basis, the arguments of Levinas and Agamben circulate in an entirely imaginary historical space. In the years that preceded this work of the French philosopher, the campaign that in the West raged against Marxism and against Bolshevism was conducted explicitly in the name of biology. For that wretched doctrine, "the very existence of superior biological values is a crime."[128] "A battle to the death" was underway "between biology and Bolshevism."[129] The latter not only furiously opposed "the new eugenic truth" and "the new biological revelation"[130] but assumed an "antiracial" attitude and incited the "colored races,"[131] requiring society in one way or another to unburden itself of failures.

Catastrophe can be foiled only by reaffirming by every means biological truth against the ravings of Marxists and Bolsheviks. Expressing himself this way, we find an American intellectual celebrated by two U.S. presidents (Warren G. Harding and Herbert Hoover) and then solemnly welcomed to Berlin by Hitler.[132] These were the years in which the regime of white supremacy dominant in the U.S. South exercised such an attraction to Nazism that its principal ideologue spoke of the North American Republic as a "splendid country of the future" that had the merit of having formulated the happy "new idea of a racial state," an idea that should be put into practice "with the strength of youth" in Germany itself, enforcing it against not only Black and yellow peoples but also against Jews.[133] As we see, it makes no sense to contrast the liberal West with Marxist and Nazi biological determinism. The chapter of history we have discussed here is imperially ignored by Levinas and Agamben, who deduce *a priori* the meaning of the Third Reich from an idea that pretends to be profound but which, entirely abstracted from real history, is entirely empty.

While on the one hand they paint a caricature of historical materialism, on the other, Levinas and Agamben offer a vision of the Third Reich that we could define as Hollywood-esque. The Nazis are immediately recognizable for their crudeness, intent only on speaking of blood, race, and arms, and entirely incapable of articulating a discourse that references interiority, soul, spiritual or cultural values. In reality, having already refuted these stereotypes are the great intellectuals who were attracted to the Third Reich: Heidegger, Schmitt, etc. Above all, one must reflect on the personality of the Führer himself. As the most authoritative biographers have made clear, from the years of his earliest development, he cultivated "the dream of a great artist." The most brutal exercise of power did not prevent him from excluding from the list of authentic leaders those who were without any artistic sensibility, nor from making appeals to teachers to work hard to "arouse in men the instinct for beauty." It was "what the Greeks considered essential."[134]

The Nazi bosses did not disdain paying homage to moral conscience, to "the voice perceptible in silence," of which Goethe and Kant wrote, or to the "categorical moral law," or even to "freedom," to the "feeling of responsibility," or to the "culture of the soul" that it implied.[135] As long as the colonial peoples were excluded from the civil community, moral community, and human community. And so a policy of enslavement of servile races and of annihilation of Jewish-Bolshevik agitators that incite them to an insane revolt could go hand in hand with paying homage to the categorical imperative and the celebration of the moral, artistic, cultural, and spiritual values of the West and of the white and Aryan race. So if we want to understand the Third Reich, we must start with the reprise and the radicalization of the colonialist tradition (and of the racism intrinsic to it), that is, with the very problem ignored and erased by Levinas and Agamben.

This is not to underestimate the novelty of these two authors. The theory of totalitarianism and biopolitics put the Third Reich and the Soviet Union on the same plane, but Marx, if not spared, had not been directly implicated. Now, instead, as a starting point of the parabola that resulted in the Third Reich, which was trying to build a colonial and slave empire in Eastern Europe and reaffirming the supremacy of the white and Aryan race, we are presented with the philosopher who not only denounced the colonialist system in its entirety but also denounced Black slavery with fiery words and expressed his indignation over the sympathy certain important sectors of the liberal British world had for the secessionist and slavery-based Confederacy. On the other side, we find the liberal world, which for centuries had been amply involved in the world colonialist-slavery system and with the regime of white supremacy in the U.S. South, which was still in power in the mid-twentieth century, and which Nazi leaders admired, now immersed in a cleansing bath. It is a total misunderstanding of real history, a history that mostly took place under the banner of an exalted pathos of Europe and of the West, and to which Nazism was anything but foreign.

10. Negri and Hardt and the Esoteric Celebration of Empire

The esoteric history of racism and biopolitics is an indirect apologia for the liberal West, whose role as the protagonist of the history of colonial expansion and the racism connected to it is hushed up or greatly underestimated. With Negri and Hardt, the picture changes. The apologia becomes direct and esoteric. And emphatic. This might seem like a polemical judgment. To refute this impression, engaging in a sort of intellectual experiment, or, if one likes, a game, may be useful. Let's compare two pieces by authors who compare the United States favorably to Europe. The first celebrates "the American Experience," emphasizing "the difference between a nation conceived in liberty and dedicated to the proposition that all men are created equal, and the nations of the old world, which certainly were not conceived in liberty."[136]

And now, let's see the second:

> Was not American democracy, in fact, founded on the democracy of exodus, on affirmative and nondialectical values, and on pluralism and freedom? Did not these values, along with the notion of new frontiers, perpetually re-create the expansion of its democratic basis beyond every abstract obstacle of the nation, ethnicity, and religion?... When Arendt claimed the American Revolution to be superior to the French because the American was an unlimited search for political freedom and the French a limited struggle over scarcity and inequality, she not only celebrated an ideal of freedom that Europeans no longer knew but also reterritorialized it in the United States.[137]

Which of these two pieces is more apologetic? It is difficult to say; both observe the most rigorous silence about the fate of the indigenous peoples and of Blacks, the Monroe Doctrine, the subjugation of the Philippines and the merciless repression and genocidal practices against its independence movement. And even if the scale of the erasures and the apologetic zeal left us with no desire to side with either of them, we can say that the second piece is more inspired and lyrical. It came from the pens of Hardt and Negri, while the first was by Leo Strauss, the leading author for U.S. neoconservatives.

With little variation, this intellectual experiment and this game can be repeated over and over and always with the same result. What is the real meaning of the revolt against the government of London by the English colonies in America that resulted in the founding of the United States? We have seen the enthusiasm expressed by two authoritative exponents of Western Marxism. Now, let's read the analysis of an American scholar:

> The American Revolution was not a social revolution like the French, Russian, Chinese, Mexican or Cuban Revolutions. It was a war of independence. Moreover, it was not a war of independence of natives against alien conquerors, like the struggles of the Indonesians against the Dutch or the Vietnamese or the Algerians against the French, but instead a war of settlers against the home country. Any recent parallels are in the relation of the Algerian colons to the French Republic or the Southern Rhodesians to the United Kingdom.[138]

At least as far as the relations with the colonial peoples and those of colonial origin are concerned, the founding of the United States resembled more a counter-revolution than a revolution. A conservative author, Samuel Huntington (who was, at the time, a rising and authoritative U.S. historian), recognized this, but it is blasphemy to the authors of *Empire*!

Let's continue with the comparison. In our own times, eminent *liberal* scholars describe the history of their own country as the history of a *Herrenvolk democracy*, that is, a democracy that existed only for the *Herrenvolk* (significantly, they have recourse here to the language of Hitler), for the "people of the masters," and that, on the other hand, it did not hesitate to enslave Blacks and exterminate the native peoples from the face of the Earth. "Only in the United States was there a stable and direct link between the property in slaves and political power. Only in the United States did slave owners play a central role in founding a nation and creating representative institutions."[139] *Empire* instead speaks in reverent tones of the "American democracy" that breaks with the "transcendent" vision of power of the European tradition and, for the authors, referring to Arendt, constitutes the "invention of modern politics itself" or "the establishment of freedom."[140]

Scholars who cannot be suspected of anti-Americanism have had no difficulty recognizing that "from the first day of its existence, the United States is an imperial power."[141] And that "there were no more self-confident imperialists than the Founding Fathers" of the North American Republic.[142] Hardt and Negri, instead, always speak about "*European* colonialism" and European imperialism: "imperialism was an extension of the sovereignty of the European nation-states beyond their own boundaries. Eventually, nearly all the world's territories could be parceled out, and the entire world map could be coded in European colors."[143]

In conclusion, let's take a central figure in the worldwide rise of the United States, Woodrow Wilson. Among the scholars of history and international politics, it is almost taken for granted to write of "Wilsonian nationalism."[144] This was a president who carried out a record number of military interventions in Latin America in the name of the Monroe Doctrine and tended to side with white supremacy domestically and internationally and to support the oppression of the colonial peoples and those of colonial origin.[145] But, for Hardt and Negri, Wilson becomes a champion of the "internationalist ideology of peace" far from the "European-style imperialist ideology."[146]

Marx's observation about Bakunin comes to mind: for all his anti-statist radicalism, he spared England, "the really capitalist state," the one that constituted the "point of the spear of bourgeois society in Europe." Hardt and Negri's polemic against the principle of the sovereign state spares the country that grants itself a monstrously expanded sovereignty that authorizes it to intervene in every corner of the world, with or without the authorization of the Security Council of the United Nations. This is the country that, far from building an alternative to European militarism, represents, as Sartre put it, "that super-European monstrosity."[147]

PART V

Revival, or the Last Gasp of Western Marxism?

1. Žižek's Anti-Imperialism

Compared to 1989 and the years immediately following, compared with the period in which the discourse on the unlamented death of Marx had become almost common sense, the ideological framework of our own times today appears quite different. Interest in that great thinker and revolutionary is evident and growing. Authors who, in one way or another, refer to him enjoy considerable prestige and popularity at times. Must we, therefore, speak of a revival of Western Marxism?

Recently, the most illustrious exponent of what he likes to coquettishly self-describe as "libertarian Western Marxism"[1] welcomed 2011 as "the year of dreaming dangerously, of the revival of radical emancipatory politics all around the world."[2] The author [Žižek] hurried to call attention to the disillusion that quickly followed. But let's leave aside the subsequent developments to concentrate on 2011, which was celebrated in such flattering terms. Yes, it was the year in which new protest movements (Occupy Wall Street, the *indignados*, etc.) seemed to spread like oil stains, but it was also the year in which NATO unleashed a war against Libya that, after having led to tens of thousands of deaths, ended with the horrible lynching of Qaddafi. The neocolonial character of the aggression was recognized by authoritative organs of the Western press. Nevertheless, Hillary Clinton abandoned herself to exultation so unbalanced ("we came, we saw, he died!" exclaimed the then-secretary of state) as to arouse moral reservations even in a Fox News reporter, for whom this was disquieting enthusiasm for a war crime. Unfortunately, the infamous neocolonialist enterprise we are discussing here did not meet any resistance from Western Marxism. In Italy, it was even considered legitimate, at least to a historic figure of this ideological current.

Still, in 2011, in Tel Aviv and other Israeli cities, hundreds of thousands of *indignados* went to the squares to protest high prices and unsustainable rents, but they were careful not to question the persistent and accelerated colonization of Palestinian territories. The "indignation" called attention to the rising difficulties of popular strata of the Jewish community but did not pay any attention to the interminable tragedy of the people under military occupation. A professor at the Jewish University of Jerusalem described the tragedy in a prestigious US-American journal: at least as far as the occupied Palestinian territories are concerned, Israel is an ethnocracy and, in the final analysis, a racial state.

The colonization of the land expropriated by force from the Palestinians continues uninterrupted. Those who dare protest are "treated harshly, sometimes imprisoned for long periods, sometimes killed in the course of the demonstrations."[3] All this occurs in the context of "a malevolent campaign to make life as miserable as possible for the Palestinians there . . . in the hope that they will go away."[4] It is an ethnic cleansing, even if diluted over time. We see here an ethnocracy so harsh as to be "all too reminiscent of dark precedents in the history of the last century."[5] And yet, those *indignados* protesting the high cost of living they faced, but indifferent to the cruel ethnocracy imposed on the Palestinians, were celebrated by two illustrious Marxist authors as champions of a new society based on "our relation to the commons."[6]

And so, was 2011, the year "of the revival of radical emancipatory politics all around the world," as Žižek put it, or of the revival of the ideal of a society based "on our relation to the commons" as Negri and Hardt put it, or was it the year in which colonial and neocolonial misdeeds were greeted with silence or conniving even in the traditional areas of the left? Completely erasing the fate of colonized peoples from their balance sheet, Žižek, Hardt, and Negri reproduce the basic limitation of Western Marxism by diluting it even further. From this point of view, the success that Žižek especially has enjoyed in our own times brings to mind, rather than a revival, the last gasp of Western Marxism.

The removal of the colonial question is an integral part of the theoretical and political platform of the Slovenian philosopher. Far from the wished-for and dreamed-of totally Other, capitalism completely dominates the world. It makes no sense to distinguish the imperialist and colonialist powers from those countries that only a short time ago liberated themselves from colonial domination, and that still, through trial and error, seek to overcome backwardness and achieve full independence economically and build for themselves political institutions adequate to their socioeconomic conditions and to their geopolitical situation. Žižek is no less hostile than Arendt to the category of the Third World. Indeed, he is more radical in his opposition to it. His irony is cutting against those countries that, despite identifying with a revolutionary ideology and sometimes with Marxism, fly the banner of anti-imperialism: today's predominant class struggle is no longer between "the capitalists and proletariat in each country"[7] but instead occurs internationally, between states rather than social classes; in this way, the Marxian "critique of capitalism itself"[8] is reduced to and deformed into "a critique of 'imperialism,'" which loses sight of what is essential, and that is the capitalist relations of production.[9]

Once the terrain has been cleared of the categories of the Third World, imperialism, anti-imperialism, and so forth, the only sensible distinction, as far as the present is concerned, would be that between "authoritarian capitalism" and that which is not authoritarian. In the former category, the first place goes to China, but Vietnam and perhaps Cuba also can be placed there, after the latter's recent opening to the market and the private sector economy (which at least tend toward capitalism). In any case, the countries of "Latin America," marked by a "populist capitalism" and inclined toward *caudillismo* and authoritarianism, also end up there.[10] Looking closely, this represents the distinction disdained by the Slovenian philosopher, that of the Third World on the one side and the capitalist West (with its persistent colonial tendencies) on the other. Only now, this distinction is reintroduced to the exclusive glory of the liberal West, which becomes the model to which the Third World countries must aspire.

In conclusion, Žižek's vision is not any different from the self-consciousness of the dominant classes in Europe and in the United States. The discovery of this convergence is not in itself a refutation of it. However, the refutation is provided by the Slovenian philosopher himself. He comments on the directive that Kissinger imparted to the CIA to destabilize Salvador Allende's Chile ("make the economy scream") and emphasizes how this same policy has continued to be used against Hugo Chávez's Venezuela.[11] Žižek avoids, however, a question that imposes itself: why would the Venezuela of Chávez and Maduro be considered more "authoritarian" than the country that tries by every means to destabilize it and to subjugate it and that seeks to exercise its dictatorship over Latin America and over the world? Certainly, from the point of view of the self-consciousness of the liberal West, the despotism exercised against the colonial peoples is irrelevant. Based on this logic, on the occasion of his first inaugural address, Bill Clinton celebrated the United States as the oldest democracy in the world. No attention was given to the enslavement of Blacks or to the expropriation, deportation, and decimation of the indigenous peoples. Žižek proceeds by a similar abstraction, a rather arbitrary one, in which he does not even ask whether the authoritarianism of Washington is not in some way the cause of the authoritarianism of Caracas.

We can make a general assessment here: it is quite strange to find a critic of capitalism who spares the worst aspects of this system, which are quite evident, according to Marx, in the colonies. A critique of waged work silent on forced labor would lack credibility. But the history of forced labor in its many forms is, in large part, the history of colonial oppression. And it is, without a doubt, misleading for a critic of "authoritarianism" such as Žižek to invite us to pass over the authoritarianism enacted against peoples, by a great power or by a coalition of powers, who are subjected to devastating embargoes, or bombardment and military occupation.

2. Žižek, the Degradation of the Anticolonial Revolution, and the Demonization of Mao

The lack of attention to the struggle between colonialism and anticolonialism also emerges from the chapters of history described by the Slovenian philosopher. Of the revolution of the Black slaves of Saint-Domingue/Haiti, he observes that it ended in "regression into a new form of hierarchical rule" after the death of Dessalines in 1806.[12] The observation is just if we look only at domestic politics. Internationally, the picture looks very different. Despite failing to find a stable form to transcend autocracy, the power of the ex-slaves continued to play a revolutionary role. It was Alexandre Pétion, president of Haiti from 1806 to 1818, who got Simon Bolivar to commit himself to the immediate liberation of slaves in return for support for the struggle of Latin America for its independence from Spain. Obstinately defending the institution of slavery was the "democratic" republic of North America, which, with a policy of embargo and naval blockade, sought to impose starvation or capitulation on Haiti, the country that, notwithstanding the despotism of its political regime, still embodied the cause of abolitionism and of freedom for Blacks. To resort to the criterion that Žižek makes central for the reading of the present, we would have to say that Haiti represented "authoritarian capitalism" while the United States represented more or less "democratic" capitalism. But this reading helps us understand very little of the present or the past, and indeed, does violence to both.

No less one-sided is the judgment of the Slovenian philosopher on the Soviet Union after the death of Lenin. I will limit myself here to reproducing a lapidary condemnation: "this is why Heidegger is wrong when he reduces the Holocaust to the industrial production of corpses: it was not that, Stalinist Communism was that."[13] Let's leave aside the taste for provocation by an author who sometimes prefers fireworks displays to arguments. This is not what is essential. We have seen eminent historians characterize Hitler's aggression in the East as the greatest colonial war of all time, a colonial war that, as we know, Stalin prepared for even before coming to power. So the least we can say is that the theorist of "libertarian Western Marxism" doesn't have an anticolonialist bias! Just as he ignores the international role of Haiti, the embodiment of the cause of abolitionism notwithstanding its despotic regime, so he does not pay any attention to the international role of the Soviet Union of Stalin, which, frustrating the attempt by Hitler to reduce Eastern Europe to the "German Indies," sounded the death knell for the world colonialist system (at least in its classical form).

The pose Žižek assumes on another, more recent chapter of history, this time regarding China, is especially significant. Referring to the grave economic crisis and the terrible famine provoked or gravely exacerbated by the Great Leap Forward in 1958–59, he discusses with distracted disinterest "Mao's ruthless decision to starve tens of millions to death in the late 1950s."[14] When for the first time I came across this statement, I was stunned. Was the Italian translation perhaps imprecise or too emphatic? But no! The original English is unequivocal and even more chilling than the translated version. In the Italian, we find the phrase "ten million people," but the original has it as "tens of millions." Probably, the Italian translator had tried to safeguard the prestige of the author being translated, reducing the scale. In any case, we must acknowledge something: the recurring motif of the campaign committed to demonizing, together with the leader who exercised power in Beijing for more than a quarter of a century, the People's Republic of China itself, the republic founded by the greatest anticolonialist revolution in history, such a motif is echoed without any critical caution by the most famous exponent of "libertarian Western Marxism"!

However, the accusation does not find supporting evidence among the most serious authors. Even the *Black Book of Communism*, while insisting on the colossal proportions of the disaster, recognizes that "undoubtedly it was not Mao's intention to kill so many of his compatriots."[15] There also were eminent Western statesmen who refused to jump on the bandwagon of the incipient Cold War against the great

Asian country. In an interview with the weekly *Die Zeit*, the German ex-Chancellor Helmut Schmidt emphasizes the unintentional nature of the tragedy that the Great Leap Forward led to.[16] Henry Kissinger also argued similarly: certainly, it was "one of the worst famines in human history," and yet, Mao sought to maximize the "industrial and agricultural development" of China, wanting to rapidly catch up to the West, and therefore provide a widespread and generalized condition of well-being. So, summing up, according to the illustrious U.S. scholar and politician, Mao "had once again called on the Chinese people to move a mountain, but this time the mountain did not move."[17]

Although marked by honesty and intellectual seriousness, the above-mentioned positions are limited. They ignore the historical context in which the Great Leap Forward took place and which follows the long struggle between colonialism and anticolonialism. We have already seen the concern expressed by Mao on the immediate eve of the proclamation of the People's Republic of China. The country, notwithstanding the glorious struggle for national liberation now concluded, risked being economically dependent on the United States and thus becoming a semi-colony.

In effect, the Truman administration's directives were clear and merciless. Already in a desperate condition because of decades of war and civil war, the People's Republic of China (which was not admitted to the United Nations) was encircled and threatened militarily. It now had to be subjected to an economic war that would have brought it to a "catastrophic economic situation," "toward disaster," and "collapse." That would have provoked the political defeat of the Chinese Communist Party as well, which up to that moment had only governed more or less extended rural areas and therefore suffered from total "inexperience" in the "field of urban economics." It was this extreme economic fragility and potential fall into (or return to) the semi-colonial dependence that Mao sought to escape, making an appeal for a military-like mass mobilization of tens of millions of peasants, who, despite being illiterate, through their revolutionary enthusiasm would have brought about a prodigious acceleration of economic development.

In reality, with his impatience and inexperience in the "field of urban economics," the Chinese leader fell into the trap prepared by his enemies. The result was catastrophic. A fact, however, is worth noting: at the start of the 1960s, a figure in the Kennedy administration, Walter W. Rostow, bragged about the triumph of the United States, which could slow the economic development of China by "decades." And so the terrifying famine that followed the Great Leap Forward was put on the ledger of the presumed homicidal rage of Mao rather than on the Machiavellian policy pursued by Washington.[18]

In conclusion, Margolin, Schmidt, and Kissinger are at fault for not fully placing the disastrous utopian experiment of Mao in the historical context of the colonial tragedy that opened with the Opium Wars and was still going on in the years of the Great Leap Forward. Instead, Žižek, by removing the struggle between colonialism and anticolonialism and Mao's troubled race to escape from the desperate mass misery that had resulted from colonial aggression and domination, puts it all on the ledger of the homicidal folly of the Chinese leader.

3. Harvey and the Absolutization of Inter-Imperialist Rivalry

Openly vilified by Žižek, the anticolonial revolution is entirely absent from the work of David Harvey, another exponent of Western Marxism. The picture he paints, starting with the contradictions of capitalism from the mid-twentieth century on, is eloquent testimony: "the overall result, as Lenin so accurately predicted, was fifty years of inter-imperialist rivalry and war in which rival nationalisms featured large."[19] Can the great historical crisis that broke out in 1914 and came to a provisional resolution in the defeat of the Third Reich be characterized only by the conflict between opposing imperialist powers? Was the war that saw the "indigenous people" of Eastern Europe strenuously resist Hitler's attempt to subjugate and enslave them an inter-imperialist war? Like the Great Patriotic War, Harvey also ignores the Chinese people's war of resistance against Japanese imperialism, not to mention the "minor" national wars of resistance (in Yugoslavia, Albania, France, and Italy) that accompanied the Second World War and contributed to the defeat of the Third Reich. The only conflict that Harvey refers to is "inter-imperialist rivalry and war."

Harvey wrongly cites Lenin, whom we have seen in 1916 evoke national wars not only in the colonial world but in the heart of Europe itself, anticipating the scenario that would happen a little more than two decades later. The British Marxist scholar instead reads the Second World War according to a scheme that we have come to know: you go from the Great Depression to the explosion of "inter-imperialist rivalries." In other words, to overcome the devastating economic crisis that broke out in 1929, "it took the travails of war between capitalist states."[20] But how do we explain the fact that Hitler came to power posing as a champion of the cause of white supremacy in Europe and the world? He was quite aware that, inspired by the appeal by Lenin and the October Revolution to the "slaves of the colonies" to break their chains, the world anticolonialist revolution had begun. It was a question of containing it and pushing it back by any and every means.

It is this anticolonialist revolution that Harvey ignores when he looks at both past and present. To be precise, as far as the present is concerned, there is a particular discrepancy. When he analyzes the conflicts of our own time, the British Marxist scholar describes them correctly. But, when drawing conclusions, he subsumes under the category of inter-imperialist rivalry and war contradictions and processes that are quite different. Harvey emphasizes the role of the United States in the coup d'état in Chile in 1973 that overthrew Allende and in Venezuela in 2002, which, for a brief time, overthrew and imprisoned Hugo Chavez. In both cases, Harvey does not hide his sympathy for the popular resistance against imperialist aggression.[21] Unfortunately, he does not ask what kind of contradiction existed between Chile and Venezuela on the one hand and the United States on the other.

And having analyzed (correctly) the relations between Washington and Beijing, he poses no questions either. We read: the United States wants "the power to cut off the oil flow to its opponents" in general and China in particular.[22] The United States is not disposed to peacefully resign itself to the shift pushing the center of the world economy toward East Asia; it feels a strong temptation to use its military power to maintain its shaky hegemony. In sum, it is tending "to make the transition from informal to formal empire."[23] According to the British scholar, the Chinese leadership seems fully aware of all this. The economic reforms introduced in 1979 serve "to upgrade its technological capacities" and "to better defend itself against external aggression."[24]

Staying with this description, it is a question of measures that also constitute an insurance policy against imperialist projects hatched by the great powers responsible for having imposed "a century of humiliation" on a fifth or a fourth of the population of the world through colonial or semi-colonial oppression. But, from the general picture painted by the exponent of Western Marxism, there emerges a very different conclusion: in passing from the twentieth to the twenty-first century, "echoes of the geopolitical competition that became so destructive in the 1930s begin to be heard."[25] We risk "a return to Lenin's scenario of violent competition between capitalist power blocs."[26] History is the repetition of identity; it is the eternal rivalry between capitalist and imperialist powers. The cautionary warning by Lenin that the British Marxist scholar ignores comes to mind: one cannot adequately understand imperialism if one loses sight of "the enormous importance of the national question."[27]

4. Ah, if Only Badiou Had Read Togliatti!

Among the most recent exponents of Western Marxism, Alain Badiou seems to be the most equipped to overcome the limits of this current of thought. He had the rare courage to speak of 1989–1991 as a "second Restoration."[28] This is true with particular clarity internationally speaking. The collapse of the Soviet Union was certainly not seen as a moment of liberation by the Palestinian people, who saw themselves exposed to Israeli colonial expansionism, now without any defense, or by the Cuban people, who only through great sacrifices have been able to defend their independence from Washington's attempts to restore the Monroe Doctrine. It was after the fall of the Soviet Union that the U.S. neoconservatives dreamed of imposing an empire of planetary dimensions. To speak of the upheaval of 1989–1991 as a "second

Restoration" would, therefore, seem to pave the way for the rediscovery of the colonial and neocolonial question.

Unfortunately, this rediscovery is nowhere to be found in Badiou either. In conducting his meritorious battle against neoliberalism and for incisive measures against austerity, misery, and growing inequality and social polarization, he formulates a thesis that is intended to be radical: "justice is far more important than freedom."[29] And what we have here "is the paradigm of classical revolutionary politics, whose goal is justice,"[30] starting with "the great Jacobins of 1792," that is, "our great ancestors, the Jacobins."[31] The Jacobins were uninterested in the cause of freedom? At the end of the eighteenth century, the "Black Jacobins" of Saint Domingue, with the support of the Jacobins who governed Paris, were the main actors in one of the great battles for freedom in world history. They overthrew slavery and colonial domination, defended these conquests, and defeated Napoleon's powerful army. From this revolution came Haiti, the first country to abolish slavery and ban the slave trade, which still flourished in the nearby North American republic, which was committed to using any means to strangle the country run by ex-slaves. Badiou is right to define the Jacobins as "ancestors" of the communist movement. In effect, the Jacobins were the first to inflict two mortal blows on the world colonialist-slavery system, and later on came the Bolsheviks and the communists. At least from this point of view, each of them should be considered a champion of the cause of freedom.

It goes without saying that the dominant ideology sees things quite differently. At the start of the Cold War, Isaiah Berlin offered an anthem to the West: even if there are areas of misery that block "positive freedom" (access to education, to health, to free time), "negative freedom" is still guaranteed to all, liberal freedom itself, the sphere of the autonomous, inviolable individual.

He explained this in an essay published in 1949, while in many U.S. states sexual contamination and marriage of members of the white race with other races was forbidden by law. Berlin makes no mention of these laws to confine the people of color to a servile caste, just as he does not take any account of the world colonialist system. Did the people under colonial domination and exposed to tyrannical power and the arbitrary will of their rulers at least enjoy "negative freedom"? Clearly, Berlin ignored the fate the West imposed on colonial peoples and those of colonial origins and did not take into account that the bans on interracial sexual relations and marriage, even if they were aimed at maintaining the permanent segregation of the race considered inferior, ended up heavily weighing as well on the negative freedom of the members of the privileged white race themselves. To advocate for negative freedom for all were the communists, who were on the front lines in the struggle against segregation and racial discrimination and who, because of this, suffered terrible persecution at the very moment that Berlin celebrated the liberal West.[32]

But paradoxically, Badiou signs on to the arbitrary erasure of the fate of the colonial peoples and those of colonial origin. Otherwise, how can we explain the statement in which the main actors of the revolt against the world colonialist-slavery system were more interested in the cause of "justice" than "freedom"? Even if judging by differing and contrasting values, Berlin and Badiou share the thesis that liberals are the theoreticians and guardians of "negative freedom." Both erase the frightful clauses of exclusion that characterize liberal discourse on "negative freedom."

Arguing in a manner we have already seen, the French philosopher takes up again a common theme of Western Marxism from the preceding decades. One thinks of the critique of liberalism made at one time by Crawford B. Macpherson, of it being, in reality, synonymous with "possessive individualism."[33] In this definition, both the noun and the adjective are in error (if, I mean, we do not remove the colonial question). Let's start with the noun: in the North American Republic and in the European colonies, the fate of an individual was determined from start to finish by their racial appearance, which constituted an insuperable barrier between the white race of the masters and the colonial people of color. An individual's merit played no role or was a very minor one. This is anything but individualism! Regarding the adjective, the superstitious capitalist cult of property was not extended to the colonial peoples. This is a point that Marx strongly insisted on:

The profound hypocrisy and inherent barbarism of bourgeois civilization lie unveiled before our eyes, turning from its home, where it assumes respectable forms, to the colonies, where it goes naked. They are the defenders of property, but did any revolutionary party ever originate agrarian revolutions like those in Bengal, in Madras, and in Bombay? . . . While they prated in Europe about the inviolable sanctity of the national debt, did they not confiscate in India the dividends of the rajahs, who had invested their private savings in the Company's own funds?[34]

And in the cases of the Irish and Scottish peasants, even in these cases of colonial and semi-colonial peoples located in Europe, the government in London did not see any occasion in which it needed to act in the face of "the most shameless violation of the 'sacred rights of property.'"[35]

One could object that colonialism is now in the past. But one need only look at the people of Palestine. An arbitrary power can expropriate, jail, and execute them extra-judicially. There is no aspect of public and private life of the members of a colonial people that escapes the control, intervention, and bullying of the occupation forces. Of course, in our times, classical colonialism constitutes the exception, not the rule. But we must not forget the weekly extrajudicial executions ordered, as the *New York Times* of May 30, 2012, informs us, by the president of the United States and carried out in every corner of the world, almost always aimed at citizens of the Third World. Citizens of the Third World are also the collateral victims who so often accompany extrajudicial executions. And that is not all. What freedom or security of property do the citizens of a country enjoy when they can be bombed, invaded, or reduced to starvation at the sovereign whim of the West and its leading country, which can act without even waiting for authorization by the UN Security Council?

As authoritative organs of the Western press inform us, when the United States (or the British or the French) secret services decide to destabilize a country deemed rebellious, the first operation carried out is this: the threat of being brought before the International Criminal

Court is made against the functionaries that do not come over to their side, which is so not nonpartisan that, while it can rage against the head of state of a country that has been attacked and defeated, it cannot investigate the latest acts by U.S. soldiers or contractors, whatever the crimes committed by them or that they have been accused of! This double standard is a constituent of the colonial tradition, and the struggle between colonialism and neocolonialism on the one hand and anticolonialism on the other, even if it assumes new forms, is anything but over. This means that, even in our own times, struggling against colonialism and neocolonialism, Marxists can advance the cause of negative freedom, in a universal sense.[36]

In the first place, what defines the intolerably inhuman nature of capitalist society is not the "propertied" or "possessive" nature of its "individual" (Macpherson), nor the priority it accords to "freedom" rather than to "justice" (Badiou), but rather the tyranny and terror unleashed on the colonies (Marx) or the "barbaric discrimination between human creatures" that Togliatti referred to, based on the lessons of Marx and Lenin.[37] Confined by Anderson and by many others before him to Eastern Marxism, the leader of the Italian Communist Party had the merit to refuse every contrast between "freedom" and "justice."

Certainly, in advocating for one or the other, it is important to consider objective conditions. Even for the classic authors of liberalism, a situation of war or civil war makes security a priority over freedom. It remains the case that Togliatti saw in communism the movement that certainly fought for "social rights" but also, at the same time, rejecting the "barbaric discrimination between human creatures," shows that it takes "the right of freedom" even more seriously than does the liberal tradition, and exactly for this reason it considers it a "patrimony of our movement," and of the communist movement as a whole. One wants to sigh, ah, if only Badiou had read Togliatti!

5. Transformation of Power into Love, Critical Theory, the Fused Group, and the Renunciation of Power

Western Marxism's break with the anticolonial revolution is also the refusal to take up the problems arising from taking power. Even on this issue, there is a contrast between Western and Eastern Marxism. Addicted to the role of opposition and critique, and to varying degrees influenced by messianism, the former look with suspicion and disapproval at the power that the latter are called upon to wield by the victory of the revolution. It is power as such that is the object of indictment by the young Bloch:

> Dominance and power in themselves are evil, but it is necessary to confront power in terms of power, as a categorical imperative with revolver in hand, wherever and as long as power cannot otherwise be destroyed, wherever and as long as everything diabolical still balks so violently at the (undiscovered) amulet of purity, and thereafter finally discharge authority, the "power" even of the good, the lie of vengeance and its right, as methodically as possible.[38]

If, even for a brief period, the young German philosopher did consider the management of power, others found themselves disoriented and alarmed by this very prospect. Immediately after the October Revolution, those who defended its legitimacy and historical necessity asserted that the Bolsheviks could not renounce the power they had acquired in the struggle against the war since this would prolong the senseless carnage. It was an argument that did not impress the majority tendency of the Italian Socialist Party. Lenin "had to energetically refuse power."[39] Even in Italy, it was absurd to pose the problem of the conquest of power: "the liquidation of the war must be done by those who wanted it. From the misery it leaves us, we must profit *by our critique*, by our work of propaganda and of preparation."[40] One wonders at the tendency to identify the work of the socialist party and the socialist movement as "critique" rather than as a struggle to transform the sociopolitical reality (by taking power). "Critique" later became the keyword of critical theory, whose approach found its classic formulation in the peremptory *incipit* of *Negative Dialectics* by Adorno:

> Philosophy, which once seemed outmoded, remains alive because

the moment of its realization was missed. The summary judgment that it had merely interpreted the world is itself crippled by resignation before reality, and becomes a defeatism of reason after the transformation of the world failed. . . . Praxis, delayed for the foreseeable future, is no longer the court of appeal against self-satisfied speculation but, for the most part, the pretext under which executives strangulate that critical thought as idle, which a transforming praxis most needs.[41]

The anticolonial revolution and the overthrow of the world colonialist-slavery system founded on the negation of the universal concept of humanity and on the reification of the majority of humanity, but in the view of the exponent of critical theory the "transformation of the world" had "failed" and "philosophy" missed its "realization," only because everything was taking place according to an unexpected process, unforeseen and distorted, a process that was far from calling into question power as such.

Unlike Adorno, Sartre is a passionate champion of action, praxis, and political commitment. And yet, the philosopher of *engagement* has something in common with the exponent of critical theory. Recurrently and throughout *The Critique of Dialectical Reason* he seeks the reason why the "fused group," that is, the main actor of the revolution, tends to fall back in a way that is difficult to resist into a "practico-inert" structure that is hierarchical and authoritarian. Only the initial moment of the revolution is exultant and magical, when a power considered intolerable by public opinion at large is overthrown, but certainly not so is the consolidation of the new power and the construction of the new order. Power corrupts.

It is an approach that, in different ways, we find among not a few exponents of Western Marxism. In reconstructing its evolution, after having declared that he has never had any interest in the Third World, the Italian theorist of *operaismo*, Mario Tronti, proceeds:

But we welcomed the fact that the twentieth-century workers had disrupted the long and glorious history of the lower classes with their desperate rebellions, their millennial heresies, their recurrent and generous attempts–always painfully repressed—at breaking their chains.[42]

In this case, far from exercising power, the subaltern classes cannot even overthrow the *ancien régime*. But the repeated defeats do not result in any rethinking, they do not lead to a critique of millenarianism, and they are only partly a cause of suffering. From a different perspective, they are the revival of the revolutionary project's ambitious grandeur and the cause's purity and nobility. Power continues to be an element of contamination.

Let's read now the two authors of *Empire*: "from India to Algeria, from Cuba to Vietnam, *the state is the poisoned gift of national liberation*." Yes, the Palestinians can count on the sympathy and support of Western Marxism. But, from the moment in which "the Palestinians are institutionalized," one can "no longer be at their side." The fact is that "as soon as the nation begins to form as a sovereign state, its progressive functions all but vanish."[43]

And so, we can be sympathetic to the Chinese, Vietnamese, Palestinians, or any other people only so long as they are oppressed, humiliated, and without any power—that is, as long as they are in the hands of colonialism and imperialism. We can support their struggle for national liberation only as long as it continues to be defeated! The defeat or the inconclusiveness of a revolutionary movement is the precondition for certain exponents of Western Marxism to celebrate themselves and enjoy being rebels who, in any circumstance, refuse to contaminate themselves with constituted power!

The tendency described here has found a home in a recent book, which has been quite successful among Western Marxists and whose title invites us to *Change the World Without Taking Power*.[44] To renounce power, to concentrate on the critique of the existing order, and avoid the distractions and compromises that the prospect of taking power inevitably leads to seems a noble and high-flying approach. But, in light of this new truth, how small seem, retrospectively, the great struggles of the colonial peoples, the subaltern classes, and women to end the three great forms of discrimination (race, class, and gender) that excluded these three groups from enjoying political rights and the possibility of influencing the composition and direction of the organs of power. Small also appear the struggles for emancipation of the colonial peoples that, among other things, were clearly struggles for power. And no less small, then, are the struggles for emancipation of our own times.

There are many, even beyond those on the left, that denounce the fact that in the West, democracy has been revealed to always be more of a plutocracy, the power of great wealth and finance that can avail itself of an electoral system that, in varying ways, makes it difficult or impossible for the popular classes to gain control of the representative organs and of the highest political offices. What does all this matter if the real problem is to "change the world without taking power"? Plutocracy also makes itself felt internationally. Churchill acknowledged this in his own time when he said, "the government of the world must be entrusted to satisfied nations, who wish nothing more for themselves than what they have. If the world-government were in the hands of hungry nations, there would always be danger."[45] In organs like the World Bank and the International Monetary Fund, it is the masters of yesterday and today who make the law. These forces seek to exclude even the UN, demanding for the West alone (the "satisfied nations" of which Churchill spoke) the power to unleash war in every corner of the globe, even without authorization by the UN Security Council. The new truth proclaimed by Holloway is, in fact, the truth of religions. Immediately after the defeat of the Jewish national revolution, crushed by Roman imperialism, Jesus proclaimed, "my kingdom is not of this world." The self-dissolution of Western Marxism here is reconfigured as the abandonment of the terrain of politics and its ending up in religion.

6. The Struggle against the Phrase, from Robespierre to Lenin

Moreover, the discomfort and diffidence toward power are not manifest only in the West. In Russia, the adversaries of Marxism criticized its followers, even the most revolutionary, for being only talkers incapable of governing and running a country and so inclined to seek refuge from the responsibilities of power. On the immediate eve of the October Revolution, to convince his own party comrades to overcome their hesitations, Lenin, in an article, reported on the derisory portrait that the adversaries of the Bolsheviks painted of them:

> The Bolsheviks, except for a few fanatics, are brave only in words. They would not attempt to take "full power" on their own accord. Disorganizers and disrupters *par excellence*, they are really cowards who in their heart of hearts are fully aware of both their own intrinsic ignorance and the ephemeral nature of their present successes.... Irresponsible by their very nature, anarchists in method and practice, they should be regarded only as a trend of political thought, or rather, as one of its aberrations.[46]

Knowing how things turned out, we can smile today at this portrait, but we must not forget its history. For centuries, conservative and liberal cultures have denounced the "abstractness" of intellectual supporters of radical social and political transformation. To nurture utopias and dreams of social palingenesis—the recurring theme of the liberal-conservative indictment—can only be the work of intellectuals with no experience exercising power. Indeed, neither do they have any experience in the administration of large private property. They were, at best, good-for-nothings who made a living by their education and were immersed in an artificial world of books, ideas, and utopias never put to the test of reality and practice. They were "beggars of the pen," according to Burke's disparaging definition. So how could they expect to govern a state or exercise a task beyond their abilities?[47]

However self-interested and full of classist spirit it might be, this criticism is not without some truth. There is no doubt that the propertied intellectuals arrived at their appointment with the crisis of the *ancien régime* having some real experience of the exercise of power. In the U.S. revolution, the slave owners played a disproportionate role, such that in the first decades of its existence, the North American republic saw an almost uninterrupted series of slave owners hold the presidency. Before the foundation of the new state, they were not limited to enjoying their slaves as a species of "peculiar" private property alongside their other property. They had exercised legislative, judicial, and executive power over their slaves. They arrived well prepared for the exercise of political power in the strict sense.

Analogous considerations hold for liberal England as well. Property in slaves was not absent, though the latter were located across the sea, but it was the great landowners that set the tone for the House of Lords and of Commons in the liberal culture. And they, given the social relations of the time, exercised some form of power over the peasants, such that sometimes, as happened in particular in the case of the gentry, the small nobility, they held the position of justice of the peace and so held judiciary power. All told, the two liberal revolutions on both sides of the Atlantic saw the rise to power of classes that had a consolidated practice of administration and governing.

The picture changes radically with the French Revolution, above all in its Jacobin phase, and with the October Revolution. In 1794, it was obviously not the slave owners who abolished slavery but rather the "beggars of the pen," the "abstract" intellectuals, who, just for this reason, were deaf to the appeals and calculations of the owners of human beasts. And in 1917, those calling on the "slaves of the colonies" to break their chains were not the beneficiaries of colonial exploitation but their antagonists, yet again the "abstract" intellectuals.

However, the merits of these social figures should not blind us to their limitations. Robespierre was forced to polemicize against the champions of exporting the revolution, thinking thereby to bring about a definitive victory "over despotism and universal aristocracy," defeating it by oratory "tribune," through "sublime" thought and "figures of rhetoric."[48] Refusing to support the humiliating pact of Brest-Litovsk, which the German imperialism of Wilhelm II imposed on Soviet Russia, seizing a conspicuous part of its national territory, a significant part of the Bolshevik Party, without considering the extreme weakness of Soviet Russia at the moment, dreamed of a European "revolutionary war" that would have resolved everything and made difficult choices unnecessary. Lenin's irony was biting in response. We can't confront a very powerful enemy through "unrestrained phrase-making," by being "intoxicated by phrases." And so, "We shall set about preparing a revolutionary army, not by phrases and exclamations." In the end, "revolutionary phrases" only express "feelings, desires, anger and indignation."[49]

But those who see in every compromise with imperialism an abdication of the revolution and morality reply, "in the interests of the world revolution, we consider it expedient to accept the possibility of losing Soviet power, which is now becoming purely formal."[50] These are words Lenin described as "strange and monstrous." He took a position on them by denouncing the persistent attitude of intellectuals inclined to see in power (with all the compromises that it inevitably entails) a source of moral contamination and who tended to prefer the role of outside opposition, "critical" but substantially unrealistic, just as, not entirely wrongly, the liberal and conservative circles had insinuated even on the eve of October.

So, in the very moment of the formation of the Communist International, the abstractions of revolutionary intellectuals made themselves felt, East and West. But at a certain point, the bifurcation between them appeared. In the East, having taken power, intellectuals and ex-intellectuals were forced to commit themselves to a trying apprenticeship. In March 1920, Lenin invited the party and state cadre to learn everything necessary to not be swept away by counterrevolution. "No, comrades, the art of administration does not descend from heaven; it is not inspired by the Holy Ghost."[51]

Developments were quite different in the East. The messianic hopes were not realized through "the transformation of power into love."[52] But this did not change the attitude of diffidence toward power, seen as a source of intellectual and moral contamination. The bifurcation between Eastern Marxism and Western Marxism comes down to a contrast between Marxists who exercise power and Marxists who were in opposition and concentrated increasingly on "critical theory," "deconstruction," and denouncing power and power relations as such.

A "Western Marxism" thus took shape, which, in its distance from power, claimed the privileged and exclusive right to rediscover an "authentic" Marxism, no longer reduced to state ideology.

Is this claim justified? If, in one respect, they may increase the clarity of vision, distance from power and disdain toward it can also obstruct vision. Undoubtedly, the challenges of leading a country strongly helped Lenin, Mao, and other leaders, and Eastern Marxism as a whole, to let go of messianic expectations and develop a more realistic vision of building a post-capitalist society. With its persistent attachment to the "phrase," Western Marxism has ended up representing two figures that are the main targets of Hegel's criticism. Since critique is satisfying, and indeed in critique one finds one's reason for being, without posing the problem of formulating practical alternatives and of building an alternative historic bloc to the dominant one, it is the very image of the conceit of what ought to exist; when one then enjoys the distance from power as a condition of one's own purity, this embodies the beautiful soul.

7. War and the Death Certificate of Western Marxism

Reduced to a religion, and indeed a religion of evasion, Western Marxism cannot provide an answer to the problems of the present, particularly the worsening of the international situation. We have seen what has happened in the past few years. On the occasion of the war against Libya in 2011, authoritative organs of the Western press recognized its neocolonial character. Neocolonial and bloody. An eminent French philosopher, very distant from Marxism, observed, "today we know that the war resulted in at least 30,000 deaths, against 300 victims of the initial repression" carried out by Qaddafi.[53] According to other estimates, the toll of the NATO intervention would be even greater. And the tragedy continues: the country has been destroyed, and people have been forced to choose between desperation at home or fleeing to the unknown, which could be fatal.

I am not aware of any exponent of "Western Marxism" or of "Libertarian Western Marxism" that denounced this horror. Indeed, a personality such as Rossana Rossanda, who, as the founder of the communist daily *Il Manifesto* can be included in the category of "Western Marxism" or "Libertarian Western Marxism," went to the very threshold of calling for armed intervention against Qaddafi's Libya. It is a threshold that Susanna Camusso, Secretary-General of the CGIL—a union federation that has left long behind its onetime links to the Communist Party and to Eastern Marxism—happily crossed over.

How did we get to this point? At the moment of the outbreak of the first war against Iraq, while the Italian Communist Party was dissolving itself, one of its illustrious philosophers, Giacomo Marramao, stated in its party newspaper *Unità*, on January 25, 1991, "throughout history, it has never happened that a democratic state made war against another democratic state." In reality, the two countries that love to celebrate themselves as the oldest democracies in the world, Great Britain and the United States, were already at war at the moment of the crisis that resulted in the founding of the North American republic, and they again clashed a few decades later in another war (the War of 1812), fought with such fury that, as we know, Jefferson called it "a war of extermination."

Even if we admit that democratic states live side by side in peace with one another, does this make irrelevant the genocide that the democratic republic of North America carried out against the Native peoples? Or the genocide the British Empire engaged in against the natives of Australia and New Zealand? On the other hand, was it not Tocqueville, the great theoretician of democracy, who revealed the true face of the colonial wars of the liberal-democratic West when he called for genocidal practices against the Algerian population? Already refuted by Togliatti at the start of the Cold War, the myth expressed by Marramao makes clear yet again the missed encounter between Western Marxism and the anticolonial revolution.

Let's now go back in time a few years. In 1999, a war unleashed by NATO without authorization by the Security Council of the United Nations did not hesitate to hit "civilian targets" nor to destroy Yugoslavia.[54] The nature of this war was very clear to its apologists: "only Western Imperialism—even if few love to call it by name—can now unite the European continent and save the Balkans from chaos."⁵⁵ And, "what good emerges from Kosovo [cut off from Yugoslavia and become the site of a gigantic U.S. military base] is what the world should now take note of; NATO can at will do everything necessary to defend its vital interests."⁵⁶ However, at the start of military operations, a major exponent of Western Marxism dared to write:

> We must recognize that this is not an act of American imperialism. It is, in effect, an international (or, to tell the truth, supranational) operation. And its objectives are not guided by the limited national interests of the United States: It is effectively aimed at protecting human rights (or, to tell the truth, human life).⁵⁷

A year later, *Empire* announced the good news: it no longer made sense to speak of imperialism as Lenin had. The world was now unified economically and politically. Even "perpetual and universal peace" had been assured!⁵⁸ This reassuring message was launched while, as we have seen, imperialism was being rehabilitated, explicitly or indirectly. It was a campaign that began with the dissolution of the "socialist camp" and of the Soviet Union itself and proceeded to grow on the wave of the wars unleashed by the West and its leading nation, without authorization by the UN Security Council, to demonstrate that no one could resist the sovereign imperial will of Washington and its closest allies and vassals.

In the euphoria of those years, the cry of jubilee intersected with the announcement of ambitious programs. The West, as authoritative scholar Barry G. Buzan observed in 1991, had "triumphed over communism and over Third Worldism."⁵⁹ And so, it could calmly remake the world. The year after, the more or less official philosopher of the Western "open society," Karl R. Popper, referring to the ex-colonies, proclaimed, "we liberated these states (the ex-colonies) too quickly and too simplistically"; it is like "abandoning a child care center to its own devices."⁶⁰ For whoever still had not understood, in 1993, the *New York Times Magazine*, a Sunday supplement of the most important newspaper in the United States, was unable to contain its enthusiasm, as seen in the title of an article written by a British author, Paul Johnson: "Colonialism's Back, and Not a Moment Too Soon."[61]

A few years later, in its March-April 2002 issue, *Foreign Affairs*, a journal close to the State Department, with its title and opening article by Sebastian Mallaby, invited all to give in to the evidence and the existing relations of force: "the logic of imperialism" or better "of neo-imperialism" was too stringent to be opposed. Still further on, a most prominent Western historian, Niall Ferguson, called for creating a "colonial office" modeled on the British Empire and, looking at Washington, sang hymns to the "most magnanimous imperial power that has ever existed."[62]

However, this program of colonial and imperial counterrevolution has encountered increasing difficulties. And so today we see increased analysis, discourse, and concern about the rising danger of a large-scale war, of a Third World War that could cross the line to become nuclear. One can then understand why the United States has for some time aspired to guarantee itself "first strike capability" and exercise the terrible power of blackmail over the rest of the world.[63] The other countries would then be forced to choose between obedience to Washington or annihilation. This aspiration explains the renunciation by President George W. Bush on June 13, 2002, of the treaty, stipulated thirty years earlier, that was "perhaps the most important agreement of the Cold War."[64] The United States and the USSR committed themselves to limiting the construction of antimissile bases, renouncing the goal of nuclear invulnerability and planetary domination that such invulnerability would have guaranteed.

The war that the United States is preparing for is against China, the country born of the greatest anticolonial revolution in history and directed by an experienced Communist Party, or against Russia, which under Putin, has wrongly, according to the White House, thrown off the neocolonial control that Yeltsin had accepted and adapted to (thanks to savage and predatory privatization, the West was in fact able to control the immense energy patrimony of the country).

This new international situation, thick with dangers, finds Western Marxism completely unprepared. Negri and Hardt's announcement of the advent of perpetual and universal peace has reduced them to servility. The discourse of Marramao, who identifies democracy with the cause of peace, is subordinate to the Western ideology of war and can only serve to legitimate the crusade of Washington against China and Russia. Likewise inadequate and misleading is the thesis dear to Harvey of eternal rivalry and "inter-imperialist war." It is certainly not with this category that we can understand the military expeditions by the West and especially by its leading nation after the triumph in the Cold War and in a period when the United States was the solitary superpower and absolutely unrivaled: the December 1989 invasion of Panama; the first Iraq war, 1991; the war against Yugoslavia, 1999; the second Iraq war, 2003; the war against Libya, 2011. In these same years, the United States intervened in Syria to accomplish the regime change that U.S. neoconservatives had called for in 2003. How can we explain why it is only the West, and above all, its leading country, the "nation chosen by God," or the "indispensable nation," wrapped in its aura of "exceptionalism," that arrogates to itself the sovereign (and imperial) right to intervene in every corner of the globe even without the authorization of the UN Security Council?

To orient ourselves in the present, we need to not lose sight of the anticolonialist revolution (mostly led by communist parties) that was the main feature of the twentieth century and the unfortunate project of rolling back the anticolonialist revolution, which is at the center of the so-called "neoconservative revolution" and of U.S. foreign policy. Born of the horrors of the carnage of the First World War, Western Marxism has shown itself to be unable to understand and oppose the large-scale war that looms on the horizon. It is the death certificate of Western Marxism.

PART VI

How Marxism in the West Can Be Reborn

1. MARX AND THE FUTURE IN FOUR ACTS

Can Marxism revive in the West, and under what conditions? To answer this question, it would help to investigate how the ideas of Marx and Engels encountered and conflicted with the actual history of the twentieth century, which they obviously did not and could not foresee. Focused on the transformation of the existing order, their discourse constantly refers to the future whose realization would be guaranteed by the proletariat (the revolutionary class *par excellence*) and the party that is the political expression of this class.

It would be good to first specify that the future those two great thinkers looked to was to unfold in four acts that were quite distinct. In the 1844 work *On the Jewish Question*, Marx writes of the North American republic as the country of "complete political emancipation." Status discrimination had been substantially eliminated (within the white community); almost all adult males, even non-property owners, enjoyed the right to vote and could be elected into the representative organs. That is to say, to use the *Grundrisse*'s language this time, the "relations of personal dependence" of the pre-bourgeois, feudal society, and sanctioned by law, had been definitively abolished, and, with the rise of capitalist society, instead, came "personal independence founded on material dependence."[1]

With the new order, legal and formal freedom and equality existed; it was instead the social relations of production and distribution of material wealth that sanctioned an even more strident inequality, starting with the "wage slavery" imposed on the workers, who were formally as free as their employers and were equal to them by law. Based on the vision delineated in *On the Jewish Question* and in the *Grundrisse*, the persistent discrimination that by law excluded certain categories of people from participation in political life would spontaneously and gradually disappear. The passage to "complete political emancipation" or to "personal independence founded on material dependence" could be considered an imminent tendency of bourgeois society itself, and this tendency would impose itself sooner or later. So the first type of future we find in Marx and Engels is that which we can call the future in action, the non-post-capitalist future already in action in bourgeois society itself. The future that bourgeois society itself would progressively realize during its maturation process.

The transcendence of capitalism—with the abolition of "wage slavery" and the addition of social and political emancipation to political emancipation—refers to another kind of future. The *Critique of the Gotha Program* foresees and hopes for, after the political overthrow of the bourgeoisie's power, a period of transition under the banner of the "revolutionary dictatorship of the proletariat" and of the incipient socialist transformation.[2] Marx believed this problem was already on the agenda when he was writing. And so we have to deal with it in the near future. The period of transition goes on until communism. To cite Marx's words in the *Manifesto of the Communist Party*, "in place of the old bourgeois society, with its classes and class antagonisms, we shall have an association, in which the free development of each is the condition for the free development of all."[3] The advent of communism presupposes the definitive defeat of capitalism and its total transcendence. In this case, we are in the presence of the remote future. When communism is imagined and configured as a society that is completely free of contradictions and conflicts and, therefore, can even do without the state, the remote future becomes a utopian future. In conclusion, after the future in action due to a dialectic internal to bourgeois society that realizes "complete political emancipation," the building of the post-capitalist order embraces three types of future: the near future, the remote future, and the utopian future.

It is worth noting immediately that things went quite differently than had been foreseen by Marx and Engels. In the West, "complete political emancipation" was not in any way the result of a spontaneous dialectic internal to bourgeois society. The first great form of discrimination, the proprietary monopoly of political rights and the exclusion of the non-propertied, was only abolished thanks to a prolonged struggle by the workers' movement, inspired by socialists and Marxists. That is true also for the overcoming of the second great form of discrimination, that against women, which, together with denying them political rights, prevented them from participating in the liberal professions, enclosing them in domestic slavery and in the lower-status and lower-paid segments of the labor market. Above all, the history of the third great form of discrimination is important here, that against colonized peoples and those of colonial origin. In the democratic North American republic, far from seeing a gradual evolution of bourgeois society, the abolition of Black slavery was the result of a Civil War that brought more deaths for the U.S. population than the two world wars put together. Moreover, the defeat suffered by the South did not signal the end of servile relations of production, which in the colonies continued to exist on a large scale well into the twentieth century.

In conclusion, centuries of developing the world capitalist system, long hegemonized by countries of stable liberal traditions, have not completed political emancipation. In elaborating an abstract theoretical model by definition, Marx could well state that it was the very internal dialectic of bourgeois society that moved in the direction of "complete political emancipation." In reality, this tendency was neutralized by a still stronger tendency of capitalist colonial expansionism. This brought about monstrous forms of inequality and unfreedom not only in the colonies but also in the capitalist metropoles themselves. In the United States, which to Marx was the country *par excellence* of "complete political emancipation," even after the Civil War, Blacks continued to be deprived of political rights and often also of civil rights.

This was demonstrated by the practice of lynching organized as a mass spectacle and signs in front of some public parks in the U.S. South that banned entry to "dogs and negroes." As we know, in China, then reduced to a colony or semi-colony, the Chinese were banned by the master race [the colonizers] on the signs along with dogs and were exposed to every form of discrimination and outrage, even when, in search of work, they emigrated to the United States!

2. The Long Struggle against the World Colonial-Slavery System

We are forced to rethink the picture painted by Marx of history and the theory of emancipation. For him, before the decisive revolution that would bring about social emancipation, the starting point was identifying with the U.S. American Revolution, which brought about the country of "complete political emancipation," and with the French Revolution, which put political emancipation on the agenda for all of Europe. In reality, we have seen that the revolt of the colonies resulting in the founding of the United States was more of a counterrevolution so far as the relations with the colonized peoples or those of colonial origin were concerned. These relations must be the center of our attention for two reasons: it is in the colonies that the harshest system of power emerged, often involving slavery and even genocide against the subject peoples, and suffering under this system of power was the vast majority of humanity.

We must then take note of the fact that it was the revolution of the Black slaves of Saint-Domingue led by Toussaint Overture that inflicted the first blow against the world colonialist-slavery system. If we want to continue to identify the French Revolution as the starting point of the gigantic conflict between emancipation and de-emancipation that runs through contemporary history, we will have to date it differently from the traditional way, finding in 1789–1791 the beginning of the gigantic upheaval, and so intersecting in a single process the overthrow of the *ancien régime* in France and the uprising against slavery and colonial subjection in Saint Domingue.

We can describe the nature of the world colonialist-slavery system, giving the floor to witnesses and authors who are anything but extraneous to the liberal West. Here is a liberal British historian in the middle of the nineteenth century calling attention to the "reign of terror" imposed by England on India in moments of crisis, a "reign of terror" to which "all the injustice of former oppressors, Asiatic and European, appeared as a blessing."[4] Things went no better for the colonies located in Europe. The friend and companion of Tocqueville on his voyage in America, Gustave de Beaumont, referring to Ireland, speaks of "a religious oppression beyond all imagination." The bullying, the humiliations, and the suffering imposed by English "tyranny" on this "enslaved people" demonstrate that "in human institutions, there is a level of egoism and folly, of which it is impossible to define its limits." Of the domination exercised by the British Empire over this unhappy island, he speaks of the extreme limits of evil, of an absolute evil. It is a description that, in our own days, is reserved for the Third Reich.[5]

Let's see what happened in the United States. That terror loomed over the Black slaves is not astounding. A traveler described the situation in Virginia immediately after the revolt of 1831 led by Nat Turner: "Military service (by the white patrollers) is carried out night and day, Richmond resembles a besieged city. . . . The Negroes . . . don't risk communicating with each other for fear of being punished." More interesting is to note how the terror ended up affecting the white community itself. Here is the testimony of an important Union politician on the prevailing climate in the South in the years preceding the Civil War: the abolitionist party is not absent but "is forced into submission by fear." Those who oppose slavery "do not dare even to exchange opinions with others who think as they do, out of fear of being betrayed." The historian of our own times who records this testimony concludes that, because of lynchings, violence, and threats of every kind, the South silenced not only all opposition but even the mildest dissent. Beyond the abolitionists themselves, those who were and felt threatened were those who distanced themselves from this merciless witch hunt. All were forced by the terror "to keep their mouth shut, to kill their own doubts, to bury their own reservations." There can be no doubt that this describes the efficacy of totalitarian terror and totalitarianism.[6]

Herbert Spencer, the liberal philosopher, describes how colonial expansionism (of which the traditionally liberal countries are often the protagonists) works: "after the expropriation of the defeated comes their extermination." Not only the "Indians of North America" and the "Natives of Australia" are to pay this price. Resort to genocide was had in every corner of the British colonial empire. In India, "death was inflicted on entire regiments" guilty of "having dared to disobey the tyrannical commands of their oppressors." Around fifty years later, Spencer felt obligated to increase the dosage: "we have entered an epoch of social cannibalism in which the strongest nations are devouring the weakest." We should realize that "the white savages of Europe are overcoming the dark savages everywhere." In effect, liberal Belgium reduced "the indigenous population [of the Congo] from twenty to forty million in 1890 to eight million by 1911." Moreover, we have seen the genocide the United States practiced to strangle the Philippines' independence movement.[7]

Genocide was not only practiced but was calmly and cheerfully theorized. We have seen Theodore Roosevelt theorize at the end of the nineteenth century, against rebellious colonial peoples, "a war of extermination," one that would not spare "women and children." It is eloquent testimony coming from the U.S. president and statesman who stated in an 1896 speech, "I don't go so far as to think that the only good Indians are dead Indians, but I believe nine out of every ten are. And I shouldn't like to inquire too closely into the case of the tenth."[8] But there is little to joke about. In the North American republic, the voices calling for the "extinction of the misfit" and for a "divine law of evolution" and who declare that on the agenda is a "final solution to the Negro problem" were growing, which would happily substantially replicate the already carried out final solution to the U.S. American Indian problem.

It is arbitrary to separate the darkest pages of the twentieth century written by Nazism and fascism from the history of colonialism.

Hitler sought to imitate Great Britain and the United States. He aimed to establish the "German Indies" in Eastern Europe or to promote a form of colonial expansion similar to what had happened in the West of the North American republic. It is in the course of the colonial and racial oppression of the latter against the indigenous and Black people that there emerged what would become the keywords of Nazi ideology: underman / *Untermensch* and ultimate solution / *Endlösung*. The German colonial empire would have to be built on the forced labor of the "indigenous" people, the Slavs, reduced to conditions of slavery.

Even this program based itself on a long-term history that went well beyond Germany. With the end of the U.S. Civil War, the Black slaves were now replaced by "coolies," semi-slaves from India or China. Independently of the coolies, colonial expansionism, even that of liberal countries, brought with it the imposition of modern forms of slavery or semi-slavery on the subject peoples. It is for this reason that Lenin, regarding the conflict between the great capitalist and colonialist powers in the First World War, spoke of the "war between slave owners, for the consolidation and reinforcement of slavery." Was this a polemical exaggeration? During the war, in Egypt, peasants, surprised in the bazaar, were "arrested and sent to the closest mobilization centers." To use the words of the conservative British historian A. J. P. Taylor, "around fifty million Africans and 250 million Indians" were forced by England to fight and die en masse in a war of which they knew nothing."[9]

If the definition of slavery is the power of life and death exercised by the master, Lenin's characterization is fitting. Over their subject peoples, the great colonialist powers exercised the power of life and death. This power hung over the more or less servile labor force from their colonies that Britain and France sent to the front to dig trenches or do other heavy and dangerous work. In particular, this latter practice inspired the Third Reich, which, with a further level of brutality, forced a gigantic mass of slaves to work or to die of exhaustion and hunger to maintain the productive apparatus needed to conduct the war.

Even regarding racial ideology, the continuity is clear. Here is a "profession of racial faith" from the early twentieth century:

1. Blood will tell. 2. The white race must dominate. 3. The Teutonic peoples stand for race purity. 4. The Negro is inferior and will remain so. 5. This is a white man's country. 6. No social equality. 7. No political equality. . . . 10. Let there be such industrial education of the Negro as will best fit him to serve the white man. . . . 14. Let the lowest white man count for more than the highest Negro. 15. The above statements indicate the leadings of Providence.[10]

Is this a Nazi manifesto? No, it is a manifesto from the United States (before the Nazi movement was founded in Germany) by armed men in uniform who paraded around for the "jubilee of white supremacy" and that were determined to use any means to maintain "Aryan superiority" and the servile or semi-servile conditions of Black people.

As far as the Empire of the Rising Sun was concerned, in our own time a conservative historian of great success said of the Japanese that "they ended up copying everything, from Western clothes and hairstyles to the European practice of colonizing foreign people."[11] Finally, the Italian nationalists, who merged into fascism in the name of colonial expansionism, went to school "on Kipling and on Roosevelt": the British-American school of colonialism and imperialism.[12]

The horrors of the colonialist system certainly did not end with the defeat of the Third Reich and its allies. Rather than turn to Algeria and Vietnam, I will limit myself here to the example of two tragedies that are perhaps less well known. Between 1952 and 1959, the Mau Mau revolt broke out in Kenya. Utilizing the most recent historiography on the question, a prestigious liberal U.S. journal described the methods used by Britain's government to restore stability in the colony. In the Kamiti concentration camp, women "were interrogated, whipped, reduced to starvation, and subjected to hard labor that included filling common graves with corpses from other concentration camps. Many gave birth at Kamiti, but the mortality rate among babies was shocking. Women buried their babies in bunches of six at a time."[13] From Africa, let's move on to Latin America. In these same years, we find the United States not only installing ferocious military dictatorships but also committing or helping to commit "acts of genocide." The Guatemalan

Truth Commission makes this clear, referring to the fate of the Mayans, guilty of having sympathized with the opponents of the regime favored by Washington.[14]

This world made of slavery, semi-slavery, servile labor relations, monstrous forms of unfreedom, strident forms of discrimination and frightening exclusionary clauses sanctioned and tolerated by law, this world, after having undergone the first hard blows from the Jacobins in Paris and above all from the Black Jacobins of Saint-Domingue, was put into deep crisis by the communist movement, thanks to the direct action and the influence it exercised.

That influence raised alarms even in the very heart of the capitalist metropoles. One thinks of the African Americans. They were oppressed by a regime of white supremacist terrorism when the October Revolution broke out, which then immediately spread a new spirit among the peoples of colonial origin. Rather than submit to oppression as a natural condition and, in any case, an irresistible one, given the existing relations of power, they began to rebel. Here is an African American declaring in a challenging tone: "If fighting for our rights means being Bolsheviks, then we are Bolsheviks, and people should have their souls at peace."[15]

In effect, the Blacks who decided to throw off the colonial and racial yoke constituted an essential component of the Communist Party then forming. The whites who collaborated with them were also considered "foreigners" and members of inferior races and treated as such. So, what being a communist and challenging white supremacy meant "was to face the possibility of imprisonment, beatings, kidnapping, and even death."[16] Those were the years of the Great Depression and unemployment and mass misery, but despite the bitter competition that ensued in the labor market, all of that did not silence the struggle against the regime of white supremacy, and it did not break the unity between whites and Blacks engaged in that struggle, mostly organized by the Communist Party.

Jumping ahead two decades, let's now look at the forms taken by the end of the regime of white supremacy. In December 1952, the attorney general of the United States sent an eloquent appeal in a letter to the

Supreme Court, which was hearing cases on the racial integration of public schools. He stated, "racial discrimination furnishes grist for the communist propaganda mills, and it raises doubts even among friendly nations as to the intensity of our devotion to the democratic faith."[17] Washington, observes an American historian in our times, ran the risk of alienating "the colored races" not only in the East and throughout the Third World but within the United States as well. Even there, communist propaganda was having considerable success in recruiting Blacks to the "revolutionary cause," destroying their "faith in American institutions."[18] It was because of this concern that the U.S. Supreme Court declared racial segregation unconstitutional in public schools. In summary, we cannot understand how the regime of white supremacy was dismantled in the United States (itself a tenacious heritage of the world colonialist-slavery system) without noting the challenge of the October Revolution and of the communist movement.

3. Two Marxisms and Two Different Temporalities

Naturally, the fall of the world colonial-slavery system happened in tragic circumstances. In Saint-Domingue/Haiti, the conflict between supporters and opponents of colonial subjection and slavery became a form of total warfare on each side. Nothing is easier than to put both sides on the same plane and oppose each other, for example, as did the North American republic. Apparently, accounts add up, and logic is respected. U.S. democracy celebrated its superiority over the despotism of Napoleon in France and that of Toussaint Louverture in Saint-Domingue/Haiti and that of his successors. Except the reality was entirely different. Opposing the country and the people that had thrown off the yoke of colonialism and the chains of slavery were both the France of Napoleon, through a powerful military machine, and the United States of Jefferson, through an embargo and naval blockade aimed explicitly at condemning to starvation the disobedient and rebellious Blacks.

The theory of totalitarianism today embodies this formalism. It puts Stalin's Soviet Union and Hitler's Third Reich on the same plane, forgetting that the latter, in carrying out its attempt to impose colonial dominion over the Slavs and enslave them, repeatedly referred to the colonial tradition of the West and had constantly and explicitly in its view the expansionist models of the British Empire and the irresistible advance in the West of the racial policies of the North American republic.

Unfortunately, this reading of the twentieth century, which puts the most ferocious expression of the colonial-slavery system on the same plane as its most important enemy, was accomplished to a greater or lesser degree by Western Marxism and not by a few of its exponents. We have seen *Empire* fully compare the Soviet Union and the Third Reich, the former the country that called on the slaves of the colonies to break their chains and the latter the country determined to reforge them and generalize them. In this reckless historical account, the world anticolonial revolution does not play any role. And it continues to be ignored and erased by the memorable judgments with which Žižek makes Stalin into a champion of the industrial production of corpses and Mao into an Oriental despot who, on a whim, condemns to death by starvation tens of millions of his own citizens.

Historically, the socialist and communist-oriented countries, all located outside the more developed West, have had to accomplish the "complete political emancipation" that Marx attributed to the bourgeois revolution and that it has revealed itself completely incapable of accomplishing. In this sense, it is as if those countries were stopped at the stage of the future in action, that which Marx considered to be intrinsic to bourgeois society, or at the first moment of the near future, that of the expropriation of the political power of the bourgeoisie and the installation of the "revolutionary dictatorship of the proletariat."

It is a dialectic that has manifested itself not only on the political level but also on the more properly economic level. According to the *Communist Manifesto*, the introduction of "new industries" that are not strictly national in scale and that operate on the "world market" is "a question of life and death for all civilized nations."[19] It is a task that in and of itself does not go beyond the bourgeois framework. Yet, under conditions of imperialism, the countries that fail to accomplish this task become easy prey for neocolonialism. That is especially true for the countries that, because of their political orientation, are disliked by the West and that have imposed on them or are exposed to even more severe economic and technological embargoes. And again, we see the communist-oriented countries, the area of "Eastern" communism and Marxism, stopped at the threshold of the post-capitalist future. But it is precisely and exclusively this truly post-capitalist future, and only this future, that captures Western Marxism's interest, attention, and passions. Indeed, the failure to take account of messianism, rooted in the Judeo-Christian tradition and in its time stimulated by the horrors of the carnage of the First World War, leads it to concentrate mainly on the remote and utopian futures.

So then, two Marxisms are delineated according to two different temporalities. The future in action and the beginning of the near future for Eastern Marxism; the more advanced stage of the near future and the remote and utopian futures for Western Marxism. It is a problem glimpsed by Marx and Engels. They provide, not by accident, two definitions of communism. The first puts it off to the remote future (sometimes read in a utopian way), a society that has left behind the antagonisms of class and "prehistory" as such. Quite different are the vision and the temporality that emerge in a celebrated section of *The German Ideology*: "we call communism the real movement which abolishes the present state of things."[20] Or that which emerges from the conclusion of the *Communist Manifesto*: "in short, the Communists everywhere support every revolutionary movement against the existing social and political order of things."[21] In these two passages cited here, it is as if we had thrown up a bridge between the two different temporalities. When this task is ignored or disdained, it is not long before superficialities and conceits show up, which love to contrast the poetry of the remote future to the prospect of the long-term prose of immediate tasks.

There is nothing easier and more idle than this operation. Even the most intellectually and morally mediocre have no difficulty in evoking the future of the "free development of all" of the *Manifesto* to condemn or discredit the political power born of the revolution (in any determinate geopolitical situation) called on to confront the dangers that threaten it.[22] The concrete history of the new post-revolutionary society, which seeks to develop itself among the tentative contradictions, difficulties, and errors of every kind, is defined en bloc as a degeneration and betrayal of the real movement in the name of the remote and utopian futures, an attitude foreign to Marx and Engels and which deprives Marxism of any real emancipatory project.

To take such an attitude means arbitrarily amputating the plural temporalities that characterize the revolutionary project of Marx and Engels. It means a temporal amputation that is simultaneously spatial. It concentrates exclusively on the remote future, read in a utopian vein, and leads to the exclusion of the vast majority of the world and humanity that has begun to take the first steps toward modernity and has sometimes even stopped at its threshold. And so the essential condition for the rebirth of Marxism in the West is the transcendence of this temporal and spatial amputation of the revolutionary project it has carried out.

4. Restoring the Relationship with the World Anticolonial Revolution

Transcending the unfortunate temporal and spatial amputation of Marxism will not be possible if the Marxists in the West do not restore their relationship with the world anticolonial revolution, which is mostly led by communist parties and which was the principal question of the twentieth century and continues to play an essential role in the century we have entered for some years now. To restore this relationship means fully reintroducing the colonial question to the historical account of the twentieth century and twentieth-century Marxism. When Colletti broke definitively with Marxism, he amused himself by noting that he had reached a conclusion not unlike where Althusser ended up.[23] Even for the latter, failure was the legacy of the communist movement. The French philosopher bitterly observed that nowhere did the process of the "withering away of the revolutionary State" promised by the Bolsheviks take place. Indeed, added the triumphant Italian philosopher, the communists were never able in any way to solve the problem of limitations on power, contrary to what happened in the liberal West.

It is an account that can be more usefully contrasted with one by a philosopher who is not a follower of Marxism or communism but a sharp critic, even an attentive and respectful one, of both movements. As to the representation of the Cold War as a conflict between the Free World on one side and despotism and totalitarianism on the other, he objected, "Western liberalism rests upon the forced labor of the colonies and twenty wars."[24] It lacks credibility, and "any apology for democratic regimes which is silent about their violent intervention in the rest of the world, or juggles the records to make it appear a special case ... can only serve to mask the problem of capitalism."[25] And so, "the right to defend the values of liberty and conscience is ours only if we are sure in doing so that we do not serve the interests of imperialism or become associated with its mystifications."[26]

To conclude with this first point: if, in our accounts of twentieth-century history, we avoid myopia and Eurocentric arrogance, we must recognize the essential contribution made by communism to the overthrow of the world colonialist-slavery system. The merciless white supremacy that characterized the United States in the early years of the twentieth century was denounced by a few courageous people as "an all-absorbing autocracy of race."[27] This regime, which reminds us of the Third Reich, existed worldwide and constituted the principal target of the movement born of the October Revolution.

Even if it has assumed new forms with respect to the past, the struggle between anticolonialism and colonialism and neocolonialism has not ceased. It is not by accident that, following its triumph in the Cold War, the West celebrated it as not only a defeat inflicted on communism but also on Third Worldism and as the premise for its coveted return of colonialism and even imperialism. That enthusiasm and euphoria were indeed of brief duration. But this has not led to any real ideological and political rethinking. Indeed, the deprecations and cries of alarm for the sundown of the West, or for its relative weakening and weakening of its leading country, remind us of the analogous phenomenon at the beginning of the twentieth century, when extraordinarily popular authors on both sides of the Atlantic denounced the mortal peril of the "rising tide of people of color" that loomed over "world white supremacy."

Certainly, in our own time, the language has changed. There is no longer a direct reference to races and racial hierarchies. This change is a sign of the success of the anticolonial revolution in the twentieth century. On another note, however, the fresh homages to colonialism, and even to imperialism, and the persistent celebration of the West (no longer of the white race) as the exclusive site of authentic civilization and of the highest moral values are signs that the anticolonial revolution has not yet reached its conclusion. And so, Marxists in the West must restore the relationship with the world anticolonial revolution. It is right to expect that they will look with sympathy not only at a people like the Palestinians, who are still forced to struggle against a classic kind of colonialism, but also at countries that have behind them an anticolonialist revolution and that are now seeking with difficulty their own way, being cautious in particular to not fall into a semi-colonial condition of economic and technological dependence.

It is not a question of uncritically accepting the positions taken by these countries. It is enough to take into account once more the viewpoint of Merleau-Ponty: "an aggressive liberalism exists that is a dogma and an ideology of war. It can be recognized by its love of the empyrean of principles, its failure to mention the geographical and historical circumstances to which it owes its birth, and its abstract judgments of political systems without regard for the specific conditions under which they develop."[28] If the French philosopher must be considered indulgent toward Western Marxism, we can reflect on some of Machiavelli's considerations regarding the grave difficulties that inevitably block the path of those building "new orders."[29] We can even turn to a classic figure of liberalism (who is one of the Founding Fathers of the United States). In Alexander Hamilton, we read that, in a situation of geographic insecurity, it is not possible to govern by law and through the limitation of power, and that faced with "external attack" and "internal convulsions," even a liberal country has recourse to power "without limitation" and without "constitutional shackles."[30]

Third, restoring the relationship with the world anticolonial revolution means taking into account that it is not a matter of respect for the sacred history of political and social emancipation so much as the concrete form assumed by that history in the twentieth and twenty-first centuries. It has been recognized, even by acclaimed scholars in Western countries, that, thanks to the prodigious economic and technological development of China, defined as the most important event of the last five hundred years, the Columbian era has come to an end; the era during which, in the words of Adam Smith, "the superiority of forces resulted so greatly to the benefit of the Europeans, that they could commit all sorts of injustice" to the detriment of other peoples, the era which Hitler, the most fanatical champion of white and Western supremacy, tried by every means to perpetuate.

The anticolonial revolution and the destruction of the world colonialist-slavery system, which must still be brought to an end, put into a new and unexpected framework the problem of the construction of a post-capitalist society. To consider extraneous to the Marxist project of political and social emancipation the history that developed from the October Revolution and that saw at its epicenter the East means assuming the attitude Marx mocked from his youth. It is from "real struggles," he observed, that revolutionary "criticism" starts: "then we shall confront the world not as doctrinaires with a new principle: 'Here is the truth, bow down before it!' We develop new principles for the world out of its own principles. We do not say to the world: 'Stop fighting; your struggle is of no account. We want to shout the true slogan of struggle at you.' We only show the world what it is fighting for."[31] This approach toward every doctrinaire attitude is the precondition for the rebirth of Marxism in the West.

5. The Lessons of Hegel and the Rebirth of Marxism in the West

It is a philosophical problem as well as a political one. There is a need to assimilate the great lesson by which "philosophy is one's own time apprehended through thought."[32] Not by chance, the author of this definition, as his biographer notes, "was used to reading an immense number of newspapers—something that in general only a statesman can do." And so, "he could always have at hand, to support his theses, an enormous mass of factual data."[33] It is a testimony that sheds much light on the study of the great philosopher. In evidence are the classics of philosophy and ideas and German and international press clippings. The philosophical system is elaborated through an incessant confrontation with his own times. We accurately inquire into political events without ever flattening out their immediacy; we investigate the meaning of the logic and epistemology of categories that refer to the main actors of political struggle or that are implicit in their discourse. The single event is inserted into a long-term perspective. Constrained as he was to measure himself against the great texts of the philosophic tradition, his political passion, manifested by voracious newspaper reading, undergoes a process of decanting and gains historical and theoretical depth. Politics, logic, epistemology, and history all closely intersect.

Marx's writing desk is no different (although Hegel stands out first among the classics). The fitting together of events with the impulse to connect them closely with theory and praxis impeded, however, the philosopher and revolutionary from elaborating a complete philosophical system of his own and from completing that project, according to Engels, who reports that he worked long on a *Summary of Dialectics*, perhaps to revise Hegel's *Science of Logic*.[34] Now, the thesis that to philosophize is to conceptually apprehend one's own time has acquired an additional meaning. Reading one's own time is no longer only a question of conceptualizing and structuring a rigorous categorical apparatus; it is also to identify the presence of a determinate historical moment (with its contradictions and its conflicts), also in the seemingly most "abstract" conceptualizations and philosophical systems.

Western Marxism lost sight of these two theoretical moves, the birthplace of historical materialism. It, above all, in the last stages of its existence, rather than identify the steps taken in historical time, even in the apparently most abstract theoretical elaborations by great philosophers, sought with great zeal to cover them up. The nexus that connects Heidegger and Schmitt to the Third Reich is explicitly declared; just as clearly, Nietzsche's theorization of slavery as the foundation of civilization harkens back to the stances of political and intellectual circles throughout the nineteenth century that opposed and criticized the abolition of Black slavery in every way. Of course, situating an author in his time does not negate the theoretical excesses in his thought. Writing of Linguet, who in the seventeenth century called for the introduction of slavery in France as the intrinsic essence of work and the inevitable foundation of property and civilization, Marx has no difficulty clarifying his acuity and profundity. This did not mean he felt the need to immerse the French author in a bath to cleanse him of every political and ideological encrustation.[35] In this way, instead, Western Marxism proceeds: when facing the effort of historical research, it prefers the lazy arbitrariness of the hermeneutics of innocence.

No better fate has befallen the second theoretical move of historical materialism, not so much the one that invites us to see the presence of historical times in even the most abstract ideas, as much as the one that imposes recourse to the concept and the effort of the concept to understand the most immediate events. We can begin by saying that the desks of the exponents of Western Marxism have often been quite different from those of Hegel and Marx. Presumably, in 1942, Horkheimer did not have an "immense number of newspapers at his disposal." Or maybe he did not have time or the desire to read them. He could express his disapproval and his indignation about the silence imposed by the leaders in Moscow on the idea of the withering away of the state only because he was badly informed about the real situation. The *Wehrmacht* was on the verge of accomplishing the goal of transforming the Soviet Union into an immense colony forced to furnish the Third Reich with an inexhaustible quantity of raw materials and slaves. Horkheimer lacked the essential elements of historical consciousness, so his conceptualization was vacuous. Rather than a philosopher determined to conceive and promote a radical project for transforming the world starting from the contradictions and the conflicts of the present, he was a prophet who pined nostalgically or from love for a world that would be entirely new, one without any relationship to the gigantic conflict between emancipation and de-emancipation occurring at that moment. Only in this way can we understand Horkheimer's position. Otherwise, we must read him as a self-caricature or as proof of the comic effects resulting from a sense of being pushed to the extremes.

We can reach an analogous conclusion if we read *Empire* by Hardt and Negri. We have seen them announce the end of imperialism and the advent of "perpetual and universal peace," cheerfully celebrating the triumphal conclusion of the war against Yugoslavia and the demonstrated ability of the West and its leading country to sovereignly wage wars in every corner of the world, while all around journalists, ideologues, and celebrity philosophers explicitly rehabilitated colonialism and imperialism and invoked and legitimized in advance the wars needed to silence those that would dare to challenge the *pax Americana*. Once more, we are forced to ask ourselves: what newspapers were on Hardt and Negri's desks when they proclaimed the utopia of a world without war?

Marcuse is a particularly interesting case. We have seen him make clear, with precision, why a still underdeveloped country that seeks to escape colonial subjection needs a strong state economically and politically. But subjective hopes and aspirations end up overwhelming analytical lucidity. Marcuse sighs, "quantitative change would still have to turn into qualitative change, into the disappearance of the state."[36] And perhaps, "at least in some of the liberation struggles in the Third World," we find a more important novelty, the advent of a "new anthropology." To give wing to such emphatic hopes—confessed the philosopher, not without some hesitation—was some vague news that was at first sight of little relevance. It was

> a small item that I read in a report about North Vietnam, and that had an effect on me since I am an absolutely incurable and sentimental romantic. It was a very detailed report, which showed, among other things, that in the parks in Hanoi, the benches are made only big enough for two, and only two, people to sit on so that another person would not even have the technical possibility of disturbing.[37]

It is a perplexing passage, and not only due to the prodigious capacity for anthropological regeneration it attributes to the Vietnamese bench. Did it really make sense to go looking for a new anthropology of undisturbed lovers in park benches respectful of intimacy in a country exposed to massive bombardment by the U.S. Air Force? Once again, the prophet takes over from the philosopher.

And this tendency can also be read in Žižek's disdain for the anti-imperialist struggle, which, for him, distracts us from overthrowing capitalism. During the U.S. Civil War, Marx was forced to struggle against those who, in the name of the struggle for socialism, preached political indifference. In the United States, the North and the South, the capitalists were in power, and slavery was alive and well, whether it was wage slavery (also denounced by Marx) or Black slavery.[38] Those who argued this way did not grasp the gigantic emancipation implicit in the abolition of true slavery. This method of argument, widespread in Western Marxism, contrasts with Hegel, for whom the universal always assumes a concrete and determinate form and with Marx's lesson that it makes no sense to see "real struggles" as "trifles," or Lenin's warning that whoever searches for a "pure" social revolution will never find one.

6. East and West: From Christianity to Marxism

Born in the heart of the West, with the October Revolution, Marxism spread to every corner of the world, penetrating forcefully into countries and areas in backward economic and social conditions and with very different cultures. Having behind it the Judeo-Christian tradition, Western Marxism echoed, not a few times as we have seen, with messianic motivations, the expectation of a communism conceived and believed to be the end of every conflict and contradiction, and so a kind of end to history. This messianism is largely absent in a culture like the Chinese, mostly characterized in the last millennium by the attention given to mundane social reality.

The planetary expansion of Marxism was the start of a bifurcation process, which was the other side of a clamorous victory. It also historically happened to the great religions. As far as Christianity is concerned, it is not by chance that Engels repeatedly compared it to the socialist movement: the division between Orthodox on the one side and Protestants and Catholics on the other corresponds to the division between East and West. At a certain point, between the end of the seventeenth and the beginning of the eighteenth century, it seems that Christianity was also about to spread en masse into the Asian East. Jesuit missionaries exercised a notable influence in China and enjoyed great prestige, having brought advanced medical and scientific knowledge. At the same time, they adapted themselves to the country that hosted them, paying homage to Confucius and the cult of ancestors. But, with the intervention of the pope in defense of the purity of the Christian religion, the Chinese emperor reacted by barring the doors of the Middle Kingdom to the missionaries. Christianity was treated favorably when it complied with its Sinification and promoted the scientific, social, and human development of the country where it was allowed to operate. It was rejected as a foreign body when it was seen to be a religion of otherworldly salvation that in no way respected the culture and human and social relations in force in the country it operated in.

Something similar happened to Marxism. With Mao, the Chinese Communist Party promoted the "Sinification of Marxism," gaining momentum from the struggle for liberation from colonial domination, for the development of the productive forces to make possible economic and technological independence as well, and for "making young again" a nation with a thousand-year-old civilization that had undergone colonialism and imperialism in the "century of humiliation" that began with the Opium Wars. Far from being rejected by the leaders of the People's Republic of China, they proudly proclaimed the socialist and communist perspective. However, it was stripped of messianism; second, its realization was delegated to a very long historical process in which social emancipation could not be disengaged from national emancipation.

And again, it was the West that was the custodian of the orthodox doctrine, and it is again from Western Marxism that the disavowal would come. This time, the disavowal hits Eastern Marxism, which appears hardly credible and, in any case, banal from the point of view of a Marxism charmed by the beauty of a remote and utopian future whose advent seems to be independent of material conditions (such as the geopolitical situation or the development of the productive forces), being instead exclusively determined and prioritized entirely by revolutionary political will.

This disenchantment, this bifurcation, the schism of which we speak, does not take aim only at China. Western Marxism followed with participatory and impassioned attention while Vietnam was fighting an epic resistance in a colonial war that first saw France, then the United States, as antagonists, but today Vietnam is buried in oblivion while engaged in the prosaic task of economic development. Cuba no longer attracts the enthusiasm it did when it faced Washington's military aggression (unsuccessful) in 1961 and for a long time afterward. Now that the danger of military intervention is remote, the Communist leaders of Cuba aim to reinforce their economic independence. To accomplish this, they feel obligated to make some concessions to the market and private property (cautiously inspired by the Chinese model). So the island that no longer seems to be a utopia on the way to realization but reveals itself to be in the grip of its own difficulties in constructing a post-capitalist society becomes less fascinating to Western Marxists. When it was still in its first stage, the military struggle for political independence, the anticolonial revolution seldom gained from Western Marxism the sympathetic attention and theoretical interest it deserved. Now that the anticolonial revolution is in its second stage, the struggle for economic and technological independence, Western Marxism reacts with disinterest, disdain, and hostility.

Western Marxism's incapacity to consider the turning point within the turning point in the twentieth century provoked the schism between the two Marxisms. While the clouds of a new great war thicken, this schism is revealed to be more ominous than ever. It is time to put an end to it. Naturally, this will not make the cultural, social, and political differences between the East and the West disappear, nor the tasks that must be accomplished. In the West, the socialist prospect passes through a struggle against a capitalism synonymous with worsening social polarization and rising militarist temptations.

However, we do not see why these differences should transform into antagonisms. Indeed, the excommunication inflicted by Western Marxism on Eastern Marxism has resulted not in the end of the excommunicated party but of the excommunicator. Overcoming doctrinaire attitudes, the willingness to measure oneself against one's own time, and philosophizing rather than prophesying are the necessary preconditions for Marxism's rebirth and development in the West.

APPENDIX

How "Western Marxism" Was Born and How It Died*

by Domenico Losurdo
Translated by Roland Boer and Christina Petterson

1. "Western Marxism" and the Suppression of the Colonial Question

Why did Marxism, after being extraordinarily successful and even becoming the *koine* (common language) of the 1960s and 1970s, fall into such a deep crisis in the West? Of course, the historical events that we all know and which culminated in the collapse of the Soviet Union and the "socialist camp" have played an essential role in this process. And yet, as indispensable as this kind of explanation may be, it is not enough: the analysis must be deepened, and attention must be directed to internal weaknesses that Marxism exhibited in the West even in the years when its hegemony seemed unchallenged. This is especially true

---

*Lecture given by Domenico Losurdo in 2007. Originally published in *Die Lust am Widerspruch, Theorie der Dialektik: Dialektik der Theorie, Symposium aus Anlass des 80, Gebrtstag von Hans Heinz Holz*, ed. Erich Hahn and Silvia Holz-Markun (Berlin: Trafo, 2008).

in Italy. It is worth starting from a debate provoked by Norberto Bobbio in 1954. While rightly insisting on the indispensability of "formal" freedom and its juridical-institutional guarantees, Bobbio credited the socialist states with "initiating a new phase of civilizational progress in politically backward countries by introducing traditionally democratic institutions: institutions of formal democracy such as universal suffrage and the eligibility of offices, and such substantial democracy as the collectivization of the means of production." And yet, according to Bobbio's critical conclusion, the new "socialist state" has so far neither been able to appropriate the rule of law and the liberal rule-of-law mechanisms, nor to "limit power" and "pour a drop of [liberal] oil into the gear of the already completed revolution."[1]

As you can see, we are far removed from the positions that the Turin philosopher took in his late phase, when he finally became an ideologist of the war of the West. It is 1954 (two years before the Twentieth Congress of the CPSU and the Hungarian uprising), and the influence of Marxism and the prestige of the countries that invoke it are very great. For Bobbio, in addition to the "formal," there is also a "substantial democracy," and by this, he makes a judgment on socialist countries that is clearly not negative, even with regard to "formal democracy."

But how did Italian communist intellectuals react? In order to repudiate or mitigate criticism, especially of the Soviet Union and to justify its partial backwardness in this field, they could have referred to the permanent state of emergency imposed on the country of the October Revolution and to the threat of nuclear annihilation, which continued to weigh heavily upon it. Galvano Della Volpe, by contrast, pursued a completely different argumentation strategy, focusing on praising the *libertas maior*—the concrete development of the personality guaranteed by the material conditions of life. In this approach, first, the legal guarantees of the rule of law were devalued, implicitly degraded to *libertas minor*; second, Bobbio's glorification of the liberal tradition as an advocate of at least a universal validity of civil rights, of formal freedom, of *libertas minor*, of the general "limitation of power" was ultimately confirmed. In support of this view, the Turin philosopher invoked the hymn of praise to freedom that John Stuart

Mill strikes up in perhaps his most famous treatise: *On Liberty*. But it is precisely in this work that we see the English liberals justifying the "despotism" of the West against the "races" still considered as "minor," which must be forced into "absolute obedience" in order to be able to lead them on the path of progress.[2] In 1954, "despotism" and the "absolute obedience" enforced by the West were very clearly felt in the colonial world; in the United States itself, Blacks continued to be largely excluded from political rights and sometimes even from civil rights (in the southern states of the United States, the regime of racial segregation and white supremacy had not yet been eliminated). Entirely preoccupied with boasting about the *libertas maior*, Della Volpe, however, makes no effort, or is unable, to draw attention to Bobbio's blatant failure.

The displacement of the colonial question, albeit in a different form each time, is indeed largely characteristic of Western Marxism of those years. In 1961, Ernst Bloch published *Naturrecht und menschliche Würde* (Natural Law and Human Dignity). As the title already shows, we are far from Della Volpe's underestimation of the *libertas minor*; on the contrary, the author explicitly professes the heritage of the liberal tradition, which, however, is subjected to a criticism that unfortunately looks very much like a glorification. Bloch accuses liberalism of advocating "formal and only formal equality." He adds: "for in imposing itself, capitalism took an interest in an evenly expanding universalization of juridical rules."[3]

This assumption can be read in a book published in the same year that the police in Paris carried out a merciless hunt for Algerians, who were drowned in the Seine or beaten to death; and all this in broad daylight, more precisely in the presence of French citizens, who, under the protection of the rule of law, happily attended the spectacle: so much for "formal equality"! Thus, in the capital of a capitalist and liberal country, a double right applies, which excludes a specifically determined ethnic group that is subject to arbitrariness and police terror. If we then look at the colonies and semi-colonies, for example, Algeria or Kenya or Guatemala (a formally independent country but de facto a U.S. protectorate), then we see the capitalist and liberal ruling state resorting to large-scale and systematic torture, concentration camps, and genocidal practices against the indigenous inhabitants. Of all this, there is not a trace in Bobbio, Della Volpe, or Bloch.

The peoples in the colonies or of colonial origin also remain absent when Bloch, the author of *Natural Law and Human Dignity*, deals with Grotius and Locke (the appraisal of their natural-law orientation takes place without a hint of their justification for the enslavement of Blacks), or when he speaks of the American War of Independence (the homage paid to the "young free states" completely conceals the importance of slavery in the United States political-social reality and even in the Constitution of the United States).[4]

This silence is all the more remarkable because it was precisely in these years that the struggle of African Americans began to unfold in the republic across the Atlantic. This event attracted Mao Zedong's attention in Beijing, and it is interesting to compare the opinions of two so different people. While the German philosopher laments the merely "formal" character of liberal and capitalist equality, the Chinese communist politician approaches the matter quite differently. Certainly, he points out that Blacks have a much higher unemployment rate than whites, that they are confined to the lower segments of the labor market and forced to put up with reduced wages. But this is not all: Mao draws attention to the racist violence unleashed by the authorities of the southern states and the gangs tolerated and encouraged by them, and he praises "the struggle of the Black American people against racial discrimination and for freedom and equal rights."[5]

Bloch criticizes the bourgeois revolution "because equality was restricted to the political sphere"[6]; Mao, looking at African Americans, points out that "most of them are deprived of the right to vote."[7] Turned into commodities and dehumanized by their oppressors, the colonial peoples have fought memorable battles for their recognition for centuries, but with Bloch, one can read: "The proposition that men are born free and equal can already be found in Roman law; now it should also be found in reality."[8] By contrast, the above-mentioned article by Mao from 1963 concludes: "The evil colonialist-imperialist system rose with the enslaving and trafficking of the Black people, and it will certainly not come to an end without the complete liberation of the Black people."⁹

The same can be heard from Vietnam, where a great national liberation struggle was underway. It was led by Ho Chi Minh, who had already accused the Third French Republic in 1920 with the following words: "so goes justice in Indochina, for in that country there is one law for the Annamese and another for the Europeans or those holding European citizenship." They have not only "been oppressed and exploited shamelessly" but also "tortured and poisoned pitilessly" and suffer "all the atrocities perpetrated by the predatory capitalists in Indochina."¹⁰ As you can see, in the texts of Mao and Ho Chi Minh quoted here, there is neither Della Volpe's underestimation of the *libertas minor* nor the illusion (shared in various ways by Bobbio, Della Volpe and Bloch) that capitalism and liberalism would guarantee at least "formal equality" or even "political equality."

In a way, the Chinese and Vietnamese leaders recall Lenin's remark: "the most Liberal and Radical personalities of free Britain . . . become regular Genghis Khans when appointed to govern India."¹¹ In the capitalist-liberal metropolis itself, "violations of the equality of nations" are evident. In 1920, Lenin pointed to the example of "Ireland" and of the "Negro of America"; in England, as in the United States, the "guaranteed rights of national minorities" are trampled underfoot.¹² Mao, like Ho Chi Minh, also would have been able to refer to the passages in which Marx denounced liberal England's treatment of Ireland (a colony within Europe): its policy is even more cruel and terroristic than that of autocratic Czarist Russia toward Poland.¹³ As one can see, "Eastern" Marxism is understandably far more interested in denouncing the crude exclusion clauses from liberal freedom than "Western" Marxism.

2. ALTHUSSER AND THE CRITIQUE OF "HUMANISM"

Let us turn again to the debate initiated by Bobbio in 1954. There was a contribution to this debate that is noticeably different from that of Della Volpe. The discussion with the Turin philosopher was conducted in this way: "when and to what extent were those liberal principles on which the English state of the nineteenth century was established—the perfect model, I think, of the liberal regime for all those who argue like Bobbio; when have these principles ever been applied to the peoples in the colonies?" The truth is that the "liberal doctrine ... is based on a barbaric discrimination between human beings," which rages not only in the colonies, but also in the metropolis—as the fate of Blacks in the United States shows, "for a large part deprived of basic rights, discriminated against and persecuted."[14] This statement does not degrade "formal freedom" to a *libertas minor*, but at the same time it does not lose sight of the fact that it was precisely the liberal West that denied countless people the enjoyment of this freedom. The cited contribution comes from an author almost completely forgotten today—Palmiro Togliatti, then general secretary of the Italian Communist Party. Is he a representative of "Western Marxism"? In any case, it should be noted that he was not a professional philosopher but a politician by profession, and, moreover, organically connected—so, at least, his critics claim—with quasi-Eastern "actually existing socialism."

But let us focus on the expression used by Togliatti: "barbaric discrimination between human beings." This judgment is inspired by the "integral humanism," which, according to Gramsci, constitutes communism. By contrast, in 1961, we saw Bloch raise a banner in defense of "human dignity." In those same years, humanism played a central role in Sartre's passionate condemnation of colonialism, precisely on the basis of its theories and practices of dehumanization. Here, we have different forms of expression of the "humanism" that later became a specter for Louis Althusser. As is known, the young Marx condemns existing society as a negation of "positive humanism" and "fully developed humanism,"[15] of "real humanism,"[16] and formulates the revolutionary program as the "categorical imperative to overthrow all relations in which man is a debased, enslaved, forsaken, despicable being."[17] For Althusser, these formulations are ideologically naive, which would, fortunately, be overcome by the mature Marx from about 1845, when the "epistemological break" had taken place and the humanistic rhetoric that supplanted the class struggle had been replaced by historical materialism, or rather, science by history.

In reality, this alleged rhetoric is louder than ever in the *Manifesto of the Communist Party* which calls for the overthrow of a system, the capitalist one, which disregards the human dignity of the vast majority of the population. The accused are socioeconomic conditions, which for the proletarians entail "training to act as a machine,"[18] turning them from childhood into "simple articles of commerce and instruments of labor,"[19] an "appendage of the machine,"[20] in which the "living person is dependent and has no individuality," and as a mere appendage of capital, which is "independent and has individuality."[21]

However, the *Manifesto of the Communist Party* is, according to Althusser, among the "works of theoretical transition" and not among the "mature works" in the full sense.[22] Let us, therefore, consider the words with which *Capital* accuses the capitalist system: the hunt for profit leads to a "Timur-Tamerlanish prodigality of human life."[23] This is a system that is not afraid to sacrifice human lives that are still being formed and completely defenseless. Marx speaks of the "great Herodian kidnapping of children, practiced by capitalists in the infancy of the factory system, in workhouses and orphanages, by means of which robbery, unresisting material for exploitation was procured."[24] The human cost of capitalism is terrible. Think of the formation of the textile industry in England: the necessary raw material was obtained by fencing off the commons, which had fed large masses, and turning them into sheep pasture—the dispossessed people were thus abandoned to hunger and despair; in summary, Marx quotes Thomas More, who speaks of the land where they "eat up, and swallow down, the very men themselves."[25]

Bourgeois society, according to Marx, likes to celebrate itself as "in fact a very Eden of the innate rights of man," while in reality "human labor," indeed "mere man [plays] a very shabby part."[26] As soon as we move from the sphere of circulation into the sphere of production, we notice that the wage-worker, far from being recognized in his dignity as a human being, "is bringing his own hide to market and has nothing to expect but—a hiding."[27]

The critique of the processes of dehumanization inherent in capitalism becomes even stronger when Marx speaks of the fate intended for colonial peoples. With the "rosy dawn of the era of capitalist production," Africa is transformed into a "warren for the commercial hunting of black skins."[28] In Asia and in the Dutch colonial empire, "their system of stealing men, to get slaves for Java" was common, with "men stealers" who were "trained for this purpose."[29] In the second half of the nineteenth century in the United States, the Black slave was still in every way a piece of "property," and the law on the extradition of fugitive slaves turned the citizens of the North into "slave catchers."[30] Meanwhile, some southern states specialized in "Negro breeding,"[31] the "breeding of slaves."[32] Yes, "states . . . that formerly employed slaves in the production of export articles" were now becoming "states which raise slaves to export them."[33]

After the outbreak of the Civil War, slaveholders emigrated southward from areas considered unstable, taking with them their "Black chattels."[34] As can be seen, even in the writings of the "mature" Marx, the reproach was repeatedly directed at bourgeois society for degrading the vast majority of humanity to "machines," to "instruments of labor," to "commodities" that can be wasted at will, to "articles of commerce" and "articles of export," to movable goods that their master has at his disposal like pieces of luggage, like livestock that can be raised, or like hunting game of which the leather can be tanned.

The denunciation of the misanthropy of the capitalist system has by no means disappeared, and it cannot disappear because it stands at the center of Marx's thought. His frequent comparisons between modern slavery and ancient slavery, wage slavery and colonial slavery, express the permanence, characteristic of capitalism, of that reification that manifests itself in all its harshness in relation to the slave in the proper sense, who is completely degraded to a commodity or a farm animal. So scientific rigor and moral indignation are closely intertwined, and only this connection can explain the call to revolution. The description of existing society alone, however exact and merciless it may be, does not spur action for the overthrow if mediation through moral condemnation is lacking, and this moral condemnation arises in Marx from the representation of the dehumanizing processes inherent in the capitalist system. From there, the realization of a new order is perceived as a "categorical imperative" in Marx's youthful writings and in those of his maturity. If the "Theses on Feuerbach" conclude with the condemnation of philosophers who show themselves incapable of "changing" a world in which human beings are downtrodden and degraded, then *Capital* is a "critique of political economy"—as its subtitle reads—also in regard to morality: the "political economist" is criticized not only for his theoretical errors but also for his "stoical peace of mind," that is, for his inability to feel moral indignation in the face of the tragedies provoked by bourgeois society.[35] The continuity in Marx's development is evident, and what Althusser called an epistemological rupture is merely the transition to a discourse in which the moral condemnation of the misanthropy and anti-humanism of bourgeois society is expressed in a more concise and succinct way.

3. From History to "Science," or from Materialism to Idealism, from World History to Eurocentrism

The reasons for Althusser's attitude are quite understandable: these are the years in which the flag of "humanism" was waved in order to dampen the struggle against imperialism. Thus, the development that would lead later to Gorbachev's surrender had begun. Strictly speaking, the philosophical critique of humanism, insofar as humanism tended to obscure social conflict and the sharpness of such conflict, is at the same time a polemic against the "conceptions which are tainted with reformism and opportunism, or quite simply revisionist" that were widely disseminated in these years.[36] Unfortunately, this polemic arose from the wrong presuppositions. First, it should be noted that it is not only the appeal to ordinary humanity (and morality) that can make us forget class struggle but also the exhortation to science. And yet the French philosopher justifiably takes a stand against the slogan "bourgeois science, proletarian science" and acknowledges that Stalin resisted the "madness" of those "who were making strenuous efforts to prove language an [ideological] superstructure." Thanks to these "simple pages," writes Althusser, "we could see that there were limits to the use of the class criterion and that we had been made to treat science, a status claimed by every page of Marx, as merely the first-comer among ideologies."[37] Can the application of the class criterion to morality be considered without limits? Can positions that profess the unity of the human race actually be placed on a par with those which, in practice, and sometimes even explicitly in theory, dehumanize large masses of people and degrade human beings to subhumans intended merely for enslavement or destruction?

In his confrontation with a humanistic understanding of Marxism, Althusser never tires of repeating that Marx does not start from the "human" or the "individual" but from the historical structures of social relations. But, oddly enough, he takes the concept of "human" or "individual" for granted. Here, reference may be made to Nietzsche, who condemned the Paris Commune as the work of a "barbaric slave state" unleashed in the name of "human dignity" and the "dignity of human labor"[38] and then condemns "socialism" as a simple "means of agitation employed by individuals."[39] He opposed the idea that "many people are 'persons'"; "most [however] are not" persons, but rather mere "bearers and transmission instruments."[40]

In other words, the idea of the individual or of a human being as such is anything but a matter of course; it is rather the result of gigantic struggles for recognition, which were conducted precisely under the banner of the humanism so despised by Althusser. This point already applies to the wage workers in the metropolis (who have been dehumanized by the liberal tradition often enough into working tools, two-footed machines, working animals), and it applies especially to the colonial peoples. There is no point in opposing the historical structure of social relations to the idea of the human being or the individual as such, because this idea presupposes radical political and social changes. When Althusser emphasizes that humanism is ultimately bourgeois, he argues analogously to Bloch: In one case, as in the other, bourgeois society is accused of adhering only to "formal equality" and the formal inequalities and the associated profound processes that characterize capitalism are repressed.

Of course, Althusser acknowledges that there can also be a "revolutionary humanism" inspired by the October Revolution,[41] but on this point he is very hesitant, blocking out the awareness of the gigantic struggles that the "slaves in the colonies" (to speak with Lenin) waged for their recognition. This is all the more true since Althusser's theory of Marx represents only one chapter of the history of scientific thought: "before Marx, two continents *only* had been opened up to scientific knowledge by sustained epistemological breaks: the *continent of Mathematics* with the Greeks ... and the *continent of Physics* (by Galileo and his successors)."[42] This approach of necessity has two significant consequences: 1) Marx insisted many times that his theory was the theoretical expression of a real movement; now, however, the real movement is to be regarded as the product, to speak in Althusser's terms, of an "epistemological rupture," or, to speak in Della Volpe's terms, of a scientific method that heeds the teaching of Galileo and, before that, of Aristotle as a critic of Plato. We are thus witnessing an idealist distortion of historical materialism, which is now understood as the result of the genius of a single individual who set out to discover a new continent! After repeatedly accusing humanism of disguising class struggle, it is precisely Althusser who makes class struggle disappear behind the theoretical elaboration of historical materialism. 2) The idealist reversal of Marxism is, at the same time, a reinterpretation under the banner of Eurocentrism. With Engels, Lenin, and Gramsci, the French Revolution was understood to stand behind Marxism, and this ultimately—or at least potentially—referred to the gigantic struggles triggered in Santo Domingo (Haiti), culminating in the abolition of slavery in the colonies. With Althusser, however, the elaboration of historical materialism becomes a chapter of a history that takes place exclusively in the West.

4. "Western Marxism" Reads "Eastern Marxism": A Mass Misunderstanding

Although Althusser followed with deep concern the struggles of peoples living under colonial conditions and looked with sympathy at China, which was hoping to place itself at the head of the anti-imperialist movement, he was nevertheless unable, apparently, to grasp the theoretical significance of these struggles. This is a generally characteristic phenomenon. In the course of the 1960s and 1970s, a massive misconception characterized the Marxist-oriented left in Europe and the United States. The great support for Vietnam seemed to combine effortlessly with the veneration of authors who regarded movements for national liberation as definitively obsolete. In his 1966 work, *Negative Dialectics*, Adorno dispenses with the Hegelian thesis of the "people's spirit," that is, of the essential importance of the nation and the national question. It is "reactionary" and retrograde "in view of the Kantian generality of his period, of visible humanity"; it is affected by "nationalism" and "is in the epoch of telluric conflicts and the potential of a telluric arrangement of the world utterly provincial." Worse still, nationalism is a cult devoted to a "fetish," a "collective subject" (the nation), in which "more completely the subjects disappear... without a trace."[43] This position subsequently delegitimized the war waged by the Algerian National Liberation Front, by a people and a country that was undoubtedly more provincial, backward, and less cosmopolitan than the France against which they had risen. In any case, it became impossible for Adorno to comprehend the great struggles unfolding right before his eyes, starting with the National Liberation Front of Vietnam.

Let us consider how "Eastern Marxism" argues in relation to this issue. Three years after the appearance of *Negative Dialectics*, Ho Chi Minh died. In his last testament, he calls his compatriots to "patriotic struggle" and to a commitment to "national salvation." He then draws the following personal balance sheet: "all my life, I have served the Fatherland, the revolution and the people with all my heart and strength."[44] Already in 1960, on the occasion of his seventieth birthday, the Vietnamese leader recalled his intellectual and political development as follows: "at first, it was patriotism, not yet communism, which led me to have confidence in Lenin, in the Third International." Strong emotions were aroused above all by the appeals and documents that supported and promoted the liberation struggle of the colonial peoples and emphasized their right to constitute themselves as independent states. In response to Lenin's "Theses on the National and Colonial

Questions," Ho Chih Minh writes: "what emotion, enthusiasm, enlightenment and confidence they communicated to me! I wept for joy."[45] As for Mao Zedong, one need only think of his declaration of 1949, on the eve of the founding of the People's Republic of China: "ours will no longer be a nation subject to insult and humiliation. We have stood up.... The era in which the Chinese people were considered uncivilized is now ended."[46]

The attitudes of the two great revolutionaries can easily be understood. They base themselves on Lenin, who characterized imperialism as follows: it is a system in which some alleged "model nation" grants itself "the exclusive privilege of forming a state," which they deny to the peoples of the colonies.[47] Indeed, "a few chosen nations" want to create their own "prosperity" by plundering and dominating the rest of humanity.[48] In addition to economic plunder and political oppression, the hierarchization of nations is also characteristic of imperialism. The exploited and oppressed peoples are simultaneously branded as incapable of governing themselves and of constituting themselves as a state; the struggle to shake off this stigma is a great struggle for recognition.

However, in those years, the reverence for Ho Chi Minh, Mao, or Castro did not lead to any distancing from the national nihilism peculiar to Western Marxism. Not even Sartre was able to resist national nihilism despite his strong commitment to the fight against colonialism. As a central chapter of his *Critique of Dialectical Reason* shows,[49] for Sartre, the various human conflicts ultimately arise from "scarcity" (*rareté*). The result of this approach is devastating. To the extent that the situation of scarcity causes a struggle for life and death, it ultimately justifies in a certain way those responsible for oppression: they now appear as protagonists of a tragic struggle for survival, which fatefully imposes itself on the present and can be ended in the future only by an extraordinary development of the productive forces. Vice versa, the oppressed seem to be driven only by the desire to escape unbearable living conditions. But if language, culture, national identity, and dignity play no role whatsoever, it is impossible to understand why social strata that enjoy a comfortable standard of living or live in prosperity to a greater or lesser extent also participate in the struggle against national oppression. As one can see, sympathy for the "damned of this earth" and indignation at the crimes of colonialism and imperialism in Algeria or Vietnam, however meritorious they are, do not in themselves guarantee an adequate understanding of the national question.

A few decades later, Hardt and Negri would explain the deeper reason for this contradictory attitude: "from India to Algeria and Cuba to Vietnam, the state is the poisoned gift of national liberation." Yes, the Palestinians can count on our sympathy, but once they are "institutionalized" one can no longer stand by "their side." For "as soon as the nation begins to form as a sovereign state, its progressive functions all but vanish."[50] This means that sympathy for the Vietnamese, the Palestinians, or other peoples can only be felt as long as they are oppressed and humiliated; a liberation struggle is supported only to the extent that it is unsuccessful! The defeat or futility of a revolutionary movement is a prerequisite for the rebel to be able to boast and enjoy his rebelliousness as a rebel who is under no circumstances willing to engage with the dirty work of institutionalized power!

The leaders of the peoples fighting for their liberation clearly argue in a very different way. In September 1949, on the eve of the communist seizure of power, Mao Zedong drew attention to Washington's wish that China "will live on U.S. flour" and thus eventually "become a U.S. colony."[51] The struggle to increase production thus became a continuation of the struggle for national independence.

In truth, the *Manifesto of the Communist Party* had already pointed out that "the proletariat will use its political supremacy" and control of the means of production "to increase the total of productive forces as rapidly as possible," and in particular, to develop "new industries" that no longer have a national basis and "whose introduction becomes a life and death question for all civilized nations."[52] Nevertheless, the general problem to which Marx and Engels drew attention acquires a very special urgency in the East. Having shaken off the colonial yoke, the countries and peoples that have become independent are striving to consolidate themselves economically: they no longer want to depend on the alms or arbitrariness of their former masters; they consider it absolutely necessary to break the monopoly of the more powerful countries on more advanced technology.

In fact, we find the same orientation that we had already found with Mao in Vietnam. While the war for independence and national unity was still in full swing, Le Duan, the First Secretary of the Workers' Party of North Vietnam, declared that the most important task after the assumption of power was a "technical revolution." Since "the productive forces play the decisive role," it is therefore a matter of making a thorough effort aimed at "changing the backward state of our national economy and pushing forward the development of productive forces."[53]

In the West, on the other hand, when the movement to support the Vietnamese revolution was growing stronger, and the influence of China was becoming more noticeable, a completely different tone was heard among the Marxist left. In Italy, Mario Tronti published a book that rapidly became a great success. One of his central theses: the socialist revolution "will abolish work. And in so doing, it will abolish class domination. The abolition of work by the working class and the violent destruction of capital are one and the same."[54] Tronti published his essay in 1966, the year in which the "Cultural Revolution" was breaking out in China. And at this point the comedy of misunderstandings reaches its peak.

The "Cultural Revolution" was unleashed with a specific slogan: "grasp revolution; promote production." Among Western Marxists, there was no lack of sympathetic or even enthusiastic opinions in support, but they dropped the second part of this slogan. However, as late as 1969, on the occasion of the Ninth Congress of the CPC, Lin Biao, at that time the designated successor of Mao Zedong, emphasized:

> As the *16-Point Decision* indicates, "The Great Proletarian Cultural Revolution is a powerful motive force for the development of the social productive forces in our country." Our country has seen good harvests in agricultural production for years running and there is also a thriving situation in industrial production and science and technology. The enthusiasm of the broad masses of the working people both in revolution and production has

soared to unprecedented heights. Many factories, mines and other enterprises have time and again topped their production records, creating all-time highs in production. The technical revolution is making constant progress.... "Grasp revolution; promote production"—this principle is absolutely correct.[55]

Lin Biao affirmed this point persistently:

We must . . . energetically promote production and fulfill and overfulfill our plans for developing the national economy. It is certain that the great victory in the Great Proletarian Cultural Revolution will continue to bring about new leaps forward on the economic front and in our cause of socialist construction as a whole.[56]

One of the main accusations against the deposed president of the PRC, Liu Shaoqi, was "the doctrine of trailing behind at a snail's pace,"[57] that is, the inability to understand that the "Cultural Revolution" would accelerate the development of the productive forces and would lift the country at breakneck speed to the level of the most advanced capitalist countries. It was not by chance that the "Cultural Revolution" revived and relaunched the Great Leap Forward of 1958, through which China had hoped to catch up with the most advanced capitalist countries in a flash.

We should not forget that as early as 1937, Mao's essay "On Practice" had taken up a motif from the *Manifesto of the Communist Party*, emphasizing the central importance of "activity in material production" and the development of productive forces with the aim of increasing not only social wealth but also "human knowledge." Indeed, "small scale of production limited man's outlook," and because of this educational function, the activity of material production will not disappear even "in a classless society" in communism.[58] In the West, however, the "Mao Cult" could readily be combined with the expectation of an end to work; the essay "On Practice" was often quoted but with reference only to class struggle, suppressing both the struggle for production and the struggle for scientific innovation.

In Western Marxism, the populist halving of the main slogan of the "Cultural Revolution" corresponds to the halving of Mao's teaching. The latter felt obliged to eliminate two kinds of inequality: the inequality existing within the Chinese people, but also, and perhaps even more, the inequality that separated China from the most advanced countries. With a significantly accelerated development of the productive forces, overcoming the first contradiction also would have made possible the overcoming of the second. Thus, China was to rise once and for all, and the long struggle for recognition, which the oppression and humiliation of imperialism had made necessary, was to be crowned with complete success.

But in the West, the "Cultural Revolution" was distorted to become the sum total of Mao's teaching and work, and the Chinese Revolution in its entirety was reduced to a slogan: "it is right to rebel." The great revolutionary, already cut in half as outlined above, was now reinterpreted as an anarchist. Although anarchism had been defeated with much effort during the time of the Second International, it loudly returned in the movement of 1968.

5. From Foucault to Negri: The Increasing Transfiguration of Empire

In this intellectual and political climate, Marxist-oriented culture began to be beguiled and overwhelmed by authors and schools of thought that should at the time have been viewed with some critical distance. Endowed from the very beginning with Althusser's blessing,[59] Foucault advanced with his analysis of the pervasiveness or omnipresence of power not only in institutions and social relations but also in mental dispositions. Foucault's discourse was spellbinding because of its radicalism, therefore making it possible to account for the power and ideocracy in "really existing socialism," whose crisis was becoming more and more apparent. In reality, this radicalism is not merely an apparent one, but even turns into its opposite. The gesture of condemning any relationship of power, or rather any kind of power, whether in society or in the discourse about society, makes that "determinate negation," the negation of a "particular content"—which, in Hegelian terms, is the prerequisite for a real transformation of society and thus the prerequisite for the revolution[60]—very problematic or even impossible. Moreover, this effort to expose and demystify domination in all its forms shows surprising gaps precisely where domination manifests itself in all its brutality: almost no attention is paid to colonial rule.

When Jean-Paul Sartre initiated a protest in Paris against the massacre of Algerians, Foucault's friend Pierre Boulez took part, but Foucault himself did not participate. In general, the struggle against torture and the brutal repression with which the rulers tried to suppress the national liberation struggle plays no role whatsoever in Foucault's thought. As has rightly been noted, "his criticism of power remains focused on Europe."[61] Even more, colonialism and colonial ideology are largely absent from the history that Foucault draws of the modern and contemporary world. Thus, for Foucault, at "the end of the nineteenth century, we see the appearance of what might be called a state racism," and only the dawn of the Third Reich heralds the emergence of "an absolutely racist state."[62] Doubts about this periodization already emerge when we consider the abolitionists, who in the nineteenth century publicly burned the American Constitution, which they branded as a pact with the devil because it legitimatized slavery, or those who accused the 1850 laws on fugitive slaves of trying to force every U.S. citizen to "become a man-hunter." Those liable to prosecution were not only those who tried to hide or help a Black person pursued by his legitimate owners, but also those who did not participate in the capture.[63]

To partially excuse Foucault, it might be argued that he did not know about this chapter of history, but then he might at least have read Marx's comment on the fugitive slave laws: "to play the part of slave-catchers for the Southern slaveholders appeared to be the constitutional calling of the North."[64] In any case, we are not dealing here with racism that is manifested only at the level of civil society: the racial identity of a person is decided on the basis of explicit juridical and constitutional norms concerning a person's social position and his fate. As far as the United States is concerned, before the war of secession, its racial state character was even more pronounced than that of the Third Reich. According to the Nuremberg laws, while the definition of a Jew included the affiliation of one or another ancestor to the Jewish religious community, in the United States religion played no role in defining who was Black. The only decisive factor was blood: "the one-drop rule." Hitler had no slaves (neither Black nor Jewish), but almost all presidents in the first decades of the American republic were owners of (Black) slaves.

If Foucault did not deal with the history of the United States, then he might have deigned to consider the history of the secessionist confederation or that of South Africa or take an overall view. If one examines the capitalist countries together with the colonies ruled by them, it turns out that the phenomenon described by Ho Chi Minh for Indochina has a common character: there are two kinds of legislation, one for the race of the conquerors, the other for the race of the conquered. Seen in this way, the racial state accompanies the history of colonialism in its entirety like a shadow. The phenomenon is more evident in the United States only because of the spatial proximity in which the different races lived. However, Foucault is not interested in the history of the peoples in the colonies or of colonial origin.

There is also the history that the French philosopher depicts in light of racial ideology. According to him, "late in the nineteenth century," in contrast to the tradition of historical accounts that strove to legitimize sovereignty, a completely new, anti-authoritarian and revolutionary discourse prevailed, which divided society into struggling races (or classes) and introduced a "principle of heterogeneity: the history of some is not the history of others."[65] Sometime later, however, a turning point occurs: "the idea of racial purity, with all its monistic, statist, and biological implications: that is what replaces the idea of race struggle." A real revolution: "racism is, quite literally, revolutionary discourse in an inverted form." For Foucault, it is clear that "they [revolutions] had their roots in the discourse of race struggle."[66] From this picture, the centuries-long process of racialization and dehumanization that overwhelmed the colonized peoples have "literally" disappeared, as have the great struggles for recognition—beginning with the one that, in light of the radicalization of the French Revolution, led to the abolition of slavery in the colonies.

Finally, according to Foucault, "the great public ritualization of death gradually began to disappear . . . in the late eighteenth century."[67] In reality, in the United States in the first decades of the twentieth century, white supremacy was still manifested in the organized mass spectacles of the lynching of Blacks. The spectacles were announced in the local press, women and children were invited to attend and participate, and they ended with the distribution of souvenirs of the sacrificial rite.

The huge displacements that I have presented here are also reflected at the political level. When Foucault delivered the series of lectures under examination here, at the Collège de France in 1975–1976, the apartheid regime of racist South Africa was still very much alive. And about ten years earlier, Hannah Arendt had drawn attention to the prohibition of marriages between partners of different "races" and other provisions of a similar nature that continued to apply in Israel—in paradoxical analogy with the "infamous Nuremberg Laws of 1935."[68] But when Foucault sets out in search of another reality that he can place alongside the Third Reich in terms of "state racism," he succeeds in locating it only in the Soviet Union—the country which, since its foundation, had made a decisive contribution to the emancipation of the colonial peoples and which was also at the forefront of condemning the anti-Black and anti-Arab policies pursued by South Africa and Israel in 1976!

It has been noted that Foucault significantly influenced Antonio Negri. Indeed. Today, distinguished American scholars describe the history of their country as that of a *Herrenvolk* democracy, that is, a democracy that applies only to the *Herrenvolk* (the use of Hitler's language is significant) and has not hesitated to enslave Blacks and wipe out the "redskins" from the face of the earth. The book *Empire*, by contrast, speaks wistfully of an "American democracy" that breaks with the "transcendent" idea of power characteristic of the European tradition.[69] But the apologia does not end here. Take a figure as central to the history of U.S. imperialism as Woodrow Wilson. As he begins his career, Ku Klux Klan thugs are attacking Blacks in his home in the

South. But the future president takes up his pen to write an indictment of the victims in an article in the *Atlantic Monthly* of January 1901: the "negroes" are "excited by a freedom they do not understand," are "insolent and aggressive; sick of work, covetous of pleasure." In any case, "the sudden and absolute emancipation of the negroes" was a catastrophe. It had led to a "very perilous" situation, which "southern legislatures" (that is, the whites) had to face with "extraordinary steps" (lynchings and terror).[70]

Wilson will always remain faithful to this ideological-political platform under the sign of white supremacy on a national and international level. In this context belongs the heavy cudgel with which Latin America was threatened and chastised. Nor should we forget that even relations with European allies were often characterized by an ungracious *realpolitik*. It is no coincidence that the young Wilson even attracted Bismarck's attention.[71] All this did not prevent the U.S. president from intervening in the First World War in the name of the universal democratic mission of the United States: it was "a holy war, the holiest of all wars," a "transcendent enterprise" whose protagonists are the American "crusaders."

This unique combination of *realpolitik* and the idea of a religious mission sealed by a privileged and direct relationship with the Lord provoked the biting irony of Freud.[72] But it makes recourse to an iron fist against a pacifist opposition all the easier. The repression in the United States was far harsher than that carried out at the same time in Wilhelmine Germany. It is not by chance that this repression aroused the admiration of Mussolini, who was just then hurrying along the path that would lead him to *Squadrismo* and fascism.[73] In Negri and Hardt, however, we read that Wilson is characterized by "an internationalist ideology of peace," far from the "traditional European-style imperialist ideology"![74] The ideologues of "Manifest Destiny" have always insisted on the moral and political primacy of the United States, on its "exceptionalism," that it was to be the only island of freedom in an infinite ocean of despotism. The argument of *Empire* is not dissimilar.

At this point I would like to suggest a type of intellectual experiment or, if you will, a game. We will compare two quotations; they come from two noticeably different authors, but they both try to contrast the United States against Europe in a positive way. The first praises "the American experience" and emphasizes "the difference between a nation conceived in liberty and dedicated to the proposition that all men are created equal, and the nations of the old world, which certainly were not conceived in liberty."[75]

And now the second:

> Was not American democracy in fact, founded on the democracy of exodus, on affirmative and nondialectical values, and on pluralism and freedom? Did not these values, along with the notion of new frontiers, perpetually re-create the expansion of its democratic basis beyond every abstract obstacle of the nation, ethnicity, and religion?... When Hannah Arendt claimed the American Revolution to be superior to the French because the American was an unlimited search for political freedom and the French a limited struggle over scarcity and inequality, she not only celebrated an ideal of freedom that Europeans no longer knew but also reterritorialized it in the United States.[76]

Which of the two passages quoted here is more apologetic? It is difficult to say, even if the second sounds more inspirational and lyrical. The second, of course, comes from the pen of Negri (and Hardt), while the first comes from Leo Strauss, the leading ideologue of American neoconservatism! Marx's observation concerning Bakunin comes to mind. For all his anti-statist radicalism, Bakunin ultimately spares England—the "genuine capitalist state," "the true apex of bourgeois society in Europe."[77] The anarchism of our day goes even further than Bakunin in sparing the country that, in the eyes of a broad and growing worldwide opinion, has become synonymous not only with capitalism but also with militarism and imperialism—a country that also embodies for prominent U.S. historians of a liberal tendency a completely different "exceptionalism" than that invented by Strauss, Negri, and Hardt:

> Only in the United States was there a stable and direct connection

between the ownership of slaves and political power. Only in the United States did slaveholders play a central role in the formation of the state and the creation of representative bodies.[78]

At the time, Sartre denounced "that super-European monstrosity, North America."[79] *Empire*, on the other hand, not only positively opposes the United States to Europe but also supports Arendt's thesis of the clear superiority of the American Revolution over the French. In this black-and-white confrontation, of course, the deportation and decimation of the "redskins" and the enslavement of the Blacks, powerfully driven by the former revolution and abolished by the latter revolution, play no role. Hardt and Negri take no notice of the fact that Arendt had also dragged Marx into the dock together with Jacobinism; Marx as the author of the "politically most pernicious doctrine of the modern age," as the person responsible for "an actual surrender of freedom to necessity"; the latter had been influenced by "his teacher in revolution, Robespierre" and in turn had perniciously influenced "his greatest disciple, Lenin."[80] And consequently, Hardt and Negri, together with the unconditional condemnation of the two revolutions—the French and the Russian—that called into question the world system of slavery and colonial oppression, tacitly approve of the liquidation of the philosopher who, when he condemns wage slavery in the metropolis, repeatedly refers—sometimes explicitly, sometimes implicitly—to slavery in the true sense of the word in the colonies. This constitutes the self-liquidation of "Western Marxism."

6. "Western Marxism," "Eastern Marxism"

At this point, the earlier distinction or opposition between "Western Marxism" and "Eastern Marxism" formulated by Perry Anderson needs to be reexamined.[81] First and foremost, it is important to examine the different conditions in which one and the other had to act. Let us begin from 1917. In the West, Marxism was schooled primarily in condemning the destructive consequences (the slaughter and the burying of democracy) of inter-imperialist rivalry and war, while in the East, the October Revolution found an extraordinary echo thanks to the call to the "slaves in the colonies" to break the chains of oppression and national humiliation. In the West, the nation-state was the bloodthirsty Moloch that sacrificed millions of people to the greed for power and the interests of big business, in the East, it was a question of shaking off the colonial yoke and putting an end to the genocidal and enslaving practices used by the great capitalist powers against the "barbarians." In the two zones into which the world was divided, imperialism was experienced in different ways; there is no contradiction but rather a full convergence between these two aspects. But have Western and Eastern Marxism ever met? Has the first ever really grasped the second?

Another consideration. Since the initial difficulties and tragedies of the system that emerged from the October Revolution became apparent, but especially since the crisis of "real socialism" became clear, the split between Eastern and Western Marxists has led to the fact that Marxists in power and Marxists in opposition—the latter increasingly focusing on "critical theory," "deconstruction," and also the condemnation of power and of power relations in general—are alien to each other. And so "Western Marxism" was born, which increasingly understood its distance from power as a favorable condition for the rediscovery of an "authentic" Marxism that was no longer reduced to a "state ideology."

But does this proud and perhaps arrogant self-confidence have a real basis? There is another, often forgotten side of the coin. It could be said that Eastern Marxism was in a more favorable situation for understanding and appropriating an essential thesis of Marx: "the profound hypocrisy and inherent barbarism of bourgeois civilization lies unveiled before our eyes, turning from its home, where it assumes respectable forms, to the colonies, where it goes naked."[82]

Western Marxism, on the other hand, has dealt almost exclusively with the "respectable forms" of bourgeois-capitalist rule. If, however, the fate intended above all for the peoples in the colonies and of colonial origin is lost sight of, then the absolutely necessary criticism of "real socialism" results in banal liberal apologetics and in an undifferentiated liquidation of the history of communism of the twentieth century. The development of Lucio Colletti, pupil of Della Volpe, is illuminating. But no less significant is the conduct of two authors who are still considered leading figures. Speaking of Stalin's Soviet Union (but implicitly of all countries that had to bow to the logic of "socialism in one country"), Hardt and Negri write: "it is a tragic irony that nationalist socialism in Europe came to resemble national socialism . . . because the abstract machine of national sovereignty is at the heart of both."[83] In this reckless historical balance, the colonial or semi-colonial peoples continue to play no role. Here, two countries are calmly placed side by side and on an equal footing, the first of which has given a powerful impulse to the process of decolonization, while the second set out to inherit and radicalize the colonial tradition, even considering it to be applicable to Eastern Europe.

If we consider the colonial world, the historical balance of the twentieth century looks very different from what the ruling ideology would prefer (and so also today, the veterans of "Western Marxism"). If we focus exclusively on "formal" democracy, that is, on the rule of law and the classical freedoms of the liberal tradition, it must be said that the societies that emerged from the October Revolution went into a tailspin and eventually eliminated any form of democracy. And yet, at the time, they stimulated the desire for democracy and emancipation, for recognition; they stimulated the demands of the peoples in the colonies or on the periphery of the capitalist metropolis. In the case of colonies or semi-colonies, it was precisely the bourgeois-democratic metropolis that stifled democratic claims with blood.

The Soviet Union and the "socialist camp" also exerted a positive influence with regard to a population of colonial origin in the heart of the capitalist metropolis itself—African Americans. They were oppressed by a regime of terrorist white supremacy when the October Revolution broke out. But from then on, a new unrest spread among the Blacks, and without being intimidated by the witch hunts, they declared: "if to fight for one's rights is to be Bolshevists, then we are Bolshevists and let them make the most of it."[84] To take a leap of fifteen years, into the most tragic period of Soviet history: the collectivization of agriculture, imposed mainly from above and from outside, led to the spread of the Gulags on a large scale, and the Great Terror was looming on the horizon. But it is interesting to see how the country that emerged from the October Revolution continued to be perceived by African Americans. Thanks to the activity of the Communist Party of the United States, they were beginning to acquire something that the white supremacist regime had stubbornly denied them: a culture that goes far beyond the elementary education traditionally given to those who were destined to do servile work in the service of the master race. Now, in Communist Party schools in the northern United States or in Moscow schools, Blacks devoted themselves to studying economics, politics, and world history. They also used these disciplines to understand why they had been dealt such a harsh fate in a country that considers itself the refuge of freedom. Among those who attended such schools, a profound change was taking place: their "insolence" reprimanded by the regime of white supremacy is, in reality, their previously suppressed and downtrodden self-esteem. A Black woman delegate at the International Congress of Women Against War and Fascism held in Paris in 1934 was extremely impressed by the relations of equality and fraternity that emerged, regardless of the differences of language and race, in this initiative promoted by the Communists: "it was heaven on earth."

Those who managed to get to Moscow—observed a contemporary U.S. historian—"experienced a sense of freedom unheard of in the South." A Black man fell in love with a white Soviet citizen and married her, although he could not take her with him when he returned home, knowing full well what fate awaited those in the South who were guilty of miscegenation and racial "degeneration."[85] And yet, even where the regime of white supremacy raged, a new climate was spreading: the Soviet Union and Stalin especially were looked upon with hope as the "new Lincoln" who, this time, would put a complete end to the enslavement of Blacks, the oppression, the brutalization, the humiliation, the violence and the lynchings that they were continuing to suffer.[86]

These hopes were not completely disappointed. Let us think of the times when an element of a regime of white supremacy comes to an end and the circumstances in which this happens. In December 1952, the

U.S. attorney general addressed a revealing letter to the Supreme Court urging it to deal with the question of integration in the public schools: "racial discrimination furnishes grist for the Communist propaganda mills, and it raises doubt even among friendly nations as to the intensity of our devotion to the democratic faith." Washington, observes the U.S. historian who has reconstructed this story, ran the risk of alienating the "colored races" not only in the East and the Third World but in the very heart of the United States. Even there, communist propaganda met with considerable success in its attempt to win Blacks to the "revolutionary cause," making them lose "faith in American institutions."[87] There is no doubt that concern for the objective challenge posed by Stalin's USSR and the influence it exerted on the peoples in the colonies and of colonial origin played an essential role in this event.

Thus, "Eastern Marxism," unlike much of the Western variety, understood how to illuminate the colonial barbarities of capitalism very well. This is not all. Remember that Lenin praised as "excellent" the "formulation" of Hegel's logic, according to which the universal must comprise itself in "the wealth of the particular."[88] True to this approach, personalities such as Lenin, Ho Chi Minh, Mao, and Castro never constructed a contradiction between patriotism and internationalism but have always seen in the liberation struggle of oppressed nations an essential moment in the path of internationalism and universalism, of what Gramsci calls "integral humanism." Not so, however, Western Marxism.

On the one hand—think of Althusser in particular—the categories "humanity," "people," and "nation" were eyed with suspicion, as if they were a betrayal of the class struggle. An attitude of superstitious purism that forgets that the categories "socialism," "revolution," and "working class" can also be turned in a conservative and even reactionary direction (the example of the National Socialist German Workers Party of unfortunate memory may suffice here). Althusser's concern can be countered with a forceful statement by Mao: "National struggle, in the final analysis, is a question of class struggle."[89] On the other hand—think, above all, of Adorno and, today, of Negri—the struggles for national liberation, which were placed in contradiction with internationalism and universalism, were reviled. It is no coincidence that the veterans of Western Marxism today are full of contempt for the efforts of countries such as China and Vietnam to consolidate their independence also in the economic field—in such a way that, as Deng Xiaoping declared, "a real contribution to humanity" can also be made.[90] Whether for one reason or another, because of a superficial conception of the class struggle or because of an abstract conception of the general, Western Marxism has mostly failed to grasp the unity of the universal and the particular.

On the one hand, this adherence to an abstract and pure idea of the universal has prevented an adequate understanding of national liberation movements (which continue to develop even after the seizure of power); on the other hand, it has led to the fact that a fundamental cause of the crisis of the "socialist camp" could not be understood. The break between the USSR and Yugoslavia in 1948, then the Soviet invasion of Hungary and Czechoslovakia, the near-wars or outright wars between the USSR and China, China and Vietnam, and Vietnam and Cambodia—all this shows how difficult, although indispensable, it is to reconcile internationalism (the universal) with the observance of national interests, national identity, national feelings (the particular). The Communist Party of China has, in its best moments alluded to this problem.[91] Western Marxism has almost always stereotypically understood these conflicts as confrontations between Stalinist despotism and the spirit of freedom, between bureaucracy and masses, or between the revolutionary consequences of one or another opportunism or revisionism, or, even more superficially, as proof that both fighting parties had nothing to do with "authentic" socialism and Marxism.

After all, Western Marxism has enjoyed its remoteness from power, as if this were a particularly favorable situation or the only possible prerequisite for unfolding the critical potencies of Marx's theory. While the view can become more sober, the remoteness from power and contempt for power can also cloud the view; they can complicate the understanding of the great global conflicts, as well as favor an idealistic attitude and, ultimately, an escape from history. This is the only way to explain Bloch's thesis that the bourgeois revolution "limited equality to the political." Even if we want to deal exclusively with the capitalist metropolis, it is a historically untenable claim; one need only point to discrimination against women and the right to vote.

Taken as a whole, Western Marxism has involuntarily represented two fundamental figures of Hegelian philosophy over the years. Insofar as it is satisfied with criticism and derives its *raison d'être* from criticism without facing the problem of formulating viable alternatives and creating a historical bloc that represents an alternative to the ruling one, it illustrates the all-knowing nature of wanting to be; if it enjoys its remoteness from power as a condition of its own purity, it embodies the beautiful soul. Perhaps it is no coincidence that today, there is a book that enjoys great popularity among the Western Left. Its title invites us to "change the world without taking power."[92] Here, the self-dissolution of Western Marxism ends up departing from the terrain of politics and settling in the land of religion.

Notes

INTRODUCTION

Nota bene: While we accept full responsibility for any errors, we are extremely grateful to all of the people who provided insightful feedback on this text and helped improve it, including Stefano G. Azzarà, Roland Boer, Steven Colatrella, Radhika Desai, Derek Ford, John Bellamy Foster, John Harfouch, Nazia Kazi, Weber Lin, Helmut-Harry Loewen, Aymeric Monville, Immanuel Ness, Jacques Pauwels, Christina Petterson, Jasper Saah, and members of Losurdo's family.

1. V. I. Lenin, *Collected Works*, vol. 22 (Moscow: Progress Publishers, 1974), 355–56.
2. Domenico Losurdo, *La izquierda ausente: Crisis, sociedad del espectáculo, guerra*, trans. Juan Vivanco (Barcelona: El Viejo Topo, 2015), 209. Here we are using terms like colonialism, neocolonialism, and imperialism in a rather general sense, similar to Losurdo, recognizing that these have taken multiple different, and sometimes overlapping, forms throughout history. At the same time, we are focusing on the specific colonial and neocolonial dynamics of imperialism as it was understood by V. I. Lenin, meaning "the monopoly stage of capitalism" when—among other things—"the territorial division of the whole world among the greatest capitalist powers is completed." *Essential Works of Lenin*, ed. Henry M. Christman (New York: Dover, 1987), 237.
3. Churchill added, for good measure, "I will not submit to be beaten by the baboons!" Cited in W. Mark Hamilton, "The Enigma of Russia," *Churchill Bulletin* 166, April 2022, https://winstonchurchill.org/publications/churchill-bulletin/bulletin-166-apr-2022/the-enigma-of-russia/.

4. See Losurdo, *La izquierda ausente*, 207.
5. On the U.S. national security state's postwar rehabilitation of fascists to fight Communists, see Gabriel Rockhill, "The U.S. Did Not Defeat Fascism in WWII, It Discretely Internationalized It," *CounterPunch*, October 16, 2020, https://www.counterpunch.org/2020/10/16/the-u-s-did-not-defeat-fascism-in-wwii-it-discretely-internationalized-it/.
6. For information on Losurdo's political activism, see Andreas Wehr, "Der Entzauberer des Liberalismus," *Telepolis*, November 1, 2021, https://www.heise.de/tp/features/Der-Entzauberer-des-Liberalismus-6237699.html and Guido Ligouri, "Domenico Losurdo, A Marxist Philosopher Against the Current," *Verso Blog*, July 1, 2018, https://www.versobooks.com/blogs/3903-domenico-losurdo-a-marxist-philosopher-against-the-current.
7. See Domenico Losurdo, *Fuir l'histoire: La révolution russe et la révolution chinoise aujourd'hui*, trans. Ludmila Acone and Aymeric Monville (Pantin, France: Le Temps des Cerises, 2007), 221.
8. Wehr, "Der Entzauberer des Liberalismus." We are grateful to Helmut-Harry Loewen for having drawn our attention to Brielmayer's important role in Losurdo's research and writing, as well as to this text by Wehr.
9. We would like to express our gratitude to Roland Boer and Christina Peterson for sharing their translation of this lecture with us, as well as to the Losurdo family for granting us the rights to publish it.
10. See Stefano G. Azzarà, *L'humanité commune: Dialectique hégélienne, critique du libéralisme et reconstruction du matérialisme historique chez Domenico Losurdo*, trans. Aymeric Monville (Paris: Éditions Delga, 2011), 160.
11. For a fascinating and insightful analysis of the history of the Chinese reception of Western Marxism, which works through a voluminous body of literature unavailable in English, see Roland Boer, "The Chinese Reception of Western Marxism: From Wary Onlookers to Confident Participants on the World Stage," *Fudan Journal of the Humanities and Social Sciences* (September 5, 2023), https://link.springer.com/article/10.1007/s40647-023-00389-7.
12. Evald Ilyenkov, "From the Marxist-Leninist Point of View," in *Marx and the Western World*, ed. Nicholas Lobkowicz (Notre Dame, IN: University of Notre Dame Press, 1967), 391–407.
13. On Western Marxism's purity fetish, see Carlos L. Garrido, *The Purity Fetish and the Crisis of Western Marxism* (Dubuque, IA: Midwestern Marx Publishing Press, 2023).
14. See Domenico Losurdo, *Nietzsche, the Aristocratic Rebel: Intellectual Biography and Critical Balance-Sheet*, trans. Gregor Benton (Chicago: Haymarket Books, 2021).
15. Here is a non-exhaustive list of some of the important critiques of these

trends: Aijaz Ahmad, *In Theory: Nations, Classes, Literatures* (New York: Verso, 1992); Neil Larsen, *Reading North by South: On Latin American Literature, Culture, and Politics* (Minneapolis: University of Minnesota Press, 1995); E. San Juan, *Beyond Postcolonial Theory* (New York: St. Martin's Press, 1998); Adolph Reed Jr., *Class Notes: Posing as Politics and Other Thoughts on the American Scene* (New York: New Press, 2001); Benita Parry, *Postcolonial Studies: A Materialist Critique* (New York: Routledge, 2004); Antonio Y. Vázquez Arroyo, "Critical Theory, Colonialism, and the Historicity of Thought," *Constellations* 25 (March 2018): 54–70, https://doi.org/10.1111/1467-8675.12348; Martha E. Giménez, *Marx, Women and Capitalist Social Reproduction* (Chicago: Haymarket Books, 2018), 1–110, 278–362; Annie Olaloku-Teriba, "Afro-Pessimism and the (Un)logic of Anti-Blackness," *Historical Materialism* 26/2 (2018): 96–122; Gaya Markaran and Pierre Gaussens, coord., *Piel blanca, máscaras negras: Crítica de la razón decolonial* (Mexico City: Bajo Tierra and Centro Centro de Investigaciones sobre América Latina y el Caribe-Universidad Nacional Autónoma de México, 2020); Nino Brown and Derek Ford, "Teaching Politically and the Problem of Afropessimism," *Black Agenda Report*, September 29, 2021, https://blackagendareport.com/teaching-politically-and-problem-afropessimism; Tita Barahona, "Judith Butler, la pope del 'feminismo' postmoderno, y su apoyo al capitalismo yanqui," *Canarias semanal*, April 7, 2022, https://canarias-semanal.org/art/29396/judith-butler-la-pope-del-feminismo-postmoderno-y-su-apoyo-al-capitalismo-yanqui; Adolph Reed Jr., "Afropessimism, or Black Studies as a Class Project," *Nonsite* 40 (September 2022), https://nonsite.org/afropessimism-or-black-studies-as-a-class-project.
16. V. I. Lenin, *Collected Works*, vol. 16 (Moscow: Progress Publishers, 1977), 332.
17. Perry Anderson, *Considerations on Western Marxism* (London: Verso, 1989), 42 (Anderson's emphasis).
18. Ibid., 42.
19. Ibid., 20, 56, 55.
20. Ibid., 78.
21. Ibid., 78–79.
22. Ibid., 94. Anderson insists on the purported intellectual superiority of Western Marxists at numerous points in the book, writing, for instance: "The historical experience their work articulated," meaning one of practical failure, "was … in certain critical respects the most *advanced* in the world–encompassing the highest forms of the capitalist economy, the oldest industrial proletariats, and the longest intellectual traditions of socialism." Ibid., 93–94, Anderson's emphasis. In his virtual sequel to *Considerations on Western Marxism*, he criticizes the "atrophy of living socialist politics"

and claims that Marxist philosophy in the West achieved "a general plateau of sophistication far beyond its medial levels of the past." *In the Tracks of Historical Materialism* (London: Verso, 1984), 17.
23. See, for instance, Anderson, *Considerations*, 42, 118; and Anderson, *In the Tracks*, 89, 97.
24. On Lenin's contributions and "limitations," see Anderson, *Considerations*, 11–12, 19.
25. In relation to Losurdo, it is noteworthy that Anderson condemns, with no empirical evidence to support his claim, "the disastrous fixation with China as an alternative model of post-revolutionary society to the USSR." *In the Tracks*, 19, also see 88–89.
26. It is worth noting, albeit in passing, that Anderson mischaracterizes the history of the woman question and ecology in actually existing socialism. Both of these issues, and in particular the first, have been the subject of much more rigorous historical analysis in the works of Losurdo.
27. Anderson, *In the Tracks*, 96.
28. Ibid., 97.
29. Nicos Poulantzas, *Classes in Contemporary Capitalism*, trans. David Fernbach (London: Verso, 1979), 297.
30. The Editors, "Notes from the Editors," *Monthly Review* 73/1 (May 01, 2023), https://monthlyreview.org/2021/05/01/mr-073-01-2021-05_0/.
31. See Bernard Shaw, *Fabianism and the Empire: A Manifesto of the Fabian Society* (London: Andesite Press, 2017).
32. Zak Cope, *Divided World Divided Class* (Montreal: Kersplebedeb, 2015), 148.
33. *Essential Works of Lenin: "What Is To Be Done?" and Other Writings*, ed. Henry M. Christman (New York: Dover, 1987), 254.
34. V. I. Lenin, *'Left-Wing' Communism, an Infantile Disorder* (Peking: Foreign Languages Press, 1970), 13.
35. V. I. Lenin, *Collected Works*, vol. 10 (Moscow: Progress Publishers, 1978), 48.
36. Karl Marx and Frederick Engels, *Collected Works*, vol. 50 (New York: International Publishers, 2004), 164 (translation slightly modified).
37. See Losurdo, *Fuir l'histoire*, 107.
38. V. I. Lenin, *Collected Works*, vol. 28 (Moscow: Progress Publishers, 1974), 242. "Opportunism," Lenin goes on to write, "means sacrificing the fundamental interests of the masses to the temporary interests of an insignificant minority of the workers or, in other words, an alliance between a section of the workers and the bourgeoisie, directed against the mass of the proletariat. . . . Opportunism was engendered in the course of decades by the special features in the period of the development of capitalism, when the comparatively peaceful and cultured life of a stratum of privileged workingmen 'bourgeoisified' them, gave them crumbs from the table of their national

capitalists, and isolated them from the suffering, misery and revolutionary temper of the impoverished and ruined masses" (242–43).

39. See V. I. Lenin, *Imperialism, the Highest Stage of Capitalism, a Popular Outline* (New York: International Publishers, 2008).

40. See Andy Higginbottom, "Superexplotación laboral, liberación negra y pensamiento comunista," in *Teorías del imperialismo y la dependencia desde el sur global*, ed. Néstor Kohan (Buenos Aires and Ituzaingó: Amauta Insurgente, Cienflores, and Instituto de Estudios de América Latina y el Caribe, 2022), 299–322; Pablo González Casanova, "Colonialismo interno [una redefinición]," in *La teoría marxista hoy. Problemas y perspectivas*, ed. Atilio A. Boron (Buenos Aires: CLACSO, 2006), 409–34; and Antonio Gramsci's writings on the "Southern Question."

41. See Stefan Müller-Doohm, *Adorno: A Biography*, trans. Rodney Livingstone (Cambridge: Polity Press, 2005), 415 and Gabriel Rockhill, "The CIA & the Frankfurt School's Anti-Communism," *Los Angeles Review of Books*, "The Philosophical Salon," June 27, 2022, https://thephilosophicalsalon.com/the-cia-the-frankfurt-schools-anti-communism/. It should nowise be surprising that one of the core features of Western Marxism is its rejection of actually existing socialism. Looking down on it with all of the requisite colonial condescension, Western Marxists tend to denigrate it, enumerate its failures, and generally dismiss it in terms not dissimilar to those of the dominant ideology. Karl Kautsky, one of the leaders of the Second International, lost no time in contributing to this agenda only weeks after the October Revolution of 1917, claiming that "what is occurring in Russia is in fact the last of the bourgeois and not the first of the socialist revolutions." Cited in Domenico Losurdo, *Class Struggle: A Political and Philosophical History*, trans. Gregory Elliott (New York: Palgrave Macmillan, 2016), 199.

42. Michel Foucault, *Dits et écrits*, vol. 3 (Paris: Éditions Gallimard, 1994), 398 (our emphasis). For a sustained critique of Michel Foucault along these lines, see Gabriel Rockhill, "Foucault: The Faux Radical," *Los Angeles Review of Books*, "The Philosophical Salon," October 12, 2020, https://thephilosophicalsalon.com/foucault-the-faux-radical/, as well as Gabriel Rockhill, "Foucault, Genealogy, Counter-History," *Theory & Event* 23/1 (January 2020): 85–119.

43. "It is only possible to sympathize with the Vietnamese, the Palestinians or other people," Losurdo writes, "as long as they are oppressed and humiliated; it is only possible to support a liberation struggle as long as it loses!" *La cuestión communista: Historia y futuro de una idea*, trans. Juan Vivanco (Barcelona: El Viejo Topo, 2021), 196–97. He echoes, in this regard, Lenin's critical summary of Karl Kautsky's message to the workers: "Fight, but *don't dare win!*" *Collected Works*, vol. 28 (Moscow: Progress Publishers, 1981), 260.

44. Thomas Moller Nielsen, "Unrepentant Charlatanism (with a Response by Slavoj Žižek)," *Los Angeles Review of Books*, "The Philosophical Salon," November 25, 2019, https://thephilosophicalsalon.com/unrepentant-charlatanism-with-a-response-by-slavoj-zizek/.
45. On the Yugoslav Communist Party's accusations, see the BBC documentary *The Death of Yugoslavia*, https://www.youtube.com/watch?v=H3VyGPu6PKc. Regarding Žižek's weekly column for *Mladina*, see the *Encyclopedia Britannica*'s entry on him (https://www.britannica.com/biography/Slavoj-Zizek) and Ernesto Laclau, "Preface," Slavoj Žižek, *The Sublime Object of Ideology* (London: Verso, 1989), xi.
46. See the segment of the 1990 televised election debate, archived here: https://www.youtube.com/watch?v=rGfNeIRQ350. For a thorough overview and critique of Žižek's anti-communist politics, see Gabriel Rockhill, "Capitalism's Court Jester: Slavoj Žižek," *CounterPunch*, January 2, 2023, https://www.counterpunch.org/2023/01/02/capitalisms-court-jester-slavoj-zizek/.
47. Karl Marx and Frederick Engels, *Collected Works*, vol. 5 (New York: International Publishers, 1976), 49.
48. P.-A. Boutang, *L'Abécédaire de Gilles Deleuze*, 2004, transcribed here: https://www.oeuvresouvertes.net/spip.php?article910, accessed on February 27, 2023.
49. Thomas W. Braden, "I'm Glad the CIA Is 'Immoral,'" *Saturday Evening Post*, May 20, 1967.
50. See Hugh Wilford, *The Mighty Wurlitzer: How the CIA Played America* (Cambridge, MA: Harvard University Press, 2009). Also see Frances Stonor Saunders, *The Cultural Cold War: The CIA and the World of Arts and Letters* (New York: New Press, 2013) and Gabriel Rockhill, "The CIA Reads French Theory: On the Intellectual Labor of Dismantling the Cultural Left," *Los Angeles Review of Books*, "The Philosophical Salon," February 27, 2017, https://thephilosophicalsalon.com/the-cia-reads-french-theory-on-the-intellectual-labor-of-dismantling-the-cultural-left/.
51. The Church Committee Report was tightly controlled and overseen by the CIA itself, so it is highly likely that the numbers were and are much higher. The man in charge of investigating the CIA's ties to academia for the Church Committee, William Bader, was himself a former CIA officer (it is well known that company men never really leave the agency). Moreover, Braden's famous article on the subject referenced above was vetted by the CIA and shows every sign of being a limited hangout, meaning a frank admission of what activists and investigative journalists had already demonstrated, in order to try and nip the revelations in the bud and control the narrative. It is therefore likely that the CIA's involvement has been even more expansive than his straightforward admission suggests.
52. Poulantzas, *Classes in Contemporary Capitalism*, 292.

53. See *Foreign Policy* (December 2012), https://web.archive.org/web/20121201034713/http://www.foreignpolicy.com/articles/2012/11/26/the_fp_100_global_thinkers?page=0,55#thinker92.
54. Ernesto Che Guevara, *Che Guevara Reader: Writings on Politics & Revolution*, ed. David Deutschmann and María del Carmen Ariet (Havana: Ocean Press, 2013), 340.
55. For piercing critiques of the work of Hardt and Negri, see Néstor Kohan, *Toni Negri y los desafíos de Imperio* (Madrid: Campo de Ideas S.L., 2012) and Atilio A. Boron, *Imperio & imperialismo: Una lectura crítica de Michael Hardt y Antonio Negri* (Barcelona: El Viejo Topo, 2003).
56. Quoted in Wolfgang Kraushaar, ed., *Frankfurter Schule und Studentenbewegung: Von der Flaschenpost zum Molotowcocktail 1946–1995*, vol. 1: *Chronik* (Hamburg: Rogner & Bernhard GmbH & Co. Verlags KG, 1998), 252-53.
57. Losurdo, *La izquierda ausente*, 272. Žižek also openly supported NATO's bombings of defenseless civilian populations and socialist infrastructure in Yugoslavia, whose real objective was the destruction and de facto colonization of the only country in the region that had not shed what remained of its socialism: "So, precisely as a Leftist, my answer to the dilemma 'Bomb or not?' is: not yet ENOUGH bombs, and they are TOO LATE." Cited in Ian Parker, *Slavoj Žižek: A Critical Introduction* (London: Pluto Press, 2004), 35. This resounding endorsement for increasing the illegal mass murder of civilians was made in a draft article that circulated online, but he took the same basic position in a published interview: "I have always been in favor of military intervention from the West." Geert Lovink, "Civil Society, Fanaticism, and Digital Reality: A Conversation with Slavoj Žižek," *Ctheory*, February 21, 1996, https://journals.uvic.ca/index.php/ctheory/article/view/14649/5529.
58. See Losurdo, *La izquierda ausente*, 19-55.
59. For two excellent overviews of contemporary China that are very much in line with Losurdo's work, see Cheng Enfu, *China's Economic Dialectic: The Original Aspiration of Reform* (New York: International Publishers, 2019) and Carlos Martinez, *The East Is Still Red: Chinese Socialism in the 21st Century* (Glasgow: Praxis Press, 2023).
60. On this theme, see in particular Losurdo, *Class Struggle*.
61. Losurdo, *Fuir l'histoire*, 183.
62. Losurdo, *La izquierda ausente*, 317.
63. See Vicente Navarro, "Has Socialism Failed? An Analysis of Health Indicators under Capitalism and Socialism," *Science & Society* 57/1 (Spring 1993): 6–30. Also see Shirley Cereseto and Howard Waitzkin, "Capitalism, Socialism, and the Physical Quality of Life," *International Journal of Health Services* 16/4 (1986): 643-58.

64. John Ross, *China's Great Road: Lessons for Marxist Theory and Socialist Practices* (New York: 1804 Books, 2021), 17.
65. Ross, *China's Great Road*, 14. Also see the extensive data on China's extraordinary growth and people-centered economy in Enfu, *China's Economic Dialectic*.
66. Tings Chak, Li Jianhua, Lilian Zhang, "Serve the People: The Eradication of Extreme Poverty in China," *Tricontinental* (July 23, 2021), https://thetricontinental.org/studies-1-socialist-construction/. Also see Martinez, *The East Is Still Red*, 89–107.
67. "The Belt and Road Initiative at 10: Debt Trap or Development?" *Dongsheng News*, https://dongshengnews.org/en/belt-and-road-initiative-at-10/.
68. Xi Jinping, *The Governance of China*, vol. 3 (Beijing: Foreign Languages Press, 2020), 54.
69. John Bellamy Foster, "Ecological Civilization, Ecological Revolution," *Monthly Review* 74/5 (October 1, 2022), https://monthlyreview.org/2022/10/01/ecological-civilization-ecological-revolution/.
70. Ibid. On this topic, also see Martinez, *The East Is Still Red*, 135–66.
71. Foster, "Ecological Civilization, Ecological Revolution."
72. In *China's Economic Dialectic*, Cheng Enfu likewise provides an excellent analysis of Chinese development, with highly relevant critiques and proposals.
73. Losurdo, *Class Struggle*, 303. For Losurdo, the "Columbian epoch" refers to a historical period of Western dominance that was inaugurated with the European colonization of the Americas.
74. Xi Jinping, *The Governance of China*, vol. 4 (Beijing: Foreign Languages Press, 2022), 297.
75. See Slavoj Žižek, "Pacifism Is the Wrong Response to the War in Ukraine," *The Guardian*, June 21, 2022, https://www.theguardian.com/commentisfree/2022/jun/21/pacificsm-is-the-wrong-response-to-the-war-in-ukraine.
76. See Domenico Losurdo, *Antonio Gramsci: Del liberalismo al comunismo crítico*, trans. Juan Vivanco (Madrid: Ediciones del oriente y del mediterráneo, 2015).
77. For an insightful overview of some of the important work that is being done on this front, including by the author himself, see Immanuel Ness, "Anti-Imperialism and Western Marxism," *International Critical Thought* (forthcoming).
78. Lenin's critique of Kautsky focuses on his "objective position" in global class struggle, very much like Losurdo's analysis of Western Marxism. This particular passage presages key aspects of Losurdo's account, and Lenin's book is very much worth reading or rereading alongside the current work: "Kautsky takes from Marxism what is acceptable to the liberals, to the bourgeoisie … and discards, passes over in silence, glosses over all that in

Marxism which is *unacceptable* to the bourgeoisie (the revolutionary violence of the proletariat against the bourgeoisie for the latter's destruction). That is why Kautsky, by virtue of his objective position and irrespective of what his subjective convictions may be, inevitably proves to be a lackey of the bourgeoisie." *Collected Works*, vol. 28, 242–43.

PREMISE: WHAT IS WESTERN MARXISM?

1. Perry Anderson, *Considerations on Western Marxism* (London: Verso, 1976), 36, 39, 45, 116.
2. Ibid., 44.
3. Ibid., 40.
4. Maurice Merleau-Ponty, *Adventures of the Dialectic* (Evanston, IL: Northwestern University Press, 1973), 223–24.
5. Ibid., 224.
6. Ibid., 223.
7. Ibid., 222, 224.
8. Domenico Losurdo, *Antonio Gramsci dal liberalismo al "comunismo critico"* (Rome: Gamberetti, 1997).
9. See Max Horkheimer, "The Authoritarian State," *Telos*, 15:3 (1973, originally published in 1942).
10. Max Horkhheimer, "Marx oggi," in *La società di transizione*, ed. W. Brede (Turin: Einaudi, 1979), 154, 160. Untranslated work, translated here from the Italian.

PART I. 1914 AND 1917: THE BIRTH OF WESTERN AND EASTERN MARXISM

1. Giuseppe Fiori, *Vita di Antonio Gramsci* (Bari: Laterza, 1966), 128–29.
2. Georg Lukács, *Record of a Life: An Autobiography* (New York: Shocken Books, 1983), 53, 44.
3. Francesco Coppellotti. *Critical Note (Nota critica)* in Ernst Bloch, *The Spirit of Utopia,* 1st ed., 370. The first edition remains untranslated into English, therefore all references to it have been translated from the Italian of Losurdo's text. Citations in the second edition, which was translated, here, use the published English second edition and its language.
4. Ernst Bloch, *The Principle of Hope,* trans. Neville Plaice, Stephen Plaice, and Paul Knight (Cambridge, MA: MIT Press, 1995).
5. Ernst Bloch, *The Spirit of Utopia* (Palo Alto: Stanford University Press, 2000), 236, 240.
6. Mike Davis, *Late Victorian Holocausts: El Nino Famines and the Making of the Third World* (New York: Verso, 2001), 6.
7. Jacques Gernet, *Il mondo cinese: Dalle prime civiltà alla Repubblica popolare*, trans. V. Pegna (Turin: Einaudi, 1978), 615.

8. Jean Chesneaux, Marianne Bastid, and Marie-Claire Bergere, *China from the Opium Wars to the 1911 Revolution*, trans. Anne Destenay (Great Britain: Harvester Press; New York: Pantheon Books, 1977), 37.
9. Sun Yat-Sen, *The Three Principles of the People*, trans. F. W. Price (Vancouver: Soul Care Publishing, 2011), 55–57.
10. Ho Chi Minh, *On Revolution: Selected Writings 1920–1966* (New York: Praeger, 1967), 20–22.
11. V. I. Lenin, *Collected Works*, vol. 15 (Moscow: Progress Publishers, 1973), 182–88.
12. Marx's Speech on the Irish Question in *Marx and Engels, Ireland and the Irish Question* (Moscow: Progress Publishers 1971), 152; *Marx-Engels Collected Works*, vol. 21 (Moscow: Progress Publishers, 1964), 413.
13. Georg Lukács, *Epistolario 1902–1917*, ed. É. Karádi and É. Fekete (Rome: Editori Riuniti, 1984), 366, 360.
14. Walter Benjamin, *Gesammelte Schriften*, vol. 2.1, ed. R. Tiedemann and H. Schweppenhäuser (Frankfurt: Suhrkamp Verlag, 1972–99), 186.
15. Michael Löwy, *Redemption and Utopia: Jewish Libertarian Thought in Central Europe* (London: Verso, 2017), 224.
16. Bloch, *The Spirit of Utopia*, 239.
17. V. I. Lenin, *Complete Works*, vol. 27, 393.
18. V. I. Lenin, *State and Revolution* (Beijing: Foreign Languages Press, 1976), 30.
19. V. I. Lenin, *Complete Works*, vol. 20 (Moscow: Progress Publishers, 1972), 393–454.
20. Sun Yat-Sen, *The Three Principles of the People*, 26.
21. Edward Carr, *The Bolshevik Revolution 1917–1923*, vol. 3 (New York: W. W. Norton, 1953), 503–504.
22. Mao Zedong, *Selected Works*, vol. 4 (Beijing: Foreign Languages Press, 1965), 413.
23. Edgar Snow, *Red Star Over China* (New York: Grove Press, 1968), 143.
24. Mao Zedong, *Selected Works*, vol. 4, 455–56, 458.
25. Mao Zedong, *On Diplomacy* (Beijing: Foreign Languages Press, 1998), 87–88.
26. Alain Ruscio, *Ho Chi Minh* (Paris: Editions L'Harmattan, 1991); *Le Procès de la colonisation française* (Montreuil: Le Temps des Cerises, 2012), 383.
27. Jean Lacouture, *Ho Chi Minh: A Political Biography* (London: Penguin Books, 1968), 80.
28. Ho Chi Minh, in ibid., 31.
29. Ibid.
30. "The Last Testament of Ho Chi Minh," *Antioch Review* 29/ 4 (Winter, 1969–1970), 497–99.
31. Bloch, *The Spirit of Utopia*, 240, 243.

32. Ibid., 298.
33. Walter Benjamin, *Selected Works*, vol. 1: *1913–1926*, ed. Marcus Bullock and Michael W. Jennings (Cambridge, MA: Harvard University Press, 1996), 246.
34. Orlando Figes, *A People's Tragedy: The Russian Revolution 1891–1924* (New York: Random House, 1996), 771.
35. Joseph Stalin, *Economic Problems of Socialism in the USSR* (Beijing: Foreign Languages Press, 1972). Available at https://www.marxists.org/reference/archive/stalin/works/1951/economic-problems/index.htm.
36. Edgar Snow, *Red Star Over China* (New York: Grove Press, 1968), 241.
37. Mao Zedong, *Selected Works*, vol. 2, 215.
38. Mao Zedong, *Selected Works*, vol. 3, 132–33.
39. Truong Chinh, *Ho Chi Minh*, trans. I. Bassignano (Rome: Editori Riuniti, 1969), 8. Translated from Italian.
40. Enrica Collotti Pischel, *Storia della rivoluzione cinese* (Rome: Editori Riuniti, 1973), 99–100, 159–60.
41. Snow, *Red Star Over China*, 159.
42. Ibid., 167.
43. Deng Xiaoping, "Urgent Tasks of China's Third Generation of Collective Leadership" in *Selected Works*, vol. 3: 1982–1992 (Beijing: Foreign Languages Press, 1989). Available at https://dengxiaopingworks.wordpress.com/2013/03/18/urgent-tasks-of-chinas-third-generation-of-collective-leadership/.
44. Nikolai Bukharin, "Toward a Theory of the Imperialist State," in *Selected Writings on the State and the Transition to Socialism*, ed. Richard Day et al. (Armonk, NY: M.E. Sharpe, 1982), 31.
45. Walter Benjamin, "Theses on the Philosophy of History," in *Illuminations*, ed. Hannah Arendt (New York: Shocken Books, 1955).
46. Georg Lukács, *History and Class Consciousness* (Cambridge, MA: MIT Press, 1967), 136.
47. Perry Anderson, *Considerations on Western Marxism* (London and New York: Verso, 1976), 56.
48. Simone Weil, *Oppression and Liberty* (New York: Routledge, 1958), 53.
49. Max Horkheimer, "The Authoritarian State," in *Telos* 15/3 (1973): 3.
50. Mikhail Bakunin, "Equal Opportunity in Education," in *Essential Bakunin*, 1869, The Anarchist Library, https://theanarchistlibrary.org/library/michail-bakunin-equal-opportunity-in-education. The indented quote is from this source.
51. Theodor Adorno and Max Horkheimer, *Dialectic of Enlightenment* (Palo Alto: Stanford University Press: 2002), 67–68.
52. Maurice Merleau-Ponty, *Adventures of the Dialectic* (Evanston, IL: Northwestern University Press, 1973), 90.

53. Karl Marx and Frederich Engels, *Manifesto of the Communist Party*, in *The Marx-Engels Reader*, ed. Robert C. Tucker (New York: W.W. Norton, 1978).
54. Ernst Bloch, *Geist der Utopie* (untranslated 1st ed.) (Frankfurt: Suhrkamp Verlag, 1971), 316-17. Translated from the Italian.
55. Benjamin, "Theses on the Philosophy of History," 263-64.
56. Domenico Losurdo, *Antonio Gramsci dal liberalismo al "comunismo critico"* (Rome: Gamberetti, 1997).
57. Lukács, *History and Class Consciousness*, xiii-xiv.
58. Michael Hardt and Toni Negri, *Empire* (Cambridge, MA: Harvard University, 2000), 413.
59. Bloch, *The Spirit of Utopia*, 238-39.
60. Walter Benjamin, *Selected Works*, vol. 1: *1913-1926*, ed. Marcus Bullock and Michael W. Jennings (Cambridge, MA: Harvard University Press, 1996), 246, 249.
61. Ruscio, *Introduction to Ho Chi Minh: Le Procès de la colonisation française* (Montreuil: Le Temps des Cerises, 1998), 13.
62. Ho Chi Minh, *The Case Against French Colonialism by Nguyen-Ai-Quoc (Ho Chi Minh)*, trans. Joshua Leinsdorf (Edinburgh: Pentland Press, Ltd., 2017), 35.
63. Ibid., 36.
64. Ibid., 20.
65. Mao, *Selected Works*, vol. 4, 150.
66. Ibid., 315.
67. Ibid., 408.
68. V. I. Lenin, *Collected Works*, vol. 20 (Moscow: Progress Publishers, 1972), 480-84.
69. V. I. Lenin, *Selected Works*, vol. 3 (Moscow: Progress Publishers, 1977), 442-43.
70. Ibid., 714-26.
71. V. I. Lenin, *Collected Works*, vol. 18 (Moscow: Progress Publishers, 1975), 594-95.
72. V. I. Lenin, *Collected Works*, vol. 20, 235-77.
73. Bloch, *The Spirit of Utopia*, 319.
74. Lacouture, *Ho Chi Minh: A Political Biography*, 18.
75. Ruscio, 21.
76. Ho Chi Minh, *On Revolution: Selected Writings 1920-1966*, 21.
77. Bloch, *The Spirit of Utopia*, 244.
78. In Stephen Kotkin, *Stalin: Paradoxes of Power, vol. 1, 1878-1928* (New York: Penguin, 2014), 652.
79. Ho Chi Minh, *On Revolution: Selected Writings 1920-1966*, 52.
80. In Wyn Craig Wade, *The Fiery Cross: The Ku Klux Klan in America* (New York: Simon and Schuster, 1997), 203-4.

81. Snow, *Red Star Over China*, 100.
82. Antonio Gramsci. *Cronache torinesi 1913–1917*, ed. S. Caprioglio (Torino: Einaudi, 1980), 175; Antonio Gramsci, *L'Ordine Nuovo 1919–1920*, ed. V. Gerratana and A. A. Santucci (Torino: Einaudi, 1987), 520.

PART II. SOCIALISM VERSUS CAPITALISM, OR ANTICOLONIALISM VERSUS COLONIALISM?

1. V. I. Lenin, *Selected Works*, vol. 1 (Moscow: Progress Publishers, 1977), 634, 726.
2. Lenin, *Collected Works*, vol. 23, 236–53.
3. V. I. Lenin, *Collected Works*, vol. 21 (Moscow: Progress Publishers, 1975), 295–338.
4. V. I. Lenin, *Collected Works*, vol. 22, 320–60.
5. V. I. Lenin, *Collected Works*, vol. 20, 393–454.
6. V. I. Lenin, *Collected Works*, vol. 23, 28–76.
7. V. I. Lenin, *Collected Works*, vol. 22, 320–60.
8. Ibid.
9. V. I. Lenin, *Collected Works*, vol. 21, 102–6.
10. Ibid., 407–14.
11. V. I. Lenin, *Collected Works*, vol. 22, 305–19.
12. V. I. Lenin, "Imperialism: The Highest Stage of Capitalism," in V. I. Lenin, *Selected Works*, vol. 1, 702.
13. Adolf Hitler, *Mein Kampf* (London and New York: Hurst and Blackett, 1939), 492.
14. Joseph Goebbels, *The Goebbels Diaries 1942–43* (New York: Doubleday, 1948), 445.
15. Gerhard Schreiber, *La vendetta tedesca 1943–1945: Le rappresaglie naziste in Italia*, trans. M. Buttarelli (Milan: Mondadori, 2000), 21–24.
16. V. I. Lenin, *Collected Works*, vol. 27, 68–75.
17. Joseph Stalin 1954, *Works*, vol. 3, *March–October 1917* (Moscow: Foreign Languages Publishing House, 1954).
18. Lothrop Stoddard, *The Rising Tide of Color Against White World-Supremacy* (New York: Charles Scribner and Sons, 1920), 221.
19. Oswald Spengler, *Hour of Decision* (New Delhi: Gyan Books Pvt. Ltd., 1934), 213.
20. Adolf Hitler, https://www.historylearningsite.co.uk/modern-world-history-1918-to-1980/weimar-germany/text-of-the-dusseldorf-speech-of-1932/.
21. David Olusoga and Caspar W. Erichsen, *The Kaiser's Holocaust: Germany's Forgotten Genocide and the Colonial Roots of Nazism* (New York: Faber and Faber, 2010), 327.
22. Ernst Bloch, *The Spirit of Utopia*, 2nd ed. (Palo Alto: Stanford University Press, 2000, originally published in 1923), 160.

23. "Engels to Nikolai Danielson, September 22, 1892," in *Marx-Engels Correspondence* (New York: International Publishers, 1968).
24. Stephen Kotkin, *Stalin: Paradoxes of Power,* vol. 1: *1878–1928* (New York: Penguin, 2014), 66.
25. Mao Zedong, "On Coalition Government," in *Selected Works,* vol. 3 (Beijing: Foreign Language Press, 1965), 307.
26. Mao Zedong, "On the People's Democratic Dictatorship," in Mao Zedong, *Selected Works,* vol. 4, 413.
27. Mao Zedong, "The Bankruptcy of the Idealist Conception of History," in *Selected Works,* vol. 4, 453.
28. Mao Zedong, "On New Democracy," in Mao Zedong 1965, *Selected Works,* vol. 2, 344.
29. Mao Zedong, *Rivoluzione e costruzione: Scritti e discorsi 1949–1957*, ed. M. Arena Regis and F. Coccia (Turin: Einaudi, 1957/1979), 548.
30. Deng Xiaoping, "Urgent Tasks of China's Third Generation of Leadership," June 1989, *Selected Works,* vol. 3: *1989–1992*; "Uphold the Four Cardinal Principles," vol. 2, March 1979, https://dengxiaopingworks.wordpress.com.
31. "We must promote education in the four cardinal principles and adhere to the policies of reform and opening to the outside world." Deng Xiaoping, *Selected Works,* vol. 3: *1982–1992,* https://dengxiaopingworks.wordpress.com.
32. Niall Ferguson, *The War of the World: Twentieth-Century Conflict and the Descent of the West* (London and New York: Penguin, 2006), 637–38.
33. [Editor's note: We were not able to find the exact source Losurdo used for this quote. Che Guevara made statements like this on many occasions. One can be found here: Che Guevara, "Afro-Asian Solidarity," Speech for the Organization of Afro-Asian Solidarity, Algeria, February 24, 1965.]
34. Bloch, *The Spirit of Utopia*, 318–19.
35. C. L. R. James, *The Black Jacobins* (New York: Vintage, 1963), 397.
36. Hosea Jaffe, *Three Hundred Years: A History of South Africa* (Capetown: Unity Movement History Series, 1988), 144.
37. Mao Zedong, "On Protracted War," *Selected Works*, vol. 2., 149.
38. Joseph Stalin, "Report on the Work of the Central Committee to the Eighteenth Congress of the C.P.S.U.(B.)," in *Works*, vol. 14 (London: Red Star Press, 1978).
39. Mao Zedong, "The Identity of Interests Between the Soviet Union and All Mankind," *Selected Works*, vol. 2, 281–82.

PART III. WESTERN MARXISM AND THE ANTICOLONIAL REVOLUTION: A MEETING THAT DIDN'T TAKE PLACE

1. Norberto Bobbio, "Libertà e potere," *in Politica e cultura* (Turin: Einaud, 1954), 269–82, 281.

2. Norberto Bobbio, "Invito al colloquio," in *Politica e cultura* (Turin: Einaudi, 1977), 15–31, 26–27.
3. Ibid., 24, 27.
4. Norberto Bobbio, "Difesa della libertà," in *Politica e cultura* (Turin: Einaudi, 1977), 47–57, 48–49.
5. Bobbio 1977, 24.
6. Ibid., 23.
7. Norberto Bobbio, "Della libertà dei moderni paragonata a quella dei posteri," in *Politica e Cultura* (Turin: Einaudi, 1954), 160–94, 164.
8. Ibid., 280.
9. Andre Fontaine, *History of the Cold War from the Korean War to the Present* (New York: Pantheon Books, 1968), 98.
10. Palmiro Togliatti, *Opere*, vol. 5, ed. E. Ragionieri (Rome: Editori Riuniti, 1984), 866, 868.
11. Ibid., 869.
12. Norberto Bobbio, "Cultura vecchia e politica nuova," in *Politica e cultura*, 195–210, 265.
13. David Brion Davis, *The Slave Power Conspiracy and the Paranoid Style* (Baton Rouge: Louisiana State University Press, 1982).
14. Bobbio, "Della libertà dei moderni paragonata a quella dei posteri," 161.
15. John Stuart Mill, *On Liberty* (Ontario: Batoche Books, 2001), 14; Domenico Losurdo, *Controstoria del liberalism* (Rome-Bari: Laterza, 2005), chap. I, sec. 1 and 3, chap. 2, sec. 4, and chap. 7, sec. 3. Available in English: *Liberalism: A Counter-History* (London:Verso, 2014).
16. Lucio Colletti, *From Rousseau to Lenin: Studies in Ideology and Society*, trans. John Merrington and Judith White (New York: Monthly Review Press, 1973), 207.
17. Lucio Colletti, *Tramonto dell'ideologia* (Rome-Bari: Laterza, 1980), 73.
18. Ibid., 9–10.
19. Karl Marx, "The Future Results of British Rule in India," *New York Daily Tribune*, January 22, 1853, in Karl Marx and Frederick Engels, *On Colonialism* (New York: International Publishers, 1972), 86.
20. Colletti, *Tramonto dell'ideologia*, 7, 65–66.
21. Mario Tronti, *Workers and Capital* (London and New York: Verso, 2019), 335.
22. Marx to S. Meyer and A. Vogt in New York, April 9, 1870, in Marx and Engels, *Selected Correspondence* (Moscow: Progress Publishers, 1955), 237.
23. Mario Tronti, "Our Operaismo," in *New Left Review*, Feb. 2012, republished as an Afterword to Tronti, *Workers and Capital*.
24. Karl Marx, "On Proudhon," in *Der Social-Demokrat*, no. 18, February 5, 1865.
25. Mario Tronti, *Noi Operaisti* (Rome: Derive Approdi, 2009), 61.

26. Ibid.
27. Louis Althusser, *For Marx* (London and New York: Penguin Press, 1969), 94, 102; Louis Althusser, Etienne Balibar, et al., *Reading Capital* (London and New York: New Left Books, 1970), 32.
28. See Aime Césaire, *Toussaint Louverture. La révolution française et le problème colonial* (Paris: Présence Africaine, 1961).
29. Alfred Rosenberg, *Der Mythus des 20 Jahrhunderts* (Munich: Hoheneichen, 1937), 40, 127.
30. Benito Mussolini, *Opera Omnia*, vol. 29, ed. E. Susmel and D. Susmel (Florence: La Fenice, 1951), 185–89. Translation from the Italian.
31. Marco Del Bene, "Propaganda e rappresentazione dell'altro nel Giappone prebellico," in *Le guerre mondiali in Asia orientale e in Europa* (Milan: Unicopli, 2009), 92–93. Translated from the Italian.
32. W. E. B. Du Bois, "The African Roots of the War," *The Atlantic*, May 1915, https://credo.library.umass.edu/cgi-bin/pdf.cgi?id=scua:mums312-b207-i164; https://www.theatlantic.com/magazine/archive/1915/05/the-african-roots-of-war/528897/.
33. V. I. Lenin, *Collected Works*, vol. 24.
34. Antonio Gramsci, *Quaderni del carcere* (Turin: Einaudi), 567, 837, 2103; Gramsci, *L'Ordine Nuovo 1919–1920*, ed. V. Gerratana and A. A. Santucci (Turin: Einaudi, 1987), 41, 142.
35. Louis Althusser, *Lenin and Philosophy and Other Essays* (New York: New York University Press 2001), 5.
36. Althusser, Balibar, et al., *Reading Capital*, 142.
37. Louis Althusser, Introduction, in *For Marx* (London and New York: Penguin, 1969), https://www.marxists.org/reference/archive/althusser/1965/index.htm.
38. Althusser, Balibar, et al., *Reading Capital*, 143.
39. Mario Tronti, *Noi Operaisti* (Rome: Derive Approdi, 2009), 62, 17.
40. Ernst Bloch, *Geist der Utopie* (Frankfurt: Suhrkamp Verlag, 1971). Translated from the Italian (unpublished edition in English).
41. Ernst Bloch, *The Spirit of Utopia* (Palo Alto: Stanford University Press, 2000), 238.
42. Ernst Bloch, *Natural Law and Human Dignity* (Cambridge, MA: MIT Press, 1996), 38.
43. Domenico Losurdo, *Il linguaggio dell'Impero: Lessico dell'ideologia americana* (Rome-Bari: Laterza, 2007).
44. Bloch, *Natural Law and Human Dignity*, 64.
45. Mao Zedong, "Statement in Support of the Struggle of the American Black People Against Racial Discrimination," August 8, 1963, in Mao Zedong, *On Diplomacy* (Beijing: Foreign Languages Press, 1963), 377.
46. Bloch, *Natural Law and Human Dignity*, 215.

47. Mao, "Statement in Support," 377.
48. Bloch, *Natural Law and Human Dignity*, 64.
49. Mao, "Statement in Support," 379.
50. Max Horkheimer, "The Authoritarian State," *Telos* 15/3 (1973): 8, 15.
51. Ibid., 6.
52. Ibid., 8.
53. Ibid., 7.
54. Ibid.
55. Max Horkheimer, "La teoria critica ieri e oggi," in *La società di transizione* (Turin: Einaudi, 1980), 175. Translated from the Italian.
56. Max Horkheimer, *The Eclipse of Reason* (London and New York: Oxford University Press. 1947), 19.
57. Horkheimer, "La teoria critica ieri e oggi," 172.
58. Max Horkheimer, "La psicanalisi nell'ottica della sociologia," in *La società di transizione*, 138; Horkheimer, "La teoria critica ieri e oggi," 172, 178.
59. Max Horkheimer, "Marx oggi," in *La società di transizione*, 159.
60. *Infra*, chap. 6, sec. 2.
61. Horkheimer, "La teoria critica ieri e oggi," 168–169.
62. Ibid., 174–75.
63. Max Horkheimer and Theodor Adorno, *Dialectic of Enlightenment*, ed. Gunzelin Schmid Noerr, trans. Edmund Jephcott (Palo Alto: Stanford University Press, 2002), 43, 67.
64. Theodor Adorno, *Negative Dialectics* (Frankfurt: Suhrkamp Verlag, 1970), 192, 201–2.
65. Ibid., 201.
66. Theodor Adorno, *Critical Models: Interventions and Catchwords* (New York Columbia University Press, 2005), 274.
67. Adorno, *Negative Dialectics*, 180.
68. Ibid., 180.
69. Ibid, 296.
70. G. W. F. Hegel, *The Phenomenology of Mind* (New York: Harper & Row, 1967), 81.
71. Theodor Adorno, *Minima Moralia: Reflections on a Damaged Life* (New York and London: Verso, 2005), 50.
72. G. W. F. Hegel, *The Philosophy of History* (Amherst, NY: Prometheus Books, 1991), 86.
73. Immanuel Kant, *Toward Perpetual Peace and Other Writings on Politics, Peace and History* (New Haven: Yale University Press, 2006), 91–92. See also Domenico Losurdo, *Un mondo senza guerre: L'idea di pace dalle promesse del passato alle tragedie del presente*, chap. I, sec. 6–7 (Rome: Carocci, 2016).
74. Immanuel Kant, *Lectures on Ethics* (Cambridge: Cambridge University Press, 1997), 405–6.

75. Max Horkheimer, "Riflessioni sull'educazione politica," in *La società di transizione*, 124.
76. Max Horkheimer, "La lezione del fascismo," in *La società di transizione*, 40.
77. Theodor Adorno, "What Does It Mean to Come to Terms With the Past?," in *Bitburg in Moral and Political Perspective*, ed. Geoffrey Hartman (Bloomington: Indiana University Press, 1986), 122.
78. Ibid., 123.
79. Theodor Adorno, "What Does It Mean to Come to Terms With the Past?" in Theodor Adorno, *Bitburg in Moral and Political Perspective*, edited by Geoffrey Hartman (Bloomington, IN, 1986). This 1959 essay is avaailable at https://cominsitu.wordpress.com/2019/08/07/the-meaning-of-working-through-the-past-adorno-1959/.
80. Domenico Losurdo, *Il linguaggio dell'Impero: Lessico dell'ideologia americana*.
81. Stephan Grigat, "Befreite Gesellschaft und Israel: Zum Verhältnis von Kritischer Theorie und Zionismus," in *Feindaufklärung und Reeducation* (Freiburg: Caira, 2015), 20.
82. Alfred Rosenberg, *Der Mythus des 20. Jahrhunderts* (Munich: Hoheneichen, 1937), 645.
83. Max Horkheimer, "The Jews and Europe," in *The Frankfurt School on Religion: Key Writings by the Major Thinkers,* ed. Eduardo Mendieta (New York: Routledge, 2005), 226.
84. Herbert Marcuse, "The End of Utopia and the Problem of Violence" in *Five Lectures* (Boston: Beacon Press, 1970), 17.
85. Ibid., 16.
86. Herbert Marcuse, *One-Dimensional Man* (New York: Routledge, 2007), 240.
87. Herbert Marcuse, "Repressive Tolerance," https://sites.evergreen.edu/arunchandra/wp-content/uploads/sites/395/2018/07/tolerance.pdf, 1.
88. Marcuse, *One-Dimensional Man*, 51.
89. Herbert Marcuse, "The End of Utopia," an essay republished in Marcuse, *Five Lectures* (Boston: Beacon Press, 1970).
90. Infra, chap. 6, sec. 2.
91. Marcuse, *One-Dimensional Man*, 49.
92. Ibid., 49–50.
93. Ibid., 41.
94. Herbert Marcuse, "The Problem of Violence and the Radical Opposition," in Marcuse, *Five Lectures*, 87.
95. Ibid., 98.
96. Marcuse, *One-Dimensional Man,* 49.
97. Marcuse, *Five Lectures*, 95.
98. Ernst Bloch, *Zum Pulverfass im Nahen Osten*, in *Politische Messungen,*

    Pestzeit, Vormärz (Frankfurt: Suhrkamp Verlag, 1970), 421–24. Translated here from the Italian.
99. Ibid., 419–21.
100. Domenico Losurdo, *Il linguaggio dell'Impero*.
101. Marcuse, "The End of Utopia."
102. See note 73 above. Translated from Losurdo's Italian text.
103. See notes 73 and 74 above. Translated from Losurdo's Italian text.
104. See notes 73–75 above. Translated from Losurdo's Italian text.
105. This quote can be found at https://jewishjournal.com/news/worldwide/170680/the-frankfurt-exchange-part-3-herbert-marcuse-and-erich-fromms-differing-views-on-israel/
106. Mao Zedong, *The Writings of Mao Zedong 1949–76*, vol. 2, January 1956–December 1957 (New York: Routledge, 1992).
107. Lin Biao, Report to the Ninth National Congress of the Chinese Communist Party (Beijing: Foreign Languages Press, 1969), https://www.marxists.org/reference/archive/lin-biao/1969/04/01.htm.
108. Ibid.
109. Ibid.
110. Mario Tronti, "The Struggle Against Labor," *Radical America* 6/1 (May–June 1972): 22–25.
111. Mao Zedong, "On Practice," in *Selected Works of Mao Zedong*, vol. 1 (Beijing: Foreign Languages Press, 1965), 295–96.
112. Karl Marx and Frederick Engels, "Manifesto of the Communist Party," in *Marx/Engels Selected Works*, vol. 1 (Moscow: Progress Publishers, 1969), 126, https://www.marxists.org/archive/marx/works/download/pdf/Manifesto.pdf.
113. Le Duan, *On the Socialist Revolution in Vietnam*, vol. 2 (Hanoi: Foreign Languages Press, 1965), 94.
114. Jean-Paul Sartre, *Critique of Dialectical Reason* (London and New York: Verso, 2004), 130–32.
115. Frantz Fanon, *The Wretched of the Earth* (New York: Grove Press, 1963), 207.
116. Jean-Paul Sartre, Preface to *The Wretched of the Earth* (New York: Grove Press, 1963), 26.
117. Fanon, *The Wretched of the Earth*, 97–98, 101.
118. Aimé Césaire, *Toussaint Louverture: La Révolution française et le problème colonial* (Paris: Présence Africaine, 1961).
119. Sartre's term for a group of people united by a common purpose. It can refer to progressive or fascistic social movements.
120. Jean-Paul Sartre, "Existentialism Is a Humanism," in *Existentialism from Dostoevsky to Sartre*, ed. W. Kaufmann (Grand Rapids, MI: World Publishing Company, 1956), 8; *The Brotherwise Dispatch* 3/4 (Sept–Nov/2018),

originally published in *Les Temps Modernes*, 1946. Excerpted from *Literary and Philosophical Essays* (New York: Collier Books, 1962), 198–256.
121. Domenico Losurdo, *The Class Struggle: A Political and Philosophical History* (New York: Palgrave Macmillan, 2016), 228.
122. Mao Zedong, "On Practice," *Selected Works*, vol. 1, 296.
123. Ibid.
124. Sebastiano Timpanaro, *On Materialism* (London and New York: New Left Books, 1970), 120.
125. Ibid., 132.
126. Ibid., 33.
127. Ibid., 251.
128. Ibid., 43.
129. Ibid., 217.
130. Ibid., 50.
131. Ibid., 199.
132. Ibid.
133. Georg Lukács, *The Ontology of Social Being*, vol. 1 (London: Merlin Press, 1978).
134. Georg Lukács, *Lenin: A Study of the Unity of His Thought* (London and New York: Verso, 2009), 43.
135. Ibid., 47.
136. Ibid., 45.
137. Ibid.

PART IV: THE TRIUMPH AND DEATH OF WESTERN MARXISM

1. Filippo Turati, "Leninismo e marxismo," in Franco Livorsi, *Socialismo e riformismo nella storia d'Italia: Scritti politici 1878–1932* (Milan: Feltrinelli, 1979), 332.
2. Filippo Turati, "Socialismo e massimalismo," in *Socialismo e riformismo nella storia d'Italia*, 345.
3. Bloch Ernst, *Geist der Utopie* (Frankfurt: Suhrkamp, 1971), first published in 1918.
4. Karl Kautsky, *Die materialistische Geschichtsauffassung* (Berlin: Dietz, 1927).
5. Max Horkheimer, "La psicanalisi nell'ottica della sociologia," in *La società di transizione* (Turin: Enaudi, 1979), 138.
6. Richard Hofstadter, *Great Issues in American History*, vol. 3 (New York: Vintage Books, 1982) vol. 3, 414.
7. Fritz Haug, *Rosa Luxemburg und die Kunst der Politik* (Hamburg: Argument, 2007).
8. W. E. B. DuBois, "Segregation in the North," in W. E. B. Du Bois, *Writings* (New York: Library of America, 1986), 1243.

9. W. E. B. Du Bois, "The White World," in *Dusk of Dawn*, chap. 6, 678.
10. Sudarshan Kapur, *Raising Up a Prophet: The African-American Encounter with Gandhi* (Boston: Beacon Press, 1992), 107, 109, and 112.
11. Mohandas K. Gandhi, *The Collected Works of Mahatma Gandhi* (New Delhi: Publications Division Government of India, 1999), 98 vols.,. vol. 80, 200, available at https://www.gandhiashramsevagram.org/gandhi-literature/mahatma-gandhi-collected-works-volume-80.pdf.
12. Hannah Arendt and Karl Jaspers, *Correspondence 1926–1969* (New York: Harcourt Brace, 1992), 386.
13. Frantz Fanon, *The Wretched of the Earth* (New York: Grove Press, 1963), 90.
14. Ibid., 101.
15. J. J. Heydecker and J. Leeb, *Der Nürnberger Prozess*, vol. 2 (Köln: Kiepenheuer & Witsch, 1985), 531 and 543.
16. Hannah Arendt, *The Jewish Writings* (New York: Shocken Books, 2007), 182.
17. Hannah Arendt, "Imperialism: Road to Suicide: The Political Origins and Use of Racism," 1946, in *Erstveröffentlichungen*, 255–56. This essay is available at https://www.commentary.org/articles/mortbarrgmailcom/imperialism-road-to-suicide/.
18. Arendt, *The Jewish Writings*, 359 and 181.
19. Ibid., 360.
20. Ibid., 315.
21. Hannah Arendt, "Antisemitismus und faschistische Internationale," in *Essays & Kommentare*, vol. 1 (Berlin: Edition Tiamat, 1989), 45 and 48.
22. Hannah Arendt, "Organized Guilt and Universal Responsibility," *Jewish Frontier*, January 1945, 23.
23. Arendt, "Imperialism: Road to Suicide," 254.
24. Hannah Arendt, Albert Einstein, Sidney Hook, and Seymour Melman 1948/2007, "New Palestine Party Visit of Menachem Begin and Aims of Political Movement Discussed," Open Letter to the *New York Times*, December 4, in Arendt, *The Jewish Writings*, 417–19.
25. Hannah Arendt, *The Origins of Totalitarianism* (New York: Harcourt Brace, 1973), 176.
26. Ibid., 160.
27. Ibid., 176.
28. Ibid., 175.
29. Ibid., 186.
30. Ibid., 186.
31. Ibid., 212.
32. Ibid., 213 and 479.
33. Elizabeth Young-Bruehl, *Hannah Arendt: For Love of the World* (New Haven: Yale University Press, 2004), 158.

34. G. Mann, "Vom Totalen Staat," *Die Neue Zeitung-Die amerikanische Zeitung in Deutschland*, October 20–21, 1951.
35. Arendt, *The Origins of Totalitarianism*, 232–33.
36. H. Stuart Hughes in A. Gleason, *Totalitarianism: The Inner History of the Cold War* (Oxford: Oxford University Press, 1995), 112.
37. Ian Kershaw, *The Nazi Dictatorship* (London: Bloomsbury Publishing, 1985), 28.
38. Gleason, *Totalitarianism*, 112.
39. Ian Kershaw, *To Hell and Back: Europe 1914–1949* (London: Penguin, 2015), 112 and 117.
40. Toni Negri and Michael Hardt, *Empire* (Cambridge, MA: Harvard University Press, 2000), 112.
41. Arendt, "Imperialism: Road to Suicide," 264.
42. Arendt, "Antisemitismus und faschistische Internationale," 44–45.
43. Hannah Arendt, "Herzl and Lazare," in Arendt, *The Jewish Writings*, 338–40.
44. Hannah Arendt, "Organized Guilt and Universal Responsibility" in *Erstveröffentlichunge*n, 212. Available at https://hannah-arendt-edition.net/textgrid/data/3p/pdf/III-004-organizedGuilt.pdf.
45. Hannah Arendt, "Die vollendete Sinnlosigkeit," in *Essays & Kommentare*, 1950, vol. 1, 9.
46. Theodore Roosevelt, *The Letters*, ed. E. E. Morison, J. M. Blum, J. J. Buckley (Cambridge, MA: Harvard University Press, 1951), 377.
47. Domenico Losurdo 2015, *Il revisionismo storico: Problemi e miti*, expanded ed. (Rome-Bari: Laterza), chap. 5, sec. 5.
48. Lothrop Stoddard, *The Revolt Against Civilization: The Menace of the Under Man* (New York: Charles Scribner), 151–52.
49. Ibid., 233, 86–87, and 212.
50. Arendt, *The Origins of Totalitarianism*, 458.
51. Ibid., 457.
52. Ibid., 457–58.
53. Ibid., 458.
54. G. Aly and S. Heim, *Vordenker der Vernichtung: Auschwitz und die deutsche Pläne für eine neue europäische Ordnung* (Frankfurt: Fischer, 2004).
55. See Mark Mazower, *Hitler's Empire* (London: Penguin Books, 2009) on the slave trade; David Olusoga and Caspar W. Erichsen, *The Kaiser's Holocaust: Germany's Forgotten Genocide and the Colonial Roots of Nazism* (London: Faber and Faber, 2010) on the colonial war in the East; and C. P. Kakel III, *The American West and the Nazi East: A Comparative and Interpretive Perspective* (London: Palgrave Macmillan); and C. P. Kakel III, *The Holocaust as Colonial Genocide: Hitler's "Indian Wars" in the "Wild East"* (London: Palgrave Macmillan, 2013) on the Nazi "West."

56. Domenico Losurdo, "Psicopatologia e demonologia: La lettura delle grandi crisi storiche dalla Restaurazione ai giorni nostri," *Belfagor: Rassegna di varia umanità* (March 2012): 151–72.
57. Arendt, *Origins of Totalitarianism*, 308.
58. Ibid., 309.
59. Ibid., xxvi.
60. Ibid., 311.
61. Domenico Losurdo, *Il linguaggio dell'Impero: Lessico dell'ideologia americana* (Rome-Bari: Laterza, 2007), chap. 3, sec. 5.
62. M. Mukerjee, *Churchill's Secret War: The British Empire and the Ravaging of India during World War II* (New York: Basic Books, 2010), 246–47.
63. Adolf Hitler, *Tischgespräche*, ed. H. Picker (Berlin: Ullstein, 1989), 453–54.
64. Hannah Arendt, *On Revolution*, 1963, 65.
65. Alexis de Tocqueville, *Œuvres complètes*, vol. 3, pt 1, 229, cited in Domenico Losurdo, *Liberalism: A Counter-History* (London: Verso, 2011), 235.
66. Losurdo uses the word *"emancipazione"*—emancipation—to describe the struggles of the 1960s and 1970s in the United States, but since "emancipation" in the United States refers specifically to the abolition of slavery in 1865, we have translated it as "liberation" here, using a term closely identified with the movements of that time. -Trans.
67. Hannah Arendt, "On Violence," in Hannah Arendt, *Crises of the Republic* (New York: Harcourt Brace, 1972), 123.
68. Hannah Arendt, interview, "Thoughts on Politics and Revolution" in *Crises of the Republic*, 209–10.
69. Hannah Arendt, *On Revolution*, 112.
70. Ibid., 66n4. The reference that Losurdo refers to is a quote of Monroe from his notes on the Debates at the Constitutional Convention.
71. Hannah Arendt, "Reflections on Little Rock," *Dissent* (1959), 45–56.
72. James Bryce, *Studies in History and Jurisprudence* (New York: Oxford University Press, 1901), 325.
73. Niall Ferguson, *Civilization: The West and the Rest* (New York: Penguin, 2011), 129.
74. Louis Althusser, Etienne Balibar, et al., *Reading Capital* (London: New Left Books, 1970), 27, 45, and 103.
75. G. W. F. Hegel, *The Science of Logic* (New York: Cambridge University Press, 2010), sec. 21.38, 33.
76. B. H. F. Taureck, *Michel Foucault* (Hamburg: Rowohlt, 2004), 40 and 116.
77. Michel Foucault, *Discipline and Punish* (New York: Vintage, 1991), 7.
78. Michel Foucault, *Society Must Be Defended* (New York: Picador, 1997), 247.
79. Foucault, *Discipline and Punish*, 3-7.
80. C. Vann Woodward, "Dangerous Liaisons," *New York Review of Books*, February 19, 1998.

81. Foucault, *Discipline and Punish*, 9.
82. Foucault, *Society Must Be Defended*, 80 and 69.
83. Ibid., 81.
84. Ibid., 81
85. Ibid., 81.
86. This quote can be found here: https://www.academia.edu/21582830/Foucault_Michel_Historical_Discourse_and_Revolution.
87. Ibid., 81–82.
88. Domenico Losurdo, *Liberalism: A Counter-History* (London: New Left Books, 2011), 101 and 161.
89. Karl Marx, "The North American Civil War," first published in *Die Presse* No. 293, October 25, 1861; available in *Marx and Engels and the US Civil War*, Internationalist Group/League for the Fourth International at https://www.marxists.org/history/etol/newspape/internationalist/pamphlets/MARX-on-Slavery-OptV5.pdf.
90. Foucault, *Society Must Be Defended*, 260.
91. George M. Frederickson, *Racism: A Short History* (Princeton: Princeton University Press, 2002), 124.
92. E. J. Sieyès, *Écrits politiques*, ed. R. Zapperi (Paris: Éditions des archives contemporaines, 1985), 99.
93. Augustin Thierry, *The Formation and Progress of the Tiers Etat, or Third Estate in France* (London: Henry G. Bohn, 1859), 23.
94. Ibid., 27 and 44.
95. Tzvetan Todorov, *The Conquest of America: The Question of the Other* (Norman: University of Oklahoma Press, 1999), 5.
96. Losurdo's thoughts on Nolte are summarized here: https://www.versobooks.com/blogs/news/2809-domenico-losurdo-ernst-nolte-and-the-development-of-revisionism.
97. Franklin D. Roosevelt to Henry Morganthau Jr., August 19, 1944, in Henry Morganthau III, *Mostly Morganthau: A Family History* (New York: Ticknor and Fields, 1991), 365.
98. This comment and its source can be found here: https://www.marxists.org/history/etol/newspape/themilitant/1936/v02n19/komsomol.html.
99. Hannah Arendt, *Eichmann in Jerusalem* (New York: Viking Press, 1963), 35.
100. Foucault, *Society Must Be Defended*, 242.
101. Ibid., 244.
102. Ibid., 253.
103. Ibid., 253.
104. Ibid., 249.
105. Ibid., 254.
106. Todorov, *The Conquest of America*, 175.

107. John Hope Franklin, *From Slavery to Freedom* (New York: Knopf, 1947), 106.
108. Karl Marx, *Capital*, vol. 2 (Chicago: Charles Kerr & Co., 1909), 559.
109. John A. Hobson, *Imperialism: A Study*, 1902, chap. 4, sec. 3, https://www.marxists.org/archive/hobson/1902/imperialism/index.htm.
110. Benjamin Franklin, *The Autobiography of Benjamin Franklin*, 154.
111. Benjamin Franklin to John Fothergill, March 14, 1764, Philadelphia, Yale University Library, available at https://founders.archives.gov/documents/Franklin/01-11-02-0025.
112. See http://nietzsche.holtof.com/Nietzsche_the_will_to_power/the_will_to_power_book_IV.htm.
113. Clive Ponting, "Churchill's Plan for Racial Purity," *The Guardian*, June 20, 1992.
114. Michel Foucault, *The Birth of Biopolitics* (New York: Palgrave, 2004), 182, 187, and 189.
115. Slavoj Žižek, *In Defense of Lost Causes* (London: Verso, 2008), 97, 165, and 338.
116. Giorgio Agamben, Alain Badiou, Daniel Bensaid, Wendy Brown, Jean-Luc Nancy, Jacques Rancière, Kristin Ross, and Slavoj Žižek, *Démocratie, dans quel état?* (Paris: La Fabrique, 2009).
117. Giorgio Agamben, "Introduzione" to Emmanuel Levinas, *Alcune riflessioni sulla filosofia dell'hitlerismo* (Macerata: Quodlibet, 2012), 9.
118. Ibid., 25–26, 33–3, and 28.
119. Ibid., 32–33 and 29–30.
120. Domenico Losurdo, *The Class Struggle: A Political and Philosophical History* (New York: Palgrave-Macmillan, 2016), 227.
121. Karl Marx, "Preface" to *A Contribution to the Critique of Political Economy*, in *The Marx-Engels Reader*, ed. Robert Tucker (New York: W. W. Norton, 1978), 4.
122. Emile Durkheim, "The Materialist Conception of History," in Durkheim, *The Rules of Sociological Method* (New York: Free Press, 1982), 169.
123. Ibid., 169–70.
124. Emile Durkheim, "The Rules of Sociological Method," in Durkheim, *The Rules of Sociological Method*, 50.
125. Durkheim, "The Materialist Conception of History," 171.
126. Ibid., 171.
127. G. W. F. Hegel, *Elements of the Philosophy of Right* (Cambridge: Cambridge University Press, 1991), 227.
128. Lothrop Stoddard, *The Rising Tide of Color*, 220.
129. Lothrop Stoddard, *The Revolt Against Civilization*, 223.
130. Ibid., 86; Stoddard, *The Rising Tide of Color*, 309.
131. Stoddard, *The Rising Tide of Color*, 220.

132. Losurdo, *Il linguaggio dell'Impero,* chap. 3, sec. 5.
133. Alfred Rosenberg, *Der Mythus des 20 Jahrhunderts, Hoheneichen* (Munich: Hoheneichen Verlag, 1930), 673.
134. Domenico Losurdo, *Nietzsche, il ribelle aristocratico: Biografia intellettuale e bilancio critico* (Turin: Bollati Boringhieri, 2002), chap. 24, sec. 6.
135. Rosenberg, *Der Mythus des 20 Jahrhunderts, Hoheneichen,* 339 and 336.
136. Leo Strauss, "Progress or Return?" *Modern Judaism* 1 (1981): 21.
137. Toni Negri and Michael Hardt, *Empire* (Cambridge, MA: Harvard University Press, 2001), 380–81.
138. Samuel Huntington, *Political Order in Changing Societies* (New Haven: Yale University Press, 1968), 134.
139. David Brion Davis, *The Slave Power Conspiracy and the Paranoid Style* (Baton Rouge: Louisiana State University Press, 1982), 33.
140. Negri and Hardt, *Empire,* 164.
141. Sergio Romano, *Il declino dell'impero americano* (Milan: Longanesi, 2014), 7.
142. Niall Ferguson, *Colossus: The Rise and Fall of the American Empire* (London: Penguin, 2005), 33.
143. Negri and Hardt, *Empire,* xii.
144. Romano, *Il declino dell'impero americano,* 39.
145. Domenico Losurdo, *Un mondo senza guerre: L'idea di pace dalle promesse del passato alle tragedie del presente* (Rome: Carocci, 2016), chap. 7, sec. 1.
146. Negri and Hardt, *Empire,* 174.
147. Jean-Paul Sartre, Preface to *The Wretched of the Earth* (New York: Grove Press, 1963), 26.

PART V: REVIVAL, OR THE LAST GASP OF WESTERN MARXISM?

1. Slavoj Žižek, *In Defense of Lost Causes* (London: Verso, 2008), 203–4.
2. Slavoj Žižek, *The Year of Dreaming Dangerously* (London: Verso, 2012), 127.
3. David Shulman, "Israel in Peril," *New York Review of Books,* June 7, 2012.
4. Ibid.
5. Ibid.
6. Michael Hardt and Toni Negri, "Declaration," 2012, https://criticallegalthinking.com/2012/06/14/declaration-hardt-negri/.
7. Slavoj Žižek, "Mao Zedong: Marxist Lord of Misrule," 2007, https://www.lacan.com/zizmaozedong.htm.
8. Ibid.
9. Ibid.
10. Žižek, *In Defense of Lost Causes,* 362.
11. Domenico Losurdo, *Class Struggle: A Political and Economic History* (New York: Palgrave-Macmillan, 2016), 291.

12. Slavoj Žižek, *The First Time as Tragedy, Then As Farce* (London: Verso, 2009), 125.
13. Žižek, "Mao Zedong: Marxist Lord of Misrule."
14. Žižek, *In Defense of Lost Causes*, 169.
15. Stéphane Courtois, Andrzej Paczkowski, et al., *The Black Book of Communism* (Cambridge, MA: Harvard University Press, 1999), 523.
16. Helmut Schmidt, Interview with G. di Lorenzo ("Verstehen Sie das, Herr Schmidt?"), *Zeitmagazin*, September, 13, 2012.
17. Henry Kissinger, *On China* (New York: Penguin Press, 2011).
18. Domenico Losurdo, *Il revisionismo storico: Problemi e miti*, expanded ed. (Rome-Bari: Laterza, 2015), chap. 6, sec. 10.
19. David Harvey, *The New Imperialism* (New York: Oxford University Press, 2003), 46.
20. Ibid., 76.
21. Ibid., 8.
22. Ibid., 25.
23. Ibid., 4.
24. David Harvey, *A Brief History of Neoliberalism* (New York: Oxford University Press, 2005), 122.
25. Harvey, *The New Imperialism*, 71.
26. Ibid., 75.
27. Lenin wrote a great deal on the national question. See https://www.marxists.org/archive/lenin/works/subject/nation/index.htm.
28. Alain Badiou, *The Century* (Cambridge: Polity Press, 2007), 26.
29. Alain Badiou, "The Enigmatic Relationship Between Philosophy and Politics," in *Philosophy for Militants* (London: Verso, 2012), 30.
30. Ibid., 33.
31. Ibid., 34 and 31.
32. Domenico Losurdo, *Il linguaggio dell'Impero: Lessico dell'ideologia americana* (Rome-Bari: Laterza, 2007), chap. 7, sec. 7.
33. C. B. Macpherson, *The Political Theory of Possessive Individualism* (Oxford: Clarendon Press, 1962).
34. Karl Marx, "The Future Results of British Rule in India," *MECW* [Marx Engels Collected Works], vol. 12,. 217, available at https://www.marxists.org/archive/marx/works/cw/index.htm. First published August 8, 1853; reprinted in the *New-York Semi-Weekly Tribune*, No. 856, August 9, 1853.
35. Karl Marx, *Capital*, vol. 1 (New York: Vintage, 1977), 889.
36. Domenico Losurdo, *La sinistra assente: Crisi, società dello spettacolo, guerra* (Rome: Carocci, 2014), chap. 2, sec. 3, and chap. 6, sec. 3.
37. We can assume that this is taken from Palmiro Togliatti, 1973-84, *Opere*, edited by E. Ragionieri (Roma: Editori Riuniti, 1973-84).

38. Ernst Bloch, *The Spirit of Utopia* (Palo Alto: Stanford University Press, 2000), 242.
39. Filippo Turati, "Leninism and Marxism in Socialismo e riformismo nella storia d'Italia," in *Scritti politici 1878–1932*, ed. F. Livorsi (Milan: Feltrinelli, 1979), 333.
40. Filippo Turati, "Socialismo e massimalismo," in *Socialismo e riformismo nella storia d'Italia* (1919/2000), 347.
41. Theodor Adorno, *Negative Dialectics* (Frankfurt: Suhrkamp Verlag, 2001), 6.
42. Mario Tronti, "Our Operaismo," *New Left Review* 73, Jan/Feb 2012, https://newleftreview.org/issues/ii73/articles/mario-tronti-our-operaismo.
43. Toni Negri and Michael Hardt, *Empire* (Cambridge, MA: Harvard University Press, 2000), 134 and 109.
44. John Holloway, *Change the World Without Taking Power* (London: Pluto, 2005).
45. Noam Chomsky, *Deterring Democracy* (Boston: South End Press, 1991), ix.
46. V. I. Lenin, "Can the Bolsheviks Retain State Power?," in Lenin, *Collected Works*, vol. 26, October 14, 1917 (Moscow: Progress Publishers, 1965). Appeared originally in the magazine *Prosveshcheniye* 1–2. https://www.marxists.org/archive/lenin/works/1917/oct/01.htm.
47. Losurdo, *Il revisionismo storico*, chap. 2, sec. 11.
48. M.Robespierre, *Œuvres* (Paris: Puf, 1950–67), vol. 8, 80-81.
49. V. I. Lenin, "The Revolutionary Phrase" and "War or Peace?," in Lenin's *Collected Works* (Moscow: Progress Publishers, 1972), vol. 27, 19–29 and 36–39.
50. V. I. Lenin, "Strange and Monstrous," in *Collected Works*, vol. 27, 68-75.
51. V. I. Lenin, Delivered March 16, 1920, first published in the book *Ninth Congress of the Russian Communist Party: Verbatim Report*, Moscow, 1920. Verified with the shorthand notes, *Collected Works*, vol. 30, 439–90, available at https://www.marxists.org/archive/lenin/works/1920/mar/29.htm.
52. See Ernst Bloch, *The Principle of Hope* (Cambridge: MIT Press, 1995).
53. Tzvetan Todorov, "La guerra impossibile," *La Repubblica*, June 26, 2012.
54. Niall Ferguson, *The Cash Nexus: Money and Power in the Modern World* (London: Penguin Press, 2001), 413.
55. R. D. Kaplan, "A NATO Victory Can Bridge Europe's Growing Divide," *International Herald Tribune*, April 8, 1999.
56. J. Fitchett, "Clark Recalls 'Lessons' of Kosovo," *International Herald Tribune*, May 3, 2000.
57. M. Hardt, "La nuda vita sotto l'Impero," *Il manifesto*, May 15, 1999.
58. Negri and Hardt, *Empire*, 16.
59. See Barry Buzan, "New Patterns of Global Security in the Twenty-First Century," *International Affairs* Vol. 67, No. 3 (July, 1991), pp. 431-451.

60. In an interview Losurdo did in 2017 with the magazine *Opera* (revistaopera.com.br) in connection with his book *War and Revolution*, he references Karl Popper's statements. He gives the following source: Karl Popper, "Kriege führen für den Frieden" [Waging Wars for Peace]. Interview with *Der Spiegel*, March 22, 1992.
61. Paul Johnson, "Colonialism's Back, and Not a Moment Too Soon," *New York Times Magazine*, April 18, 1993.
62. Domenico Losurdo, *La lotta di classe. Una storia politica e filosofica* (Roma-Bari: Laterza, 2013), chap. 9, sec. 1.
63. S. Romano, *Il declino dell'impero americano* (Milan: Longanesi, 2014), 29.
64. Ibid., 24.

PART VI: HOW MARXISM IN THE WEST CAN BE REBORN

1. Karl Marx, *Grundrisse* (New York: Vintage, 1973), 158.
2. Karl Marx and Frederich Engels, *Critique of the Gotha Program* in *The Marx-Engels Reader*, ed. Robert Tucker (New York: W. W. Norton, 1978), 538.
3. Karl Marx and Frederich Engels, *Manifesto of the Communist Party*, in *The Marx-Engels Reader*, 491.
4. Thomas B. Macaulay, *Critical and Historical Essays*, vol. 3 (London: Longman, Brown, Green and Longman, 1848), 390, available at https://oll-resources.s3.us-east-2.amazonaws.com/oll3/store/titles/365/1227.03_Bk.pdf.
5. Gustave de Beaumont wrote a two-volume work, *Ireland: Social, Political, Religious*, published in 1839. It is not improbable that Lusordo's quotes in this paragraph are from this source, given that it describes the horrific treatment of the Irish by England. The two volumes are available at https://oll.libertyfund.org/titles/taylor-ireland-social-political-and-religious-vol-1-1839.
6. The "historian of our own times" is very likely C. Vann Woodward. See C. Woodward, "Dangerous Liaisons" in *New York Review of Books*, February 19, 1998, and C. Vann Woodward, *The Origins of the New South* (Baton Rouge: Louisiana State University Press, 1971).
7. On Spencer's denunciations of British colonialism, see the following and the sources cited therein: https://mises.org/mises-daily/herbert-spencer-freedom-and-empire#footnote9_81unae7.
8. See Theodore Roosevelt, *The Letters*, E. E. Morison, J. M. Blum, J. J. Buckley, eds. (Cambridge: Harvard University Press, 1951).
9. For Taylor's work on the First World War, see A. J. P. Taylor, *The First World War: An Illustrated History* (London: Penguin, 1963).
10. C. Vann Woodward, *The Origins of the New South* (Baton Rouge: Louisiana State University Press, 1971), 355–56.

11. Niall Ferguson, *Civilization: The West and the Rest* (Penguin: London, 2011), 306.
12. Benedetto Croce, *Storia d'Italia dal 1871 al 1915* (Bari: Laterza, 1967), 251.
13. Domenico Losurdo, *Il revisionismo storico: Problemi e miti* (Rome-Bari: Laterza, 2015), chap. 6, sec. 2.
14. M. Navarro, "U.S. Aid and Genocide," *International Herald Tribune*, February 27–28, 1999.
15. J. H. Franklin, *Negro: Die Geschichte der Schwarzen in den USA* (Frankfurt: Ullstein, 1983).
16. Robin D. G. Kelley, *Hammer and Hoe: Alabama Communists During the Great Depression* (Chapel Hill: University of North Carolina Press, 1990), xiii and 30.
17. Amicus Brief in the case of *Brown v. Board of Education*. This can be found at https://startrekprof.sdsu.edu/410b/amicusbriefbrownvboard.htm.
18. Domenico Losurdo, *Liberalism: A Counter-History* (London: Verso, 2005), chap. 10, sec. 6.
19. Marx and Engels, *Manifesto of the Communist Party*.
20. Marx and Engels, *The German Ideology*, in *The Marx Engels Reader*, 162.
21. Marx and Engels, *Manifesto of the Communist Party*, 500.
22. Ibid., 491.
23. L. Colletti, *Ideologia e società* (Bari: Laterza, 1969), 78–79 and 74–75.
24. Maurice Merleau-Ponty, *Humanism and Terror: An Essay on the Communist Problem* (Boston: Beacon Press, 1969), 1.
25. Ibid., 179–80.
26. Ibid., xxiii.
27. Woodward, *Origins of the New South*, 353.
28. Merleau-Ponty, *Humanism and Terror*, xxiv.
29. Niccolò Machiavelli, "The Prince," in *The Prince and the Discourses* (New York: Modern Library, 1940), chap. 6.
30. Alexander Hamilton, Federalist Paper no. 23. Available at https://avalon.law.yale.edu/18th_century/fed23.asp.
31. Karl Marx, "For a Ruthless Criticism of Everything Existing," letter to Arnold Ruge, 1844, in *The Marx-Engels Reader*, 14-15.
32. G. W. F. Hegel *The Philosophy of Right* (Kitchener, Ont.: Batoche Books, 2001), 19.
33. K. Rosenkranz, *Vita di Hegel*, (Florence: Vallecchi, 1966), 432.
34. *Marx Engels Collected Works*, vol. 36 (Moscow: Progress Publishers. 1975), 3.
35. Karl Marx, *Theories of Surplus Value*, vol. 1, chap. 7 (Moscow: Progress Publishers, 1971).
36. Herbert Marcuse, *One-Dimensional Man* (New York: Routledge, 2007), 47.

37. Herbert Marcuse, "The End of Utopia and the Problem of Violence," in Marcuse, *Five Lectures* (Boston: Beacon Press, 1970), 82.
38. Domenico Losurdo, *Class Struggle: A Political and Philosophical History* (New York: Palgrave Macmillan, 2016), 62 and 334.

APPENDIX: HOW "WESTERN MARXISM" WAS BORN AND HOW IT DIED
1. Norberto Bobbio, *Politica e cultura* (Turin: Einaudi, 1977), 164, 167n280.
2. John Stuart Mill, "On Liberty," in *Collected Works of John Stuart Mill*, vol. 18, ed. J. M. Robson (Toronto: University of Toronto Press, 1977), 224.
3. Ernst Bloch, *Natural Law and Human Dignity*, trans. Dennis Schmidt (Cambridge, MA: MIT Press, 1986), 136.
4. Bloch, *Natural Law*, 64–65.
5. Mao Zedong, "Statement in Support of the Struggle of the American Black People Against Racial Discrimination," in *On Diplomacy* (Beijing: Foreign Languages Press, 1998), 377.
6. Bloch, *Natural Law*, 63.
7. Mao, "Statement in Support," 377.
8. Bloch, *Natural Law*, 63–64.
9. Mao, "Statement in Support," 379.
10. Ho Chi Minh, "Speech at the Tours Congress (1920)," in *Selected Writings of Ho Chi Minh 1920–1969* (Hanoi: Foreign Languages Press, 1977), 16.
11. V. I. Lenin, "Inflammable Material in World Politics," in *Collected Works*, vol. 15 (Moscow: Progress Publishers, 1963), 184.
12. V. I. Lenin, "Preliminary Draft Theses on National and Colonial Questions for the Second Congress of the Communist International," in *Collected Works*, vol. 31 (Moscow: Progress Publishers, 1966), 147.
13. Karl Marx, "Record of a Speech on the Irish Question Delivered by Karl Marx to the German Workers' Educational Society in London on December 16, 1867," in *Marx Engels Collected Works*, vol. 21 (Moscow: Progress Publishers, 1985), 318–19.
14. Palmiro Togliatti, "In tema di libertà," in *Opere*, vol. 5, ed. Luciano Gruppi (Rome: Editori Riuniti, 1954), 884, 866.
15. Karl Marx, *Economic and Philosophic Manuscripts of 1844*, in *Marx Engels Collected Works*, vol. 3 (Moscow: Progress Publishers, 1975), 342, 296.
16. Karl Marx and Friedrich Engels, *The Holy Family, or Critique of Critical Criticism*, in *Marx Engels Collected Works*, vol. 4 (Moscow: Progress Publishers. 1975), 7.
17. Karl Marx, "Contribution to the Critique of Hegel's *Philosophy of Law*: Introduction," in *Marx Engels Collected Works*, vol. 3 (Moscow: Progress Publishers, 1975), 182.
18. Karl Marx and Friedrich Engels, *The Manifesto of the Communist Party*, in

Marx Engels Collected Works, vol. 6 (Moscow: Progress Publishers, 1976), 501.
19. Marx and Engels, *The Manifesto of the Communist Party*, 302.
20. Ibid., 490–91.
21. Ibid., 499.
22. Louis Althusser, *For Marx*, trans. Ben Brewster (London: Verso, 2005), 34–35.
23. Karl Marx, *Capital: A Critique of Political Economy, Vol. I*, in *Marx Engels Collected Works*, vol. 35 (Moscow: Progress Publishers, 1996), 269n1.
24. Marx, *Capital*, 406n2, translation modified.
25. Ibid., 710n1.
26. Ibid., 186, 54.
27. Ibid., 186.
28. Ibid., 739.
29. Ibid., 740.
30. Marx, "The North American Civil War," in *Marx Engels Collected Works*, vol. 19 (Moscow: Progress Publishers, 1984), 37.
31. Marx, *Capital*, 447.
32. Marx, "Marx to Engels in Manchester, London, 29 October 1862," in *Marx Engels Collected Works*, vol. 41 (Moscow: Progress Publishers, 1996), 420.
33. Marx, "The North American Civil War," 39.
34. Marx, "The Situation in North America," in *Marx Engels Collected Works*, vol. 19 (Moscow: Progress Publishers, 198), 257.
35. Marx, *Capital*, 717.
36. Louis Althusser, Étienne Balibar, et al., *Reading Capital: The Complete Edition*, trans. Ben Brewster and David Fernbach (London: Verso, 2015), 219.
37. Althusser, *For Marx*, 23.
38. Friedrich Nietzsche, *The Birth of Tragedy and Other Writings*, trans. Robert Speirs (Cambridge: Cambridge University Press, 1999), 86–87, 125.
39. Friedrich Nietzsche, *The Will to Power: Selections from the Notebooks of the 1880s*, trans. R. Kevin Hill and Michael Scarpitti (Harmondsworth: Penguin, 2017), 437.
40. Nietzsche, *The Will to Power*, 505.
41. Althusser, Balibar, et al., *Reading Capital*, 203.
42. Louis Althusser, *Lenin and Philosophy and Other Essays*, trans. Ben Brewster (London: NLB 1971), 38–39.
43. Theodor Adorno, *Negative Dialectics*, trans. Dennis Redmond (London: n.p., 2001), 413–16.
44. Ho Chi Minh, "Testament," in *Selected Writings of Ho Chi Minh 1920–1969* (Hanoi: Foreign Languages Press, 1977), 359, 362.
45. Ho Chi Minh, "The Path Which Led Me to Leninism," in *Selected Writings*

        of Ho Chi Minh 1920–1969 (Hanoi: Foreign Languages Press, 1977), 252, 251.
46. Mao Zedong, "The Chinese People Have Stood Up!," in *Selected Works of Mao Zedong*, vol. 5 (Beijing: Foreign Languages Press, 1977), 17, 18.
47. V. I. Lenin, "The Right of Nations to Self-Determination," in *Collected Works*, vol. 20 (Moscow: Progress Publishers, 1965), 437.
48. V. I. Lenin, "Declaration on the Rights of the Working and Exploited People," in *Collected Works*, vol. 26 (Moscow: Progress Publishers, 1966), 424.
49. Jean-Paul Sartre, *Critique of Dialectical Reason*, vol. 1: *Theory of Practical Ensembles*, trans. Alan Sheridan-Smith (London: Verso, 2004) 122–52.
50. Michael Hardt and Antonio Negri, *Empire* (Cambridge, MA: Harvard University Press, 2000), 134 and 109.
51. Mao Zedong, "The Bankruptcy of the Idealist Conception of History," in *Selected Works of Mao Zedong*, vol. 4 (Beijing: Foreign Languages Press, 1961), 453.
52. Marx and Engels, *The Manifesto of the Communist Party*, 504, 488.
53. Lê Duẩn, "In the 1962 Plan Our Industry Must Serve the Development of Agriculture with Still Greater Efficiency," in *The Socialist Revolution in Vietnam*, vol. 2 (Hanoi: Foreign Languages Press, 1965), 109.
54. Mario Tronti, *Workers and Capital*, trans. David Broder (London: Verso, 2019), 311.
55. Lin Biao, *Report to the Ninth National Congress of the Communist Party of China (Delivered on April 1 and Adopted on April 14, 1969)* (Beijing: Foreign Languages Press, 1969), 58–59.
56. Lin, *Report*, 61.
57. Lin, *Report*, 45.
58. Mao Zedong, "On Practice," in *Selected Works of Mao Zedong*, vol. 1 (Beijing: Foreign Languages Press, 1961), 295–96.
59. Althusser, Balibar et al., *Reading Capital*, 26.
60. G. W. F. Hegel, *The Science of Logic*, trans. George di Giovanni (Cambridge: Cambridge University Press, 2010), 33
61. Bernhard Taureck, *Michel Foucault* (Hamburg: Rowohlt, 1997), 40n116.
62. Michel Foucault, *Society Must Be Defended: Lectures at the Collège de France, 1975–76*, trans. David Macey (New York: Picador, 2003), 82, 260.
63. Domenico Losurdo, *Liberalism: A Counter-History*, trans. Gregory Elliott (London: Verso, 2011), 101.
64. Marx, "The North American Civil War," 37.
65. Foucault, *Society Must Be Defended*, 77, 69.
66. Ibid., 81.
67. Ibid., 247.
68. Hannah Arendt, *Eichmann in Jerusalem: A Report on the Banality of Evil* (Harmondsworth: Penguin, 1994), 7.

69. Hardt and Negri, *Empire*, 164.
70. Woodrow Wilson, "The Reconstruction of the Southern States," *Atlantic Monthly* 87 (January 1901): 1–15, 6.
71. August Heckscher, *Woodrow Wilson. A Biography* (New York: Scribner, 1991), 44n298.
72. Domenico Losurdo, *Il linguaggio dell'Impero: Lessico dell'ideologia americana* (Rome: Laterza, 2007), 55, 109–110.
73. Domenico Losurdo, *Democrazia o bonapartismo: Trionfo e decadenza del suffragio universale* (Turin: Bollati Boringhieri, 1993), 161–62, 180–82.
74. Hardt and Negri, *Empire*, 174.
75. Leo Strauss, "Progress or Return? The Contemporary Crisis in Western Civilization," *Modern Judaism* 1/1 (1981): 17–45, 22.
76. Hardt and Negri, *Empire*, 380–81.
77. Karl Marx, "Notes on Bakunin's Book *Statehood and Anarchy*," in *Marx Engels Collected Works*, vol. 24 (Moscow: Progress Publishers, 1989), 499, 498.
78. David Brion Davis, *The Slave Power Conspiracy and the Paranoid Style* (Baton Rouge: Louisiana State University Press, 1982), 33.
79. Jean-Paul Sartre, Preface, in Frantz Fanon, *The Wretched of the Earth* (New York: Grove Press, 1963), 26.
80. Hannah Arendt, *On Revolution* (London: Penguin, 1990), 64–65.
81. Perry Anderson, *Considerations on Western Marxism* (London: New Left Books, 1976).
82. Karl Marx, "The Future Results of British Rule in India," in *Marx Engels Collected Works*, vol. 12 (Moscow: Progress Publishers, 1975), 221.
83. Hardt and Negri, *Empire*, 112.
84. John Hope Franklin and Evelyn Higginbotham, *From Slavery to Freedom: A History of African Americans*, 9th ed. (New York: McGraw-Hill, 2010), 362.
85. Robin Kelley, *Hammer and Hoe: Alabama Communists during the Great Repression* (Chapel Hill: University of North Carolina Press, 1990), 94–96.
86. Ibid., 100.
87. C. Vann Woodward, *The Strange Career of Jim Crow* (New York: Oxford University Press, 1966), 131–34.
88. V. I. Lenin, "Conspectus of Hegel's Book *The Science of Logic*," in *Collected Works*, vol. 38 (Moscow: Progress Publishers, 1968), 99.
89. Mao, "Against Racial Discrimination," 379.
90. Deng Xiaoping, "To Uphold Socialism We Must Eliminate Poverty (26 April, 1987)," in *Selected Works of Deng Xiaoping*, vol. 3 (Beijing: Foreign Languages Press, 1987), 221–23, at 222.
91. Domenico Losurdo, "Flight from History? The Communist Movement between Self-Criticism and Self-Contempt," *Nature, Society, Thought: A*

Journal of Dialectical and Historical Materialism 13/4 (2000): 457–511, 488–90.

92. John Holloway, *Change the World Without Taking Power: The Meaning of Revolution Today* (London: Pluto Press, 2002).

Index

Adorno, Theodor, 21, 25, 116–23, 130; on critical theory, 200–201; on Israel, 126; on nationalism, 246
Africa, 88–89
African-Americans, *see* Blacks
Agamben, Giorgio, 177, 179–81
Algeria, 117, 146, 160, 246
Algerians, 110, 237, 252
Allende, Salvador, 98, 189, 194
Althusser, Louis, 102, 105–8, 224; on anticolonialism, 245–46; on Foucault, 163; on humanism, 240, 244–45, 261; on young Marx, 240–45
American Revolution, 182–83, 204–5, 208; Marx on, 215; Negri and Hardt on, 256, 257
anarchism, 17, 49, 251; Timpanaro on, 134–37
Anderson, Perry, 13–18; on Western and Eastern Marxism, 37–38, 41, 87, 141, 257

anticolonialism, 102–5; Sartre on, 134–37; Timpanaro on, 137–39
anti-humanism, 102, 105
anti-Semitism, Arendt on, 144–52
Applebaum, Anne, 171
Arabs, 128; in Israel, 127
Arendt, Hannah, 144–51, 154–63, 254; on American Revolution, 256, 257; Negri and Hardt on, 182
Aristotle, 245
Azzarà, Stefano, 12

Badiou, Alain, 24, 195–99
Bakunin, Mikhail, 58–59, 138, 184, 256
Beaumont, Gustave de, 216
Begin, Menachem, 147
Belt and Road Initiative (BRI; China), 31
Benjamin, Walter: on inequality, 64; messianism of, 61; on militarism, 48, 49; on money economy, 54; on technology, 58

Bergson, Henri, 104–5
Berlin, Isaiah, 196–97
Bidault, Georges, 94
biological racism, 170, 172, 178
biopolitics, 171–77
Bismarck, Otto von, 255
Blacks, 95; breeding of, during slavery, 173–74; deprived of political rights in United States, 214–15; discrimination against, in United States, 220–21; in Haiti, 102–3; Horkheimer on, 114–15; liberation struggle among, in United States, 161; lynchings of, 71, 164–65, 254; Mao on, 238–39; on natural law, 237; Popular Front policy and, 88; slavery of, 162–63; Soviet Union, Communist Party, and, 259–60; in United States, 96, 110–11, 114–15, 237
Bloch, Ernst, 83, 238; on bourgeois revolution, 263; on capitalism, 53–54, 63–64; on First World War, 44, 60; on Germany's colonial aims, 86–87; on human dignity, 240; on Israel, 126–27; legacy of, 108–11; Lenin rejected by, 69; on liberalism, 237; on militarism, 70; on political power, 200; on powers of state, 48, 49; on Soviet Union, 142–43; on United States, 70–71
Bobbio, Norberto, 92–96, 236, 239–40
Bolivar, Simon, 190
Bolshevik Party (Soviet Union), 205–6
Boulez, Pierre, 164, 252
Braden, Thomas, 25
Brest-Litovsk, Treaty of (1918), 79

Brielmayer, Erdmute, 11–12
Britain, *see* Great Britain
British Empire, 148, 216; genocide in, 217
Bukharin, Nikolai, 44, 57
Burke, Edmund, 204
Burkina Faso, 16
Bush, George W., 210
Buzan, Barry G., 209

Calley, William, 117
Camusso, Susanna, 208
capitalism: biopolitics in, 175; Bloch on, 53–54, 63–64; Marx on future of, 213–14; Marx on human cost of, 241–42; Thatcher on, 28
Central Intelligence Agency (CIA), 11, 25–26
Chamberlain, Houston S., 103
Chavez, Hugo, 194
Chen Yi, 56
Chile, 189, 194
China (People's Republic of China), 15, 45–46, 100–101; Cultural Revolution in, 130–34, 249–51; under Deng, 29–30; economic development in, 30–32; famine in, 191–93; invaded by Japan (1937), 82, 83, 91, 104, 157–58; Jesuits in, 232; under Kuomintang, 55; modernization in (after Second World War), 84–85; Taiping Revolt in, 62; United States policy toward, 210
Chinese (people), 215
Chinese Communist Party (CCP), 31, 56, 133, 232, 262; on Cultural Revolution, 130–31; founding of, 46, 50; during war with Japan, 82
Chinese Revolution (1911), 51, 65

Index 301

Christianity, 232
Churchill, Winston, 9, 158, 176, 203
Civil War (U.S.), 214, 231
Clinton, Bill, 189
Clinton, Hillary, 187
Cold War, 10, 95, 114, 225; Western Marxism during, 143
Colletti, Lucio, 97–98, 224–25, 259
colonialism: Adorno on, 116–18; anticolonialism and, 102–5; Arendt on, 155–62; in China, 65, 84; in differences between Western and Eastern Marxism, 69–72; Faucault on, 164, 172; Hardt and Negri on, 184; Lenin on, 74–75; Lukács on, 139–40; Marcuse on, 123–24; national question and, 77–79; Nazism and, 144, 148–49; in Palestine, 198; Popular Front policy on, 88–90; Sartre on, 134–37; Žižek on, 190–93
Columbus, Christopher, 19
communism, 24; Arendt on, 156; definitions of, 223; Eurocommunism, 141; Lenin on future of, 66–67; as threat to capitalism, 220
Communist International, 70; Eastern and Western Marxisms in, 206–7; Popular Front policy of, 88–90
communist parties: of China (*see* Chinese Communist Party); Eurocommunism in, 141; Italian, 10–11, 92–95; of Soviet Union, 112; of United States, 220, 221, 260; of Vietnam, 38, 133; world anticolonial revolution led by, 224
Congo (Belgian), 217

Congress for Cultural Freedom (CCF), 25
Congress of the Peoples of the East (Baku, 1920), 77
conscription, 48
Cope, Zak, 17
critical theory, 22, 115–16, 200–201
Croce, Benedetto, 170
Cromer (Lord), 148, 150–51, 158
Cuba, 86, 99, 233
Cultural Revolution (China), 29, 130–34, 141, 249–51

Damiens, Robert-Francois, 164
Danielson, Nikolai F., 83–84
Davis, David Brion, 96
Deleuze, Gilles, 24
Della Volpe, Galvano, 92, 239; on *libertas maior*, 95–97, 236; on scientific method, 105, 245
Deng Xiaoping, 32, 56, 262; China under, 29; on science, 57; on socialism in China, 85–86
Dew, Thomas R., 173
Dien Bien Phu, Battle of (1954), 94
Disraeli, Benjamin, 148
Du Bois, W. E. B., 89, 104, 144
Dulles, John Foster, 94
Durkheim, Emile, 178–79

East: science and technology in, 59–60; during Second World War, 80; struggle against inequality in, 63–66
Eastern Europe, 15
Eastern Marxism, 12–13, 233, 257–63; Anderson on, 16, 41; boundaries between Western Marxism and, 66–68; Merleau-Ponty on, 39–40

Eden, Anthony, 121–22
Egypt, 121–22, 127
Einstein, Albert, 147
Eisenhower, Dwight, 128
Engels, Friedrich, 99; on Christianity, 232; on ideology as false consciousness, 19; Merleau-Ponty on, 39; on need for industrialization, 83; on Socialist League, 17
England, *see* Great Britain
eugenics, 148, 170, 175, 176
Eurocentrism, 138
Eurocommunism, 141

Fabian Society (Britain), 17
Fanon, Frantz, 120, 134–35, 137, 146
fascism, Adorno on, 116, 121
Federalist Papers, 96
Ferguson, Niall, 210
Fichte, Johann Gottlieb, 62, 136–37
First World War, 20, 42–45; Bloch on, 60; colonial populations in, 218; Eastern Marxism on, 156–57; Lenin on, 49, 74–76, 78; opposition to, 72, 73; Treaty of Versailles ending, 50; Wilson on, 255
Foster, John Bellamy, 31
Foucault, Michel, 21–22, 163–65, 251–54; on biopolitics, 171–77; on history of racism, 165–71
Fourth International, 89–90
France, Anatole, 63, 64, 110
France: Algeria under, 160; Algerians in, 110, 237; defeated in Battle of Dien Bien Phu (1954), 94; Haiti under, 102–3; history of racism in, 165–71; Popular Front policy on, 88; during Second World War, 78; slavery abolished in colonies of, 254
Frankfurt School, 13, 111
Franklin, Benjamin, 174
French Revolution, 245; Adorno on, 118; Horkheimer on, 113–14; Jacobins in, 196; Kant on, 119; Marx on, 215; slavery abolished by, 205
Freud, Sigmund, 255

Galileo, 245
Gandhi, Mohandas, 89, 145
genocide, 217
Germany: Arendt on, 144–52, 154–55; biological racism in, 170; colonial aims of, 86; Nazi theory in, 180; Non-Aggression Pact between Soviet Union and (1939), 89–90; Nuremberg laws in, 253; during Second World War, 9–10, 90; between wars, 57–58
Glucksmann, André, 22
Gobineau, Arthur de, 148
Goebbels, Joseph, 79
Gorbachev, Mikhail, 243
Gramsci, Antonio, 11, 23; Anderson on, 14, 37–38; on anticolonialism, 102; on colonialism, 104–5; on First World War, 72; on humanism, 240, 261; Italian Communist Party founded by, 10; on praxis, 178
Great Britain: American Revolution against, 182–83; Bloch on colonialism of, 69; British Empire under, 148; Irish rebellion against (1916), 74, 76; Kenya as colony

Index

of, 94; Popular Front policy on, 88–89; power of slave owners in, 205
Great Leap Forward (China), 131, 191–93, 250
Grotius, Hugo, 238
Guatemalan Truth Commission, 219–20
Guevara, Ernesto "Che," 27, 86

Haiti (Saint Domingue), 221, 245; Arendt on, 163; Black Jacobins in, 196; revolution in, 102–3, 190, 215
Hamilton, Alexander, 226–27
Hardt, Michael, 163, 210–11, 230, 248; on American Revolution, 256; on Soviet Union, 259; on United States, 182–85; on Wilson, 255; on Yugoslavia, 28
Harvey, David, 193–95, 211
Hayek, Friedrich, 176–77
Hegel, G. W. F., 164, 179, 231; Adorno on, 118–19; Lenin on, 261; Marx on, 228; on poverty, 22
Herzl, Theodor, 127, 152
Hess, Moses, 127
historical materialism, 105–6, 178, 229, 245
Hitler, Adolf, 80–83, 180–81, 227; Arendt on, 156; Du Bois on, 144; on French people, 78; "German Indies" proposed by, 97, 109, 158–59, 191, 218; racism of, 170; Randolph of, 145; slavery under, 162; socialism of, 107
Hitlerism, *see* Nazism
Hobbes, Thomas, 57
Hobsbawm, Eric, 46
Hobson, John A., 17, 174

Ho Chi Minh, 14–15, 239; in Battle of Dien Bien Phu (1954), 94; on colonialism, 69–72; at Congress of Tours of French Socialist Party, 47–48; death of, 246–47; on First World War, 91; in France, 56; on inequality, 64–65; on Lenin, 52–53; in United States, 71
Holloway , John, 203
Holocaust, 152–54
Horkheimer, Max, 111–16, 229–30; on abolition of the state, 40–41; aided by Congress for Cultural Freedom, 25; on capitalism and fascism, 123; on Hitler's supporters, 120; on Israel, 126; on nationalism, 122; national liberation struggles dismissed by, 21, 130; on Soviet Union, 40, 87; on technology, 58; on Vietnam War, 28, 143
humanism, 107–8, 239–45
Huntington, Samuel, 183

Ilyenkov, Evald, 12
imperialism: Arendt on, 149–50; Fabianism on, 17; Guevara on, 27; Hardt and Negri on, 184; Lenin on, 20–21, 49, 73, 76, 209, 247; Marcuse on, 124; neo-imperialism and, 210; Žižek on, 186–90
India, 103, 151, 158, 217
indignados, 187
Indochina, 47, 52, 94
Indonesia, 98, 99
International Criminal Court, 198–99
Ireland: Beaumont on religious oppression in, 216; Bloch on,

69; Lenin on, 239; Marx on England's treatment of, 47; rebellion against Britain by, 74, 76
Irish people, 99
Israel, 116, 126–30, 187; ban on interracial marriages in, 171, 254; *indignados* in, 187
Italian Communist Party (Partito Comunista Italiano; PCI), 10–11; Bobbio-Togliatti debate in, 92–95; problem of political power for, 200
Italy: in 1969, 100; in First World War, 72; under Mussolini, 157; nationalism in, 219; response to Chinese Cultural Revolution in, 132; during Russian Revolution, 43; after Second World War, 10–11; during Second World War, 78–79

Jacobins, 196
James, C.L.R., 88
Japan, 161, 219; China invaded by (1937), 82, 83, 91, 104, 157–58; Treaty of Versailles on, 50
Jaspers, Karl, 150–51
Jefferson, Thomas, 208
Jesuits, 232
Jesus, 203
Jews: Arendt on anti-Semitism against, 144–52; as Bolsheviks, 153–55; definition of, 166; Holocaust of, 152–53; in Israel, 127; Nuremberg laws on, 253
Johnson:, Paul, 210

Kader, Abd el, 160
Kant, Immanuel, 119
Karakhan, Lev Mikhailovich, 50

Karol, K. S., 130
Kautsky, Karl, 33, 142, 143
Kennan, George F., 143
Kenya, 94, 219
Kissinger, Henry, 189, 192
Korea, 15
Korsch, Karl, 97
Ku Klux Klan, 71, 254–55
Kuomintang (China), 55

Labour Party (Britain), Fabian section of, 17
Lasky, Melvin, 26
Latin America, 188–90, 219–20
Lazare, 152
Le Duan, 249
Lenin, V. I., 43, 200; Arendt on, 159, 257; Bloch on, 69, 87; on colonialism, 47, 74–75, 104; on despair, 13; on First World War, 49, 74–76, 78, 91; on future of communism, 66–67; Harvey on, 193, 194; on Hegel, 261; Ho Chi Minh on, 53, 246–47; on imperialism, 17, 20–21, 34, 73, 77, 209; on India, 239; on Kautsky, 33; Lukács on, 139–40; on national question, 195; New Economic Policy of, 54, 136, 139; on political power, 200, 204; on Russian Revolution, 74; during Russian Revolution, 46; after Russian Revolution, 206; on Second International, 20; on slavery, 218; on social revolutions, 9, 231; Timpanaro on, 138; Tronti on, 99; in Western and Eastern Marxism, 71; on Western Left, 18
Leninism, 142
Levinas, Emmanuel, 177–81

liberalism, 197, 226, 237
Libya, 186–87, 207–8
Liebknecht, Karl, 44
Lin Biao, 130–31, 249–50
Linguet, 229
Liu Shaoqi, 131, 250
Locke, John, 96, 114, 238
Louverture, Toussaint (Overture), 102–3, 136, 159, 215
Lukács, György, 14; on colonialism, 139–40; on conscription and militarism, 48; on Fichte, 62; on messianism, 61–63; on Russian Revolution, 43–44; on science, 58
Luxemburg, Rosa, 44, 144
lynchings, 164–65, 215, 254

Macaulay, Thomas, 151
Machiavelli, Niccolò, 226
Macpherson, Crawford B., 197
Madison, James, 96
Mallaby, Sebastian, 210
Mann, Golo, 150–51
Mao Zedong, 50–51, 247; on abolition on inequality, 132–33; on African Americans, 111; Althusser on, 102; on Blacks in United States, 110, 238–39; on capitalist development in China, 60; Cultural Revolution of, 130–32; death of, 141; famine under, 191–93; on material production, 250–51; on modernization in China, 84–85; on money economy, 55–56; on national struggle, 261; on racism in United States, 71; on social practice, 137; on start of Second World War, 90; on students studying in France, 56–57; on United States policy toward China, 248; during war with Japan, 82; Žižek on, 143, 222
Marcuse, Herbert, 63, 123–26; on Eastern totalitarianism, 143; on Israel, 129–30; on Vietnam, 230–31
Marramao, Giacomo, 208, 211
Marx, Karl: Althusser on, 106, 240–45; Arendt on, 146–47, 159, 257; on Bakunin, 184, 256; on British control over Ireland, 47; on Civil War (United States), 231; on continent history, 105; on cult of property, 197–98; current popularity of, 186; on doctrinaire politics, 227; Durkheim on, 178–79; future foreseen by, 212–15; on Hegel, 228; Ho Chi Minh on, 69; Horkheimer on, 40–41; humanism of, 240–43; Levinas on, 177–78; Lukács on, 140; Merleau-Ponty on, 39, 60; on national liberation, 97–98; on Proudhon, 101
Marxism: associated with Western Marxism, 142; Bobbio on, 93; boundaries between Western and Eastern, 66–68; expansion of, 231; Horkheimer on, 41; Levinas on, 177; Timpanaro on, 138; see also Eastern Marxism; Western Marxism
May 4th Movement (China), 50
Mayans, 220
Merleau-Ponty, Maurice, 38–40, 60, 226
messianism, 60–63, 223, 231
Mill, John Stuart, 96, 237
Molotov, Vyacheslav, 45

money economies, 53–56
Monroe, James, 161–62
Monroe Doctrine, 99, 161–62, 184
Montesquieu, 64, 96
More, Thomas, 241
Mussolini, Benito, 79, 104, 157, 255

Napoleon Bonaparte, 103
Napoleonic Wars, 79–80
Nasser, Gamal Abdel, 121–22, 127, 128
nationalism, 246
National Liberation Front (Algeria), 117, 246
National Liberation Front (Vietnam), 117, 246
national question, 76–79, 195
National Socialist Party (Germany), 154
Native Americans (Indians), 174–75, 217
NATO (North Atlantic Treaty Organization), 208–9
Nazism: American white supremacy in, 180–82; Arendt on, 146–49; Du Bois on, 144; Levinas on, 177; racial theories in, 218
Negri, Antonio, 210–11, 230, 248; on American Revolution, 256; Foucault and, 254; on Soviet Union, 259; on United States, 163, 182–85; on Wilson, 255
neo-imperialism, 210
neoliberalism, 15, 27–29
New Economic Policy (NEP; Soviet Union), 54, 136, 139
new petty bourgeoisie, 26
Nietzsche, Friedrich, 120, 175; Adorno on, 121; Althusser on, 244; on slavery, 229

Nolte, Ernst, 170
Non-Aggression Pact between Germany and Soviet Union (1939), 89–91

October Revolution (Russia, 1917), 82
Opium Wars (China), 45, 52

Padmore, George, 88
Palestinians, 187, 195, 198, 202, 248
Partito Comunista d'Italia (PCd'I), 11
Partito Comunista Italiano (PCI; Italian Communist Party), 10–11
Partito dei Comunisti Italiani (PdCI), 11
Partito della Rifondazione Comunista (PRC), 11
Partito Democratico della Sinistra (PDS), 11
Pétion, Alexandre, 190
Philippines, 109, 153, 217
Platakov (Kievski), 77
Poland, 90
Popper, Karl R., 209
Popular Front policy, 88–90
Portugal, 121, 157
Poulantzas, Nicos, 17
poverty, 161
power, political, 201–4, 206, 251–52
praxis, 178
progressivism, 39
Proudhon, Pierre-Joseph, 101
Putin, Vladimir, 210

Qaddafi, Muammar, 187, 207

racism, 71; biological racism, 172; Foucault on history of, 165–71;

state racism, 252–54; *see also* white supremacy
Radek (Parabellum), 77
Randolph, A. Philip, 144–45
Reagan, Ronald, 129
rebellionism, 22–23
Robespierre, 159, 205, 257
Roosevelt, Franklin D., 170
Roosevelt, Theodore, 153, 158, 217
Rosenberg, Alfred, 103, 170
Ross, John, 30
Rossanda, Rossana, 208
Rostow, Walter W., 193
Russia: national question in, 76–77; under Putin, 210; Revolution of 1905 in, 74; *see also* Soviet Union
Russian Revolution, 9, 45–48, 82, 206; Bloch on, 69; Italy during, 43; Lenin on, 74; Lukács on, 43–44

Saint Domingue, *see* Haiti
Sankara, Thomas, 16
Sartre, Jean-Paul, 201; anticolonialism of, 134–37; humanism of, 240; in protest against killing of Algerian, 164; in protest against killing of Algerians, 252; on scarcity, 247; on United States, 185, 257
Schmidt, Helmut, 192
Schopenhauer, Arthur, 40
science: Althusser on, 245; in China's development, 57; power of state based in, 59; in West and in East, 59–60
scientific socialism, 24
Second International (1889–1916), 20, 21
Second World War, 9–10, 39–40; Arendt on, 156; colonialism and, 109; Eastern front in, 80–83, 191; France and Italy during, 78–79; Harvey on, 193–94; Soviet Union during, 45; start of, 90–91; Western Marxism on, 157
Shanghai (China), 81–82
Sieyès, E. J., 168, 175
Six-Day War (1967), 126–27
slavery: abolished in French colonies, 254; abolished in Haiti, 196; abolished in United States, 214; in founding of United States, 184; of indigenous Americans, 172–73; in Latin America, 190; Lenin on, 218; Locke on, 96, 114; Marx on, 181, 242, 252; slave owners in power in United States, 204–5, 257; in United States, 110, 162–63, 173, 216–17
Smith, Adam, 227
Snow, Edgar, 55, 56
social chauvinism, 20–21
socialism: Anderson on, 16; Fabianism on, 17; post-World War II, 15; scientific and utopian, 24
Socialist League, 17
Socialist Party (France:), 47, 52
social revolutions: imperialism and, 76; Lenin on, 9
sociology, 179
South Africa, 89, 171, 254
Soviet Union: Anderson on, 14, 37; Arendt on, 151; Bloch on, 53–54, 108–9; civil war in, 141–42; collapse of, 10, 195, 209, 235; czarist claims on China renounced by, 50; gulags in, 171, 260; Hardt and Negri on, 259; Horkheimer

on, 40, 111–13; Marcuse on, 124–25; Marxism in, 66–68; New Economic Policy in, 54, 136, 139; Non-Aggression Pact between Germany and (1939), 89–91; during Second World War, 9–10, 80–83; Western and Eastern Marxism in, 66–68; Žižek on, 190–91; *see also* Eastern Marxism; Russian Revolution
Spain, 121; under Franco, 157
Spencer, Herbert, 217
Spengler, Oswald, 80, 158
Stalin, Joseph, 37, 41, 170; Althusser on, 106, 243; at beginning of Second World War, 90–91; Blacks on, 260; Eastern Marxism of, 68; on First World War, 44; on money economy, 54; during Second World War, 80, 191; Žižek on, 222
state, 48–49, 202
state racism, 167, 171, 252–54
state socialism, 113
Stoddard, Lothrop, 104, 153–54
Strauss, Leo, 183, 256
students, 100
Suez Canal, 121, 127–28
Sun Yat-Sen, 46, 49–50, 56, 65
Syria, 211

Taiping Rebellion (China), 45–46, 62
Taylor, A. J. P., 218
Taylorism, 67
technology: Benjamin on, 58; in Chinese economic development, 56–57; in West and in East, 59–60
Thatcher, Margaret, 28
Thierry, Augustin, 168–69

Third Reich, *see* Germany
Third World: Arendt on, 161–62; victims of colonialism in, 198; Žižek on, 188
Third Worldism, 98–101, 209
Timpanaro, Sebastiano, 137–39
Tocqueville, Alexis de, 160, 162, 163, 208
Togliatti, Palmiro: Anderson on, 37; on barbaric discrimination between human creatures, 108, 199, 240; humanism of, 102; as Italian Communist Party leader, 92, 94–96
totalitarianism, 221–22; Arendt on, 149–51, 154–55, 157–60; Randolph on, 144–45
Tronti, Mario, 63, 98–101, 107, 201–2; on abolition of work, 249
Trotsky, Leon, 44–45, 68; on Non-Aggression Pact between the Soviet Union and Germany, 89–90
Trotskyists, in United States, 90, 91
Troung Chinh, 56
Turati, Filippo, 141–42
Turner, Nat, 216

Ukraine war, 33
Union of Soviet Socialist Republics (USSR), *see* Soviet Union
United States: anti-PCI groups funded by, 10–11; Arendt on, 162; Blacks in, 237; Bloch on, 109; Civil War in, 231; colonialism of, 70–71; extraterritoriality forced on China by, 65; first strike capability of, 210; Harvey on, 194–95; history of racism in, 166–67; Mao on, 238–39; Marx

on future of, 212–15; Monroe Doctrine of, 99; in Nazi theory, 180; recent foreign policy of, 211; Revolution against Britain in, 182–83, 215; slave owners in power in, 204–5, 257; slavery in, 162–63, 216–17, 242; state racism in, 252–53; in Vietnam War, 117, 130; white supremacy in, 254

Venezuela, 189, 194
Versailles, Treaty of (1919), 50
Vietnam, 14–15, 233; France defeated by, 38; Marcuse on, 230–31
Vietnamese Communist Party, 133
Vietnam War, 99, 130, 233; Adorno on, 117; defeat of United States in, 87; Horkheimer on, 28, 143; Marcuse on, 123, 125

Weber, Marianne, 61
Wehr, Andreas, 11–12
Weil, Simone, 58
West: science and technology in, 59–60; struggle against inequality in, 63–66
Western Marxism, 257–63; Anderson on, 13–16, 41, 141; boundaries between Eastern Marxism and, 66–68; death of, 207–11; definition of, 12–13; Eurocentism in, 138; Losurdo on, 18; Merleau-Ponty on origins of, 39–40; messianism in, 60–63, 223; in new petty bourgeoisie, 26
white supremacy: international threat to, 226; lynchings and, 254; lynchings in, 164–65; Stoddard on, 153–54; U.S. foreign policy and, 180–82, 220–21, 260–61
Wilford, Hugh, 25
Wilhelm II (chancellor, Germany), 86
Wilson, Woodrow: Bloch on, 69, 70, 109; Hardt and Negri on, 184, 254–55
women: Althusser on, 106–7; in Kenya, 219; political rights won by, 214; as slaves, 173
workerism, 98–101
World War I, *see* First World War
World War II, *see* Second World War

Xi Jinping, 32

Yeltsin, Boris, 210
Yugoslavia, 23, 28, 208–9

Zhou Enlai, 56, 57
Žižek, Slavoj, 222; as anti-communist dissident, 23; anti-imperialism of, 186–90, 231; *Foreign Policy* on, 26–27; on Mao, 143; on Ukraine war, 33